The Pay-per Society

The Pay-per Society

Computers and Communication
in the Information Age
Essays in Critical Theory and Public Policy

Vincent Mosco

Ablex Publishing Corporation

Ablex Publishing Corporation
355 Chestnut Street Norwood,
New Jersey U.S.A. 07648

Cover design: Peter McArthur.
Printed and bound in Canada.

Library of Congress
Cataloguing-in-Publication Data

Mosco, Vincent
    The pay / per society.
Bibliography: p.
Includes index.
1. Computers and civilization.
2. Communication. 3. Telecommunications
systems. I. Title.
QA76.9.C66M66 1989   303.48'34   89-6665
ISBN 0-89391-604-8

For Rosie and Madeline
Remember The Story of Mosco Street

Contents

Tables and Figures

Acknowledgements

Society is changing in many ways as communication and information technologies are introduced more and more into our daily lives. This book examines these changes and the fundamental problems that confront us. In essence, *The Pay-per Society* is about the use of electronic media and computers to expand financial and social control at the expense of basic values such as democracy and human welfare.

The first part of the book demonstrates this theme by considering how different perspectives—or ways of seeing and thinking about computers and communication—sharpen our understanding of the information society. Drawing on critical theory in communication, sociology, and politics, the first five chapters try to determine the meaning of the so-called information revolution, the changing significance of democracy in a computer society, and the impact of the technology—particularly the communication and telecommunication systems—on government, labour, and efforts to create a more participatory culture. This section concludes that business and government use their concentrated economic and political power to deepen and extend the use of technology for profit and power. As a result, computers and electronic media, which hold the potential for a wide range of applications, are mainly employed to measure and monitor information transactions and

11

to package and repackage information products many times over, thereby bringing us ever closer to a Pay-per Society.

The second part deals specifically with political issues, including the military's influence on communication and information technology. This influence has grown so powerful that the term *military information society* is appropriate and especially well demonstrated by the place of computers and communication technology in the "Star Wars" program. Subsequent chapters consider the process of making government policy on the uses of computers and electronic media, emphasizing the influence of the United States, particularly on the formation of Canadian and international policy. Decisions about the structure of the Pay-per Society are shaping the international information order and determining who benefits from it.

Acknowledgements for a book can never do justice to those who influence it. Chapter Two, which details the growth of critical communications studies in North America, stands as an analytical acknowledgement to my scholarly family. There are two, more personal, acknowledgements that I would like to make here because their lessons in communication continue to resonate in my work.

Over sixty years ago, my grandmother Lucy and her husband Vincent came from the south of Italy to the United States to find work and enjoy the American dream. They settled in rural Maryland, but left when the Ku Klux Klan made their dream a nightmare. They decided to return to Italy where there was less bread, but certainly no burning crosses. Stopping on the way back in New York City, relatives convinced them to stay. The Klan, they were assured, never came to Mulberry Street. Lucy was skeptical. She agreed to stay, but armed herself with a bit of communication power. For the rest of her life she never admitted to be able to speak or understand English. It was a pleasure to observe her wield her Italian like a sword in the face of anyone who would use English as a form of authoritarian control. Lucy, I appreciated the lesson in communication.

My father was part of that generation that grew up in the Great Depression and reached maturity just in time to fight World War II. Frank always seemed to be chasing his American Dream, too many paychecks and hours of overtime away. But his chase seemed to have succeeded when on July 4, 1976, the 200th anniversary of the American Declaration of Independence, he gave a patriotic speech to a group of people gathering to celebrate the bicentennial and to raise money to keep the Fulton fish market, and the many jobs it provided, from leaving New York. After the speech, my father was arrested. For a year after that, he was made to fight what everyone knew to be, and were later proven to be, terribly false charges, laid only to stop him from helping the fish market workers and their union. But it didn't work. In spite of legal harassment (the charges were not dropped for a year) and media vilification (the tabloids of print and TV turned a community organizer into a Mafia figure), Frank continued to speak out and fight for jobs, for decent housing, and for the right to social services until he died five years later. Frank, I appreciated your lessons in communication.

When my father died, the city that arrested him, decided to make up for its mistake and honour him by renaming the Manhattan street we lived on, Mosco Street. We knew that he would have said something like, "why give me a street when you don't help the people in my neighborhood." We also know that it was an election year. But my mother and all of us agreed to the renaming and the celebration that accompanied it. Whenever my wife and children, now seven and five, visit the old neighborhood, we walk down to Mosco Street, look up at the street signs, and appreciate another lesson in communication.

I've written this book a long way from Mosco Street. For the last five years, I have lived and worked in Canada. Since five years are enough to give even a nomad roots and since I began the research for this book soon after arriving, I thought that I would publish it in my new country. However, it is important for me to acknowledge the roots of a few of the chapters. An earlier version of Chapter Two was published in *The Left Academy* edited by Bertell Ollman and William Vernoff and published by Praeger in 1986. Chapter Four is an edited and expanded version of a paper that appeared in the Winter 1988 issue of the *Journal of Communication.* Early versions of Chapter Six appeared in *Radical Science*, No. 17, and *Science as Culture* (Pilot Issue). Finally, the idea for Chapter Eight grew from my participation in a conference on "Free Trade in Culture," held at Duke University in April, 1987.

It is not without some sadness that I publish this book in what has become my country of choice, for in the week that I write these acknowledgements, it has voted in a federal election to give up some of its sovereignty to the United States. At a time when people, in such different places as Armenia and Nicaragua, Palestine and Estonia, are risking their lives for sovereignty, it is difficult to watch people voluntarily give up some of it on the promise of a few Yankee dollars. This, too, is a lesson in communication.

Vincent Mosco
Ottawa, Canada
November 26, 1988

PART I

PERSPECTIVES ON COMPUTERS, COMMUNICATION, AND THE INFORMATION SOCIETY

Chapter One

Introduction: Just in Time

The word "revolutionary" can be applied only to revolutions whose aim is freedom.—Marquis de Condorcet, eighteenth century philosopher.

The Computer on Broadway

Just in time
I found you just in time
Before you came my time was runnin' low

But now you're here
And now I know just where I'm goin'
No more doubt or fear
I found my way

Computers are studied from almost every perspective imaginable. There are books about the technology: everything from the microelectronics that make them work to the communications systems of wire, cable, microwave, and communications satellites that link computers in local, regional, national, and now, even international information networks. There are books about the computer's impact on government, business, recreation, working, shopping, education, family life, and the individual. Can computers think? Are they alive? If they are a form of life, do they enhance or diminish our form of life? Major debates revolve about these questions, most of which focus on whether the computer will have positive or negative impacts, and for whom.

These are significant, almost overwhelming concerns. It is easy to feel swamped by the sheer amount of material available on the computerization of society and on the global spread of communication media. In the face of accelerating technological change, it is a genuine challenge to introduce the subject of communication and information technology; even more challenging to convey a perspective on the debates surrounding computerization and the information society. These debates feel like being in the middle of a Broadway musical in three acts, framed by the songs, *Just in Time, Is That All There Is?*, and *The Way We Were*.

Just in Time

The show has to begin with *Just in Time*. There is an overwhelming sense among those who have a stake in the computerization of society that the technology arrived *just in time*. For bankers, it was the accelerating growth of paper records—of checks and account statements—that the arrival of the computer helped to control *just in time*. The computer permits banks to increase the number of customers, to expand their hours, and add locations without hiring new personnel. The same is true for other paperbound service industries such as insurance and retail sales. For these and others, the computer arrived just in time to overcome paper saturation and the space and time constraints that set an upper limit on the ability of these businesses to grow manageably.

For manufacturing companies, computers came just in time to manage an increasingly costly labour force and to expand their operations into a global marketplace. Computers eased the further automation of automobile assembly and lessened reliance on expensive skilled labour to perform complex design and fabrication. It also made possible the World Car, a vehicle put together with capital, labour, and raw materials in several different regions of the world. Computer communications systems arrived just in time for companies to take advantage of the most profitable sources of basic factors of productions all over the world.

For communications companies, like AT&T and Bell Canada, the computer arrived just in time to handle the growing traffic in telephone communication and still cut its workforce. Moreover, the computer helps telephone companies measure and monitor the flow of traffic, including the work of its employees, with a precision that was impossible before its application. The computer arrived just in time to tighten control of an increasingly demanding workforce by measuring every phone call an operator handles, every repair or installation a technician makes, and every keystroke that a billing clerk enters into a computer.

It is not difficult for examples to multiply. Computers arrived just in time for government to manage the growth of its social welfare function. For the military, just in time to make possible the ultimate deterrent, nuclear missiles, and, in the military view, the ultimate protective umbrella, the anti-ballistic weapons of the "Star Wars" project. For universities, computers arrived just in time to manage an information explosion and to educate a growing numbers of students of every age category. Computers arrived just in time to organize the increasingly complex household, making two-wage families easier to accommodate, and expanding opportunities for turning the home into a workplace and extended centre for leisure and learning. And so on. *Just in time.*

Is That All There Is?

The counterpoint to *Just in Time* is a song that Peggy Lee, the jazz and blues singer, made popular: *Is That All There Is?* In it, the singer looks back on the critical moments of her life—a first love, a love lost, success, failure, and, finally, her own death. Each of these events carried an enormous weight of anticipation, the exciting promise and the terror that one feels in the face of fundamental change. Yet, after each of these experiences, she responds, with icy indifference or inner strength, perhaps both, "Is that all there is?"

As a generation of people experiences a lifetime of computer communications, one begins to hear more often a new song that addresses the failure of computers and communication technology to live up to their promise of solving our problems just in time. Paper continues to pile up in offices. Managers are not all that eager to have people working at home. The promise of instant access to the world's information has not amounted to much at all. Ten times the television channels means ten times the same content. The lines at a teller window with someone there have become lines at an automated teller. The space shuttle crashed. The stock market crashes. The computer supervisor replaces the human supervisor. However, work seems as regimented as ever. Computers help create weapons to defeat the "Star Wars" shield. Nuclear power had promised to be a resource too cheap to meter. Now, nuclear power plants drive public utilities to bankruptcy. Computers promised an information explosion, too cheap to charge for. And yet, more and more people cannot read, more and more people have to decide between paying for a phone and paying for food. People now confront the computer more often with: Is that all there is? The enthusiastic technophilia that greeted the computer and electronic communications of all sorts has its counterpoint in the hostile indifference to another false promise. The computer revolution becomes just another way of saying *more of the same.*

The Way We Were

The closing act of the computerization debate looks back on the late twentieth century from some point in the twenty-first. From a vantage point a hundred years into the future, we look back on our early romance with the computer feeling the same amusement we bring to a childhood photograph. How could we have been so naive? Just in time for what? Then, we turn to what appeared to be at the time, a more mature view, a tougher view, Is that all there is, just more of the same? But this makes us uncomfortable. Something *has* changed as a result of computer communications. But not because of a sudden upheaval, an eruption in the social structure. Society's direction did *not* change. Rather, it accelerated tendencies that had been at work for hundreds of years. It deepened and extended the logic of the marketplace, and with it, the process of making all social life, including such basic components as time, space, and information, into marketable commodities. Computer communication appeared to bring nothing new because it simply accentuated certain social tendencies—commodification, markets, money, quantification, surveillance, oversight, and control over other more traditional and affective tendencies. In hindsight, we look back on what we lost and recognize the difficulty of returning to the way we were.

Ways of Seeing Information

This book sets out to describe how information and information technology are central to the processes of commodification and social control that take up more and more of the social and cultural terrain of society. Information itself is increasingly becoming a commodity as well as an instrument in society-wide commodification and control processes. Before discussing these particular ways of seeing information, it is important to describe three other concepts of information that have traditionally guided our understanding of this area: information as a discourse on technology, information systems, and information as a non-depletable, strategic resource.

Information as a Discourse on Technology

Scholars began to pay especially close attention to information after World War II. The War speeded up the development of information technologies, including the computer, microwave, television broadcasting and several related technologies. The 1950s brought the communications satellite and cost effective uses of coaxial cable and new radio spectrum-based means of distribution. As its tangible embodiment, the technology came to stand for information. Understandably, given the lack of material substance in information and the seemingly awesome and magical presence of computers, television, and communications satellites, our discourse about information became a discourse on technology. In the popular view, information came to be seen as what information technology produces. To speak of information is to speak about technology.

Much of what has been written about information takes this technological determinist view (Brand, 1987; Pool, 1983). Information *is* what comes out of information technology. The technology itself embodies sufficient power to overcome the resistance of social institutions. Political regulations or cultural nationalism may delay the diffusion of technology; but, in Pool's view, ultimately give way to the power the technology has to produce and distribute information, and to the power of information, inherent in its intangibility, to resist control and containment. From this point a view, for example, the processing power of the computer and the distributional capacity of the communications satellite or optical fibre cable make it impossible to keep information within the boundaries of one country. According to this perspective, information technology inherently promotes globalization. One can only retard the process; one cannot resist it.

Information Systems

Information systems theory provided an alternative to technological determinism because it divorced information from its carrier. This perspective grew out of a general movement to view behaviour of all sorts—cosmic, chemical, biological, machine, social, etc.—as systems; which, comprised of component parts—planets, molecules, cells, families—interact in a patterned fashion, sustained over a period of time. Systems theory has widespread roots, with particularly significant developments in biology and computing science.

The influence of research in biology began with Cannon's (1932) work on human anatomy and physiology. Cannon conceptualized the organism as an integrated system of interrelated components. His work directly influenced the development of sociological systems theory, particularly the structural-functional school established by Talcott Parsons. (1951) Later on, the growth of molecular biology, particularly the Watson-Crick model for DNA, provided positive results for the value of seeing information in systems terms. (D. Schiller, 1988).

A major contributing influence from computing science was the development of control systems theory or *cybernetics*. The cybernetic perspective, which Norbert Wiener enunciated in the late 1940s and applied to social problems in the early 1950s, identified the relationships among individual systems components in order to define and assess the value of different types of systems (Wiener, 1948 and 1954)

A key development in information systems theory was the model of communications processes introduced by Shannon and Weaver (1959). This approach sought to incorporate the communications system by modeling the process whereby a signal is encoded by a sender and decoded by a receiver. The success of the communication process depends on the quality of the signal relative to the degree of noise introduced into the system from the environment or through interpretive deficiencies in the sender or receiver. Within this model, information could stand on its own, as some *thing* distinguishable from who moves it or how it moves. So separated, information could be easily quantified. This proved particularly valuable with the development of computers because computers reduced information to a stream of measureable bits flowing through whatever transmission mechanism is used.

Information as a Resource

The advantage of information systems theory is that it identified information as a measureable entity separate from technology. The disadvantage is that the entity remained vague and abstract. In essence, systems theory could measure information but, ironically, was incapable of telling us, with some degree of concreteness, just what it is we are measuring. Is information reducible to electronic current? If so, why is it any more valuable than its electronic embodiment. This problem was addressed by numerous writers including Oettinger, who developed a significant alternative.

Oettinger's perspective viewed information as a resource that could be consumed or used to add value to existing resources by making industrial processes more productive and by enhancing the provision of services. Essentially, information is a valuable raw material in its own right and something that adds value to existing factors of production: labour, capital and other raw materials.

According to this view, information possesses unique characteristics that distinguish it from other resources, preeminently, that information is non-depletable. It can be used, but not used up. Coming as it did in the 1970s, when problems of resource depletion and control, especially oil and other fossil fuel resources, seemed almost insurmountable, this formulation particularly appealed. *Here* was an opportunity. The United States and other industrial powers, painfully dependent on increasingly unreliable fossil fuel supplies, could overcome the problems created by the loss of control over this resource by taking advantage of their leadership position in another strategic resource, information.

Aside from its practical political significance for the West, the concept of information as a resource is important because it provides advantages over both the technological and systems perspectives. The concept of an information resource is not dependent on any specific technology for production, distribution, and use. However, computers are particularly well suited for processing information; communications satellites and optical fibre cables for distributing it; VDTs are excellent display technologies. But there are numerous other means of accomplishing these tasks as well, including people, transportation highways, and paper. By treating information as a resource, we emphasize the enormous flexibility that it possesses. Information is integral to physical, biological, and social processes. Although this has always been the case, we have tended to confound information with the material substance that produced, distributed or consumed it. Separating information from its material carriers, we come to a deeper appreciation of its significance. Information is a resource common to every sector of society including economic activity, from manufacturing to services, government, education, leisure, etc.

Conceptualizing information as a resource makes it easier to identify its *strategic* significance. In this view, a world of dwindling resources, resources more than ever subject to the vagaries of politics, finds information strategically significant. Moreover, the idea of an information resource makes it easier to understand how information is central to fundamental economic change. It is hard to tease out the notion of a post-industrial information society from information systems theory. However, when we think of information as a non-depletable, strategic resource, arguments about the transition from an industrial society begin to make sense. What steel and fossil fuels were to the transition from an agricultural to an industrial society, information is to the transition from an industrial to a post-industrial, service, or information society. Proponents of the information resource notion would therefore argue that the concept is more general than technological determinism and more concrete than the conception of information that systems theorists provide.

A major question is whether the concept of an information resource is concrete enough to provide the most useful way to understand fundamental changes in society. This arises because the term *resource* covers numerous social forms. Here are four possibilities which, though by no means definitive, offer a sense of the range of forms that the concept encompasses:

1. Pure commons form
2. Commons under government trusteeship
3. Private property under individual ownership and management
4. Private property under stockholder ownership and corporate management.

A resource can be organized in the form of a *commons*. In this form, it is available to all and owned by no one. In the classic sense of the term, a resource so organized is an inalienable right of membership in a society. A resource can also be organized as a *commons under government trusteeship*. In this case, the government serves as the manager of a commons, working on behalf of the society. Public libraries or the public broadcasting system are examples of a government trustee arrangement for a commons. Again, no one has the right to alienate a part of the commons for private use. Any use of the information resource is subject to a public interest determination on the part of the trustee, acting on behalf of the entire society.

There is a fundamental difference between organizing a resource according to a commons and organizing it according to private property standards. Within legally specified limits, private property confers to ownership the right to use and dispose of property as the owner sees fit. This includes decisions about whether to use it, how to use it, the right to divide it, or to transfer ownership to another party. One can distinguish two principal types of ownership, *private property under individual owner-ship and management* and *private property under multiple (stockholder) own-ership and corporate management.* Home ownership or an individual's personal library is a good example of individual ownership. A transna-tional business like IBM is a prototypical example of corporate owner-ship.

In general terms, one of the most significant tendencies in modern society is the shift from commons organization to private corporate ownership. This is the case with all resources, including information. Conceptualizing information as a resource certainly makes it a more concrete and usable concept than that offered by systems theorists. But the idea of an information resource has nothing to say about *how* it is organized. Consequently, it ignores what is arguably the most significant movement in society over the past four hundred years: the development, first, of widespread private property ownership and, more recently, the rise of national and transnational businesses that shape the production, distribution and use of resources, including infor-mation. Consider one consequence of this fundamental shortcoming. As observed already, the idea of an information resource supports the notion of distinct developmental stages from agricultural, through manufacturing, to a service and information society. This view sees the transition from each stage to the next brought about by the social mas-tery of a new resource: steel, electronics, information, etc. This theory, basing distinct stages on fundamentally distinct resources, ignores com-petely the significance of the transition in *forms* of resource organization. It encourages the view that the service/information economy is a funda-mental departure from an industrial society.

Looking at the same history from the vantage point of *how* resources are organized, one comes to a different conclusion. The fundamental transition is not between an industrial and a post-industrial or informa-tion society, but more the transition from feudalism to capitalism. The latter is, at least by the standards of recorded history, a slow, torturous process, with, as numerous social historians have demonstrated, many counter-tendencies, including crises and resistance. Nevertheless, one can discern a direction, namely the commodification of social institu-tions, social relationships, and their fundamental resources of space, time, and information. Rather than a movement from an industrial to an information society, we experience a deepening and extending capital-ism, with the incorporation of information into the commodity form. By understanding the development as deepening and extending existing tendencies, rather than one of fundamental change, one can better appreciate the "Is that all there is?" reaction to developments in computers and communications systems.

Information is a Commodity

Two alternative formulations have appeared that can be more useful than these three for understanding information. Information is both a commodity and, within a society marked by the general tendency to commodification, information is a form of social control.

Capitalism grows by converting material whose value is determined by its use, into commodities whose value is determined by what it can bring in exchange. The history of capitalism is the history of this process, also known as the expansion of the marketplace. This has encompassed extensive expansion: the predominance of first local, then regional, national, and now global markets for commodities. Capital has also expanded intensively, by commodifying the realm of social reproduction, i.e., the home, the school, and the workplace. One need only consider the value of a home television audience to advertisers to appreciate the process of intensive commodification.

This process has increasingly taken over information. Several developments have made this possible. Two fundamental forces that accelerate this trend are changes in technology and changes in corporate and government demand. These two tendencies interact. For example, businesses recognize the profit potential in marketable information and hence promote the development of technologies that enhance marketability.

To create a commodity, we need to be able to determine what it is, preferably in precise quantitative form, and when it has been exchanged, the ability to measure transactions. The ephemeral nature of information has traditionally made it difficult to carry out both of these tasks. Since information is fundamentally formless, it was difficult to know what it was when we had it. Certainly the development of print provided the beginning of a commodity form in information with current developments in technology accelerating this process. The reduction of information to a common digital code and the ability to process and transmit this coded information instantaneously make it possible to measure information and monitor information transactions with considerable quantitative precision. These developments have augmented the possibilities for packaging and repackaging information in a marketable form. Consequently, the telephone industry can charge per minute of telephone use, as well as monitor worker conformity to average work time measured in seconds. The information and video industries can package and repackage bits of information or video material in an infinite range of marketable configurations. Similarly, audiences can be measured and their behaviour monitored to deliver increasingly refined packages of audiences to advertisers.

Companies have not lost sight of the market potential in such developments and have explored the range of opportunities to advance the commodification of information. This recognition has not been limited to companies officially defined in the information sector. Since most companies use information in a variety of ways, companies involved in every imaginable activity have been investing in ways to trade and use information to enhance the value of other products.

As a result, this book argues that it is more appropriate to refer to this as the *Pay-per Society*, rather than Post-industrial, Third Wave, Microelectronic Era, Second Self, Fifth Generation, or any of the other terms that try to capture the essence of our time. Since the driving force *is* commodification, and since we increasingly pay-per call, pay-per view, pay-per bit or screenful of information, etc., the Pay-per designation may make both analytic and popular sense. Before he became committed to the utopian fantasies of computer communications and brought us the Third Wave, Alvin Toffler coined the term Super-Industrialism to describe the impact of changes in information and communication. This term has some usefulness, particularly in its stress on historical continuity rather than disjunction, though the term "industrial" does not clearly embody the commodity form.

Information as a Means of Social Control
One of the unique values of information is that it serves as an instrument of control. But to say that information is a means of control confronts the same problem that those who define information in systems or resource terms must face. Just as a resource can be anything, so too can control. Thermostats control; computers control; parents control; prisons control; timers control; etc. The term begs the question of who or what controls whom or what, and to what end. Both terms are too abstract, lacking in concrete historical rootedness. This shortcoming raises fundamental questions about the usefulness of ahistorical systems models of control. For example, sociologist Talcott Parsons attempted to model physical, psychological, social and cultural systems along cybernetic

control principles, the outcome of which effort is a model in search of a meaning. (Parsons, 1966) It offers little more than the ideological value of making the most coercive forms of control—mental hospitals and other total institutions—appear to be as benign as thermostats.

Similarly, as part of his analysis of the evolving "post-industrial" society, Bell (1973) provided an analysis of control that differed according to the type of society in question. Agricultural society was essentially a game of control over nature and industrial society a game of control over machinery. A distinguishing characteristic of a post-industrial information society is that the control game against machines becomes a game against people. This analysis takes an important step in specifying that control is essentially social in nature. However, it is hard to accept the argument that such control was not also central to agricultural as well as to industrial society. One can make a better case for the view that machinery, like other technology, embodied both social purpose and a particular form of social relationship. In the case of machine use in nineteenth century Europe, it embodied the purpose of capital accumulation, profit and the relationship of owner to wage labourer. The skilled machinist or semi-skilled operative therefore confronted not an abstract machine, but a machine designed to embody a particular goal and particular social structural arrangements. Similarly, forms of agricultural control—e.g., slave, feudal, commercial—embody both purpose and social relations.

One cannot disagree with the view that societies contain forms of control or that information technology is one means of control. What makes the concept of control socially significant, however, is its social embodiment. In essense: control over whom and to what end? Information is a powerful means of social control in a society whose dominant tendency is commodification, even though it is not always and everywhere a means of control and commodification. In fact, these tendencies often inspire opposition on what are often described as "fairness" as opposed to "efficiency" criteria or "equity" rather than market criteria. Nevertheless, the balance of power, particularly in an age wherein the major resources of capital and force are in the hands of transnational business and government, supports the tendencies to increasing control and commodification.

"Is That All There Is?" Revisited

The most useful way of seeing information is as a marketable product or a commodity *and* as a means of social control. One can thereby understand how the experience of social change resulting from the growing use of information is one of deepening and extending established historical tendencies rather than a rupture or a revolution leading to a historical transformation. For *commodification* and *control in the service of commodification* are tendencies that are inextricably bound up with the development of capitalism, a process that is over three hundred years old.

It is noteworthy that academic research is beginning to step back from the, almost giddy, early view that information, particularly as it was driven by developments in information and communication technology, was leading to social transformation, an information revolution. Despite their different perspectives and approaches, Winston (1987), Beniger (1986), and Webster and Robins (1987) agree that these developments are part of what Raymond Williams has called "The Long Revolution," beginning with the decline of feudalism and the rise of market economies in the West. Winston's useful, if awkwardly phrased, Law of the Supression of Radical Alternatives, certainly captures the political, economic and cultural reasons why communication technologies with revolutionary potential—broadcasting, computers, communications satellites and cable television—lost that potential as they were integrated into the established social structure. They became part of what Beniger calls "the control revolution," a centuries old process of applying control systems to mechanical and human processes. Similarly, Webster and Robins look back to the images of the utilitarian philosopher Jeremy Bentham, whose eighteenth century *Panopticon* provided the model for contemporary computer surveillance systems, and to F.W. Taylor whose work on scientific management awaited developments in communication and information technology to fully realize managerial control. Although these books converge and diverge on numerous other problems, the point here is that one intersection represents a far more sober view of developments in communication and information than we have been used to seeing.

Deepening and Extending Major Tendencies: Six Dimensions

The use of communication and information to deepen the commodification and control processes in society appear in fundamental areas of social life. These areas have not been changed in any fundamental way by the accelerating growth of information and the technologies that process, distribute, and display it. Rather, this growth speeds up existing tendencies, many of which originated with the early development of capitalism. A brief sketch of these tendencies, some of which are developed in the ensuing chapters, follows. Bear in mind that sketches are valuable because they present essential details. To do this, a sketch leaves out detail and depth that is embodied in problems with realizing tendencies and with conflicting tendencies. These are certainly present in the full picture. What follows are essential details.

Markets

Communication and information systems have not changed the importance of markets in Western society. Instead, they have extended market size and scope, overcoming the space and time constraints that heretofore limited markets to a local, regional or national domain. The private market principle has been expanding geographically from the beginning of capitalism. Today, the accelerating ability to process, distribute, and receive information instantaneously, enhances the power of private markets, now dominated by large, vertically integrated, corporations to control the flow of social activity worldwide. Information and communication systems make it easier to operate and control global markets. Moreover, commodification makes information a major object of profit, valuable to produce and sell in the global marketplace.

Industrial Organization

The present application of information and communication systems has not fundamentally transformed the way we go about producing and distributing goods and services. The basic principles of the division of labour based on narrow specialization, have been deepened and extended by the growing global application of assembly line processes for the production of equipment and the provision of services. *Managerial control remains unchanged.* Rigid control principles are applied to data entry, clerical, and operator services, and the range of expanding "information work" activities. In essence, current developments lead to the creation of global factories and offices with heightened capabilities for regimentation and control.

Bureaucracy

Communication and information systems generally centralize the power to make strategic or key decisions. Major financial and managerial decision-making is concentrated in fewer hands because these systems permit fewer people to understand the breadth and the detail of a complex organization like a transnational business or government bureaucracy. At the same time, operational responsibility is deconcentrated or dispersed over a wider geographical space and over more individuals.

However, there is little evidence to support the view that bureaucratic decentralization is on the increase. *Decentralization* disperses key decision-making power over a wider range of organizational members. Though the technology makes this possible, it is largely controlled by those who would lose power from decentralization. Consequently, communication and information systems are presently used to deepen and extend the tendency to bureaucratic centralization.

Deconcentration disperses operational responsibility. Information and, particularly, communication networks make it possible to disperse activities over a wide terrain and a scattered workforce. For example, clerical workers can enter data, file, phone, etc. from a neighborhood work centre or their homes, rather than from a central office. This process is often confused with decentralization which disperses decision-making *power*, not just operational responsibility. Communication and information systems do not disperse power, only work.

The Audience

The past century has seen an accelerating use of communication and information technology to build mass audiences of consumers of information, entertainment, and, more significantly, for the products advertised to support information and entertainment programming. One can identify two types of advertising activity. *Direct advertising* promotes products or ideas by direct payment for access to an audience for a period of time. *Indirect advertising* promotes products or ideas through the content and style of programming. A beer company advertises directly—i.e., buys direct access to an audience—by paying $750,000 for a thirty second spot on the Super Bowl. The Super Bowl also indirectly advertises ideas that support a particular form of consumption by a half-time performance that features leading performers, patriotic addresses and the display of military weaponry. Essentially, advertising promotes what Gaudemar (1979) calls the process of *mobilization*. People are mobilized for the purpose of packaging their attention for sale to advertisers (commodification) and for socializing them into particular sets of acceptable values (social control).

In the late nineteenth and early twentieth centuries, advertising grew with the need to build mass demand in societies oversupplied with goods as a result of mass production. In essence, advertising creates a new category of social grouping. In addition to the *public* person, actively engaged in deciding about the conduct of life in the local, regional or national community, and the *private* person, engaged in a relationship of human intimacy; there is the *audience,* in which people essentially permit their attention to be actively marketed in return for access to entertainment and information.

Communication and information systems deepen and extend the ability to package audiences and deliver them to those, such as product advertisers, who pay for audience attention. Mass print production/distribution, broadcasting, and the cinema, advanced the production of mass audiences. New communication and information systems deepen this because they expand the commercial potential of information and entertainment by permitting the packaging and repackaging of these products for instant global distribution. They extend this process by making it possible to package a more customized audience, rather than a mass one. This permits a buyer to select an audience whose attention is worth more (because it is more capable and more likely to consume a particular product or idea) than that of many members of a mass audience. Concretely, it is better to buy an upper-middle and upper class audience for BMW ads than to buy a mass audience.

Communication and information systems which contribute to the packaging of both information / entertainment *and* audiences increase the capability to mobilize people for commodification and social control.

Time

Earlier in this century, Lee de Forest, a major contributor to the development of radio, complained about the use of his invention to "break time" into "spots" to sell products. He felt that it was better to call commercials "stains" than spots. Communication and information systems presently do no more than refine this process by making it possible to measure time more accurately and monitor the social activity that flows through time. Again, these systems and the technology that embodies them make it possible to package time more efficiently and effectively. Time itself becomes a commodity.

In his book *Turing's Man,* (1984) Bolter offers a useful distinction between the classical and the contemporary view of time. The classical view, extending well into the medieval era, called it a cyclical process, measured in the annual cycle of the seasons and the generational reproduction of families and communities. With the rise of commerce, the commodity form, and wage labour, this changed because these social developments brought about the need for more precise time measurement. The development of the clock, chronicled by Landes (1983) and others, increased that precision, as did the precise division of the earth into time zones. With capitalism, time becomes a linear process, a commodity itself, to be measured and monitored with increasing exactitude.

Space

What remains of the common lands, so central a part of the precapitalist experience? The development of capitalism is a process of extending the market principle to land by incorporating even those areas set aside for common use. Counter tendencies to the commodification process do exist. Different levels of government serve as trustees over parkland, for example. But against these exceptions stands the overwhelming trend to make land the private property of individuals and, more typically, of large businesses. Communication and information systems advance this process.

The development of earth orbiting communications satellites makes possible the rapid distribution of information and entertainment worldwide, increasing the value of "space" itself as a source of revenue. Consequently, the United States leads a movement for the private development of outer space for commercial purposes while the US military leads in the use of outer space for military control. This direction makes even a satellite orbit, particularly the geosynchronous orbit used most effectively for communication purposes, into a marketable commodity.

Similarly, a movement exists to make the electromagnetic spectrum, the resource used for the transmission of radio, television and other electronic signals, into a marketable commodity. This is not a simple job because the characteristics of the spectrum require that any spectrum commodity take into account, not only the space occupied by the signal, but also the time it is transmitted, the signal strength and several other characteristics. This has not kept economists from proposing that such packages can be developed and sold to the highest bidder, for whatever use, in the open marketplace.

Export Processing Zones provide another example of commodifying social space. The EPZ is an area set aside by governments for processing foreign goods intended for export by foreign corporations. The land is an extension of commodified space, because its sole purpose is to use labour from cheaper local workers. In order to attract foreign business, fundamental laws—governing minimum wages, benefits, occupational health and safety, environmental protection, tarriffs, etc.—are watered down, when not completely eliminated. Communications and information systems make EPZs possible because they make it cost effective for companies to manage zones distant from the headquarters or the principle markets of the company. Moreover, many of these zones are used for processing communication and information technology products, including computer hardware, and data entered in an EPZ and shipped by communication satellite worldwide.

More specifically, within the domain of information space is the development of the *teleport*. Governments have permitted large businesses to occupy parcels of land near large cities as privileged information space. Teleports mirror the use of transportation facilities such as water ports and airports. Like these, the land for a teleport is devoted to integrating a range of communications facilities—satellite earth stations, microwave towers, etc.—enabling the most cost effective data processing and transmission capabilities for large users with the need and the financial resources necessary to pay for using the teleport's facilities.

"The Way We Were," Revisited
Communication and information, embodied in computers, communications satellites, optical fibre cables, high-definition displays, and other instrumentation, are used primarily to deepen and extend centuries old processes of commodification and control. They are not creating the conditions for social transformation and revolution. One ought not to be surprised by the reaction "Is that all there is?" Nevertheless, this reaction is partial, encompassing a first reaction to the early ebullience of information society optimists. For, even though deepenings and extensions of established processes are not the stuff of social transformation, they are likely, if not countered, to exacerbate the fundamental problems inherent in them. As a result, it is similarly justifiable to anticipate a response sometime in the future that wonders why—if computers, etc. were not the instruments of fundamental social change—society has changed, why are we so unlike the way we were. One can only conclude that forces promoting a deepening and extension of established patterns, can, by slow accretion if not by social transformation, produce fundamental changes in social life. This section explores two of the consequences that, over time, can create the conditions for these fundamental changes.

Growing Disparities

The use of communication and information systems creates the potential for increasing class, gender, regional, racial and national disparities. By speeding up the commodification process, these systems realize the ability to turn more goods and services, more human interchange, into market transactions. Pay-per call, per view, per bit of information, per keystroke, etc. eliminates the benefits powerless, poor people and regions enjoyed because of the technical limitations on making every transaction a financial one. In addition, communication systems give those exerting the greatest influence on the development of information commodities—chiefly large transnational businesses—the ability to shape markets and pricing mechanisms to their maximum benefit.

In addition to technical limitations on the ability to maximize dispari ties by class, region, etc., there have been limitations set down by government principle, arrived at as a result of extensive political struggle. As a result, we have public libraries, public education, public mail service, minimum wage rates, social security, etc. The growth of our ability to use communication and information systems to measure and monitor market activity with logical exactitude, supports those who contend that market rules should replace, as fully as possible, any government or other public intervention that helps what are identified as less powerful groups. This also supports the now popular view that public policy ought to be made by those with marketplace, rather than political, power.

The result, we observe, is the growth of a movement to deregulate and privatize—i.e., turn into market systems—social institutions, including those chiefly responsible for communication and information. This contrasts sharply with an alternative policy principle: public policy made by representative bodies, not markets, should meet, not market needs, but the information needs of citizens who value information, and control over the instruments that produce and distribute it.

The interests promoting reliance on the marketplace are among the most powerful worldwide: these not only include the world's largest communication and information businesses, but also, and perhaps more importantly, businesses and other large users, like the military, which recognize the centrality of communication and information to their activity. One of the central challenges to those who would develop alternatives to the marketplace as the sole determining influence is to establish a broad policy vision. Three elements of this vision are particularly significant.

First, an alternative is based not on what the market makes available, but rather on a determination of people's real communication and information *needs* in a society where these needs are growing and changing. Just as societies assess people's needs for housing, food, clothing, etc., systematic assessment of what mix of communication and information services is vital for a sufficiently skilled citizenry to live and work in a society increasingly dependent on communication and information-based skills.

Second, an alternative would start from a broadened conception of *literacy*. It is now popular to discuss the growing problem of illiteracy in Western societies and the need to enhance reading and comprehension skills. It is also popular to talk about the need for computer literacy, though with considerable vagueness. An alternative social policy would include a commitment to verbal, visual, and information literacy.

Paramount is the traditional commitment to learning how to read; futurists who argue that computers make reading skills obsolete are essentially calling for deskilling the society. A renewed commitment to literacy means saying more than this, it means teaching people how to read and understand the range of visual material we are exposed to regularly. This requires teaching how visual material, from video to film, from posters to advertisements, is put together and presented. Visual literacy includes learning the language video-makers use to say things with visual material—everything from how camera angles speak to the different messages that different editing transmits. By learning some of the language and skill of the visual, people would better understand, question, take apart, and reassemble for themselves the messages that the visual conveys. One need not subscribe to a music video channel to appreciate the benefit of education that makes us all less taken, and taken in by, the lure of the video.

Finally, literacy means being able to "read" the systems of electronic communication and information. It is *not* necessary to learn how a computer is put together or even how to program. It *is* important to know what these systems can *do*. How do we communicate with them? What communication possibilities do they enhance or diminish? What information potential is opened or closed by the development of these systems? What is the relationship of these systems to the rest of society? What are the social costs and benefits of developing them in different ways (the market, the government, in the community)?

The third component of a social policy for overcoming disparities in communication and information calls for a strengthened commitment to *universality*. Reliance on market principles is undermining the existing commitment to universal telephone service, postal service, library service, and others. Those who oppose this trend tend to seek a commitment to universal access to a particular instrumentality like the telephone. One cannot quarrel with a public effort to maintain such access; however, in an age when long dominant technologies are changing and evolving in symbiosis with others, it is no solution simply to maintain universal access to the telephone. A useful social policy alternative would allow universal access to change as communication and information systems and people's evolving needs for access to such systems change.

Universal service should mean universal access at affordable rates to telephone networks that provide a wide range of voice, information and signalling services. These would include, in addition to local and long distance telephone, electronic access to basic information about health care, education and other community services, opportunities to respond electronically to verbal communication, and opportunities to signal for emergency services, information and other vital communications. Universal service can be defined as access to a public network that provides a range of services. A basket of these services, available to everyone at an affordable rate and determined by the widest possible public participation, would evolve with the evolution of people's needs in communication and information services. This, the basic principle guiding the development of public education, would serve as a useful alternative to the market to guide the development of communication and information services.

Social Management
The issue of privacy receives considerable attention in a society where electronic information services and information transactions are increasingly prominent. The concern that information about an individual will be made available to others without permission for some commercial or control purposes, raises the problem of maintaining some degree of individual control over the distribution of personal information.

The concern about individual privacy is laudable, though it is sometimes used to prevent access to information that might be vital to some public end, like exposing a scandal. Nevertheless, the problem runs much deeper than this. It is not so much a question of violating individual privacy, but one of social management. Electronic communication and information systems—including those that measure and monitor phone transactions, bank deposits and withdrawals, credit or debit card purchases, keystroke counts in the workplace, etc.—gather massive amounts of information about the choices of large or small, amorphous or precisely defined, collectivities, for the purpose of more effectively managing and controlling their behaviour. Such management and control can take place with full protection for individual privacy. In fact, it is more likely that such privacy protections will be provided to eliminate public reticence about using electronic communication and information systems. Major interests in social management include governments that want to determine the best means for controlling social behaviour as well as companies eager to guarantee stable growth in consumption patterns and a cooperative workforce. The growth in the ability to measure and monitor information transactions advances the capabilities and reduces the costs of managing and controlling large populations.

Social management requires—and electronic systems make possible—the extension of surveillance, in breadth, across an entire society, and in depth, into what Foucault (1980) has called the *capillary level* of the social organism. The challenge is not how to protect individual privacy; but rather, how to reduce the threat to freedom, to a self-managed life, or to a life in which people choose their own form of collective management? Powerful electronic systems that measure and monitor transactions for marketing, managing and controlling groups of people pose a slowly building threat, not by transforming the fundamentals of society, but by building on processes of surveillance, marketing and control bound only by rapidly shrinking technological limits. These systems have the potential to isolate individuals from one another so much that market driven *social atomization* erodes the social community.

Here reliance on the marketplace for policy remedies is only likely to accelerate the process of social management. Current discussion about letting the market set a purchase price for individual privacy, eliminates a human right and makes it a marketable commodity, a right for those who can afford it. We need a new definition of self- and collective-determination that would restrict the gathering of information to those areas that communities and their elected representatives have determined to be in the public interest. When information on the group behaviour of workers or consumers is made a commodity and marketed to advance profit and control, the fundamental right of self-determination is violated (K. Wilson, 1988).

The protection of self-determination in a world of electronic communication and information systems is difficult, in part because of the value of individual privacy and the difficulty in seeing harm in the gathering of what appears to be anonymous data. "Is that all there is?" is a likely early response. Former U.S. Supreme Court Justice William O. Douglas gives an appropriate answer:

> As nightfall does not come at once, neither does oppression. In both instances, there is a twilight when everything remains seemingly unchanged.
> And it is in such twilight that we all must be most aware of change in the air—however slight—lest we become unwitting victims of the darkness. (*The New York Times,* November 29, 1987: I, 38.)

Chapter Two

Communications Studies in North America:

The Growth of Critical Perspectives

Introduction.
Social Change Influences Communications Research

> We found out and it wasn't years till we did, that all the bread we
> made for Decca was going into making little black boxes that go
> into American Air Force bombers to bomb North Vietnam. They
> took the bread we made for them and put it into the radar section
> of their business. When we found that out, it blew our minds. That
> was it. Goddamn, you find out you've helped to kill God knows
> how many thousands of people without knowing it.—Keith
> Richard, The Rolling Stones, (Chapple and Garofalo, 1977: xi)

Keith Richard and other media performers have come to understand
that mass media are more than simply entertainment, more than a way
to "kill time." The mass media are tightly connected to the centers of
power in capitalist society.

Over the past two decades, communications studies have begun to
take up both the substance and the spirit of Richard's concern. Research
has identified the dense web of connections and interconnections

41

among events and forces in society, apparently unrelated. What *does* Decca Records have to do with the war in Indochina? What does the Gulf+Western corporation, with its media empire, have to do with labour camps in the Dominican Republic? What about General Electric, which owns the NBC television network, and claims to "bring good things to life," while being one of the largest weapons manufacturers in the world, a major contributor to the "Star Wars" program?

The growth of critical communications research responds to the growth of communication and information systems in the post-World War II era. Four societal developments are especially significant:

1. The growth of transnational business;
2. The spread of mass consumption;
3. The expansion of government, particularly of the military;
4. The rise of movements of national, racial, ethnic, and gender liberation.

Global Business
In the 1950s, Galbraith (1958) and others singled out the growth of large business as the major change in the post-World War II economy. The process of merger and acquisition accelerated to the point where, today, most industries are shaped by companies that control several different businesses (horizontal integration) or various stages in processes specific to one business (vertical integration). For example, Bell Canada Enterprises grew from simply providing telephone service to a company that performs management consulting, offers electronic information services and other businesses not related to telephone service. Sears is no longer simply a catalogue company with retail and mail order outlets, but sells banking and real estate services, rents cars, and performs a variety of other, largely electronic, services.

Over the past two decades, international business has grown as well because companies see the opportunity in taking advantage of profitable markets for labour, raw materials, capital, and large numbers of potential consumers.

Large, integrated companies doing business in many countries require sophisticated communication and information systems to maintain centralized control over the range of business activities scattered around the world. Business requires communications and information systems far more extensive (can reach anywhere in the world), reliable (not prone to failure), secure (not subject to interception), and cost efficient than have heretofore been available. Specifically, transnational companies need *computers* to process large amounts of data into information that is usable by any part of the company in any location. They need *telecommunications* systems, like telephone systems linked with state of the art fibre optic cable or communications satellites, to distribute messages instantaneously. These messages would include everything from the number of checks an international bank like the Bank of Montreal processes in a given day, to advertising for the latest in children's fashions. Furthermore, they need *display* systems, like high-definition screens, whether a television or a computer screen, to present messages, including information, graphics, and video, in a clear and attention grabbing fashion.

The international expansion of business, for both the production and distribution of goods and services, has brought about national and global systems of information and communication. Critical communications research pays careful attention to these developments by identifying their economic, political, social and cultural consequences, and by situating them within a general perspective on the development of capitalist society.

Mass Consumption
Alongside the expansion of transnational business, the growth of mass consumption has contributed to the formation of global networks of computers, communications satellites, and other sophisticated technologies.

Modern business, always interested in producing mass audiences of consumers, uses research and development to shape technologies that accomplish this. Television is the foremost contemporary electronic technology for cultivating audiences and delivering them to advertisers. In just over a decade, television evolved from a curiosity piece for the rich (there were just a million sets in use across North America in 1948) to a nearly universal staple in living rooms throughout the continent (Barnouw, 1975).

In essence, business used television to reshape mass leisure. Television gave advertisers the opportunity to reach huge audiences regularly, and in receptive settings, with messages about products and, generally through these products, with messages about consumption as the centerpiece of the American Way of Life. In convenience and accessibility, television built on newspapers, the cinema, and radio. Critical research has identified television's accelerationg ability to build mass audiences for mass consumption and thereby advance the ability of business to engage in social mobilization on an unprecedented scale.

The Government
The expansion of both the production and consumption ends of business was aided by, and helped to bring about, a substantial increase in government activity. The government increasingly took on the role of active manager of the conflicts and problems of an expanding, increasingly complex, world business order.

These political functions required substantial investment in government information and communications systems and, in North America, a regulatory structure to oversee the development of private forms of communication.

Military requirements generally headed the list of government communication and information priorities. Military expansion required, as much or even more than transnational business, the creation of sophisticated information and intelligence gathering and rapid, efficient, and secret communications networks worldwide. Waging war, whether to stop indigenous revolutions or to prevail in a nuclear confrontation requires complex computer / communication technologies and networks.

Government also needed a regulatory and policy structure to oversee an industry becoming increasingly vital to business and military interests, while increasingly subject to major jolts of technological change, and subject to the uncertainties of international competition. The current acceleration of global markets depending on communication and information technology raises the problems of policy and regulation to the point of creating international political organizations.

Social Liberation
Critical communications studies recognize the significance of the mass media and information technology for movements for social change. Much critical research charts the complex relationships of media to the struggles of women, of ethnic and national minorities, peace and environmental movements, and workers' struggles.

While these movements have learned how to use the media, their own and mainstream, in expanding their reach and building the movement, reliance on media, particularly newer computer technologies, produces a form of technology dependence or media consciousness that can undermine movement goals. This is particularly the case with mainstream media whose seductive appeal—the ability to reach large numbers of people instantaneously—invites co-optation and internal disruption.

Communications research has also felt the influence of international movements, such as liberation struggles in the Third World, that have used the media. International communications research has identified the efforts of Third World movements to demystify the West's ideological offensive to achieve a "free flow of information." Studies have documented how the free flow concept masks Western domination and undermines the sovereignty of non-Western peoples. Moreover, this research has supported efforts at the United Nations and other international agencies to build what Third World leaders call a New International Information and Communication Order.

Whose Research?: Administrative vs. Critical Approaches

Media Technique, Marketing, and Policy Research

The growth of transnational enterprises, the spread of a mass consumption society, the expansion of the state, and the actions of social liberation movements worldwide have all influenced the development of critical communications research. On the other hand, the nature of education in communications programs and the strategic significance of mainstream mass media and information technology research have limited the influence of the critical tradition.

Academic communications programs tend to contain a far greater vocational orientation than programs in the social sciences and humanities. In fact, Schools of Communication generally developed outside the liberal arts, with the explicit aim of training journalists, advertising and public relations specialists, film makers, and broadcasters. These programs tend to emphasize the transmission of traditional craft skills as they have been modified, in some cases substantially, by new electronic technologies. The term "critical studies" here generally refers to literary criticism and its application to film and video.

With a few exceptions, research within these programs means market studies, assessments of advertising campaigns, public opinion surveys, and other forms useful to business or to political organizations. This is an extension of the skills orientation of most communications programs. Even those who are not identified as media practitioners are schooled in skills that offer job opportunities in the research departments of media companies, or, more generally, the marketing and media divisions of large corporations. The goal is to head a marketing department, direct corporate communications, or, for the more technically-minded, take a position in the new field of Information Resources Management.

Media policy research is a less significant though growing variation on this vocational orientation. Generally concerned with the legal and economic dimensions of regulation, much of this research is constrained by the formalism that established legal structures and neo-classical economics imposes on research of all kinds. Focussing on narrow interpretations of law or the demand curves of mainstream economics leaves a blind spot that critical studies of power, social control, and national and international conflict often address. Since these issues are typically considered inappropriate for communications research, they are insufficiently addressed. Rather, mainstream policy research leads people into careers or consultancies with the legal departments of companies or with any of a number of government regulatory, commerce, public relations, or intelligence agencies that deal with the media.

Back in 1941, one of the founders of modern public opinion research, Paul Lazarsfeld, identified this mainstream conservative tradition as *administrative research,* research conducted in the service of a particular organizational interest. He distinguished administrative research from *critical research,* studies that aim to uncover how and why the media serve those in power. Lazarsfeld made this distinction explicit in an article co-authored with the noted sociologist Robert Merton. The article is particularly interesting because almost all of their massive research output—including shelves of work on public opinion, advertising campaigns, the impact of propaganda, etc.—lies squarely in the administrative tradition. As this statement indicates, they were well aware of what administrative research meant:

> But clearly, the social effects of the media will vary as the system of ownership and control varies. Thus to consider the social effects of American mass media is to deal only with the effects of these media as privately owned enterprises under project oriented management.
>
> ... Big business finances the production and distribution of mass media. And, all intent aside, he who pays the piper calls the tune. (Lazarsfeld and Merton, 1949)

Until recently, most communications research followed Lazarsfeld and Merton's pattern by ignoring their conclusion and pursuing an administrative approach. Attracted in part by lucrative research funding from business and government *and* instructed in a university training system that accepted the administrative approach as the only perspective on the field, communications scholars served power in various research pursuits. These included helping advertisers and manufacturers understand audience behaviour so that they might better influence purchasing decisions. It also included research on public opinion formation that would better enable a Canadian political party to market its candidate or a US backed dictatorship in Latin America to undermine an opposition movement. Rather than show how the media serves power, scholars were more interested in serving power themselves.

North America offered few exceptions to administrative research in the 1950s and 1960s. Nevertheless, important exceptions have become a major springboard for contemporary critical research. These include preeminently Dallas Smythe's work on the political economy and regulation of US media (1957) and Schiller's *Mass Communication and American Empire* (1969), a comprehensive analysis of how media companies in traditional (broadcasting) and new technologies (communications satellites) advanced the broader interests of American political, economic, and military control. Additionally, Guback's *The International Film Industry* (1969), gives a detailed political economic analysis of how US film companies profit from their ability to shape a global system of production, distribution and exhibition.

Critical Research in Europe and Latin America

Critical communications research which flourished in Europe and Latin America has contributed substantially to the growth of critical research in North America.

In Europe, Murdock and Golding (1974), Garnham (1979), Hamelink (1983), Nordenstreng (1974), Mattelart and Siegelaub (1979), and Webster and Robins (1986) offer good examples that have influenced the development of a critical *political economy* in North America. Specifically, these studies have emphasized social class, the power of transnational business, the militarization of technology, and the contradictory relationships of the state to the mass media and telecommunications systems in Europe.

European research has also influenced the study of media content and impact. The work of Williams (1975, 1981), Hall (1982), the Glasgow Group (1977, 1980), Mattelart and Siegelaub (1983), and Enzensberger (1974), among others, has led North Americans to question the use of traditional approaches to *cultural studies*. For example, there is widespread acknowledgement that approaches such as content analysis, which rely on numerical counts of verbal and pictoral information, are severely limited means of analyzing culture. European research is concerned with the historical, particularly class, forces that shape contemporary culture. This prompts Williams to ask about the relationship of economic upheaval in nineteenth century Britain to the rise of modern advertising (Williams, 1980: 170-195). It leads Mattelart and Siegelaub to assess the link between traditions of class opposition and struggle to the production of alternative popular culture (Mattelart and Siegelaub, 1983: 11-100).

In a similar fashion, North American scholars have drawn extensively on the contribution of Latin American research in both political economy and cultural studies. The overwhelming impact of US media companies on the mass media in Latin America has spurred the formation of several centers for media research in Latin America. Notable among these is ILET (the Latin American Institute for Transnational Studies), based in Mexico City, and IPAL (the Institute for Latin America) in Lima, Peru. These and other centers, strengthened by the support of United Nations agencies such as UNESCO, have served as international fora for discussion of problems of media and information dependency in the Third World.

Representative work on the political economy of Latin American communications draws heavily on perspectives that emphasize the structure and consequences of Latin American *dependency* on the US media system. Of particular influence is the research of Beltran and Fox (1979), Janus (1981), Rada (1981), Roncagliolo and Janus (1981), Reyes Matta (1981), Schnitman (1981), and Somavia (1981). Latin American research on mass media culture also takes off from various models of cultural imperialism. Here, Dorfman (1983) and Dorfman / Mattelart (1975) have been strong influences on North American critical cultural studies. By showing how transnational companies, from advertising firms to computer companies, have come to dominate Latin American communications, they convey a sense of the enormous transformation required to democratize communications systems. Atwood and McAnany (1986) have put together important contributions to both political economic and cultural studies in Latin American research in a collection of studies addressed an audience in the developed world.

The Political Economy of Communication

There is no ideal sorting device for categorizing critical communications research. A useful, though by no means flawless, division is to distinguish between research that concentrates on the political economy of media and work that focusses on media content and culture. Put simply, political economy starts from questions about ownership and control of media institutions, identifies processes of media production, distribution and reception, and analyzes the connections between means of communication and more general means of production and reproduction in a capitalist world economy. Cultural studies research starts with media content and form, analyzes the impact of these on consciousness and ideological production, and links the production of media to the wider ideological system.

This section on political economy focusses on three major themes in critical research: the business of communication, the relationship of the business to government, and conflicts centered on opposition to the dominant system of communication.

The Business of Communication

History
The powerful changes taking place in the world political economy of communication and the contribution of critical scholars in Europe and Latin America have helped North American researchers to build a significant body of work on the business of communication.

A major starting point of research here is the influence successive revolutions in the means of communication have had on the overall process of growth or capital accumulation. This research takes off from a point that Marx made prominent in Volume 1 of *Capital*:

> The revolution in the method of production in industry and agriculture, likewise necessitated a revolution in the general conditions of the social process of production, that is to say in the means of communication and transport. In a society whose pivots were, first, small-scale agriculture, with its subsidiary home industries, and, secondly, urban handicraft, the means of communication and transport were utterly inadequate to the requirements of the manufacturing period, with its extended division of labour and of the workers, and its colonial markets; communications and transport, therefore had to be revolutionized, and were in fact revolutionized. (Marx, 1972: 106)

Historical research has shown how capitalism incorporated communication and information technology into its fundamental processes of production. Now, capitalist economies are critically dependent on communications systems for the daily operation of domestic and international industries.

The most substantial historical work has concentrated on the means of *mass* communication. D. Schiller (1981) and Eisenstein (1979) have shown how newspapers emerged from the need for reliable business communication. The early press provided information and a record of data on prices, markets, commodities, etc. From this base, newspapers evolved to become a mass medium directed to a burgeoning working class of consumers. The press helped to create the mass consumption society so vital to the absorption of mass production, particularly critical in the late nineteenth century when capitalist economies were periodically racked by jolts of overproduction.

The press directed its mass circulation audience to products through the development of advertising. Ewen's book, *Captains of Consciousness* (1976), provides a social history of advertising that identifies the ways media restructured the social relations of consumption, drawing the home into near complete dependence on the capitalist marketplace. Ewen shows how companies wed science and technology to establish systems of *public relations* and *mass marketing* to break traditional family and household relations and thereby make the entire home a marketable commodity. In essence, market economies give rise to advertiser-funded print media that makes possible the vast expansion of production and distribution. (Leiss, Kline, Jhally, 1986) Further expansion came with successive waves of mass electronic media, chiefly film, radio, and television.

Guback (1982) and Wasko (1982) produced detailed analyses of how a few firms with close links to finance capital came to dominate US film production. In addition, these companies, through complex networks of legal, financial, and political control shaped the global film industry. As a result, transnational companies, backed completely by the US government, made Hollywood commercial feature films the world model for entertainment.

As early as 1918, the US government passed the Webb-Pomerene Export Trade Act which permitted US film companies to combine forces to fix prices and divide foreign markets, activities that, if practiced domestically, would violate anti-trust statutes. From that time on, the Motion Picture Export Association, the government backed cartel representative, has used the combined economic power of US film production and distribution companies to spread their movies and movie houses around the world.

One important means of creating a US-led transnational film culture builds on an important characteristic of film and video: the ease of reproduction after initial production. After making a profit in the dometic marketplace, US companies have distributed their movies and television programs internationally at well under the costs of production. The result of this form of "dumping" is to stifle sources of indigenous film production which cannot hope to compete with a US film that cost $10 million to produce, but which is made available in the Third World, or a more developed country like Canada, for a few thousand dollars. Moreover, US government aid programs support foreign media producers that adopt Western models and become regional distributors of US programming or produce programs, such as the *telenovela* in Latin America, that mirrors, in this case, the US soap opera.

Similar historical developments have propelled US commercial broadcasting to a dominant world influence. Building on Barnouw's important descriptive history of broadcasting (1975), Mander (1978), Mosco (1979), Smythe (1981), and Winston (1986) have shown how the three dominant broadcasting networks and their corporate and government allies built mass market commercial radio and television into the dominant mode of audience production and reproduction in North America. This research shows how successive revolutions in the means of electronic media, from AM radio through to colour television, were promoted by a small group of large firms, well integrated into corporate and military power. These companies—particularly, AT&T, General Electric, Westinghouse, RCA, CBS, and ABC—built huge commercial media empires and protected their gains by building close ties to government. The alliance with government, particularly their ability to make the link between their success and national security interests, were especially useful when corporate media power was challenged by educational, labour, and other non-profit efforts to build publicly controlled broadcasting stations and networks. As a result of their success, transnational business has been able to transform the public sphere into a marketplace in which the audience is a principle commodity.

With important exceptions, historical research on point-to-point electronic communication or *telecommunication*, is most likely to be found within books of wider scope such as those of the political economists Harold Innis (1972) and Dallas Smythe (1981) This research focusses on how telecommunications contributed to business expansion, in turn propelling more intense technological development. Significant here is: Du Boff's research, documenting the relationship of the telegraph to business demand and market growth in the nineteenth century (1984), Danilean's classic account of AT&T's rise to monopoly status (1939), and Babe's study of the Canadian telecommunications industry (forthcoming).

The rise of computers inspired renewed interest in telecommunications history. In particular, computers linked to telecommunications systems, create powerful information processing networks that permit the instantaneous global movement of electronic data and messages. Noble's work on the history of computers and related technology identifies the significance of military/corporate control over computer development for the design and use of computer systems (1984). The twin goals of extending managerial control (Webster and Robins, 1986) and automating warfare (Mosco, 1987b) continue to shape computer systems.

With historical research providing the foundation for a critical political economy of communication, researchers examined the process of business concentration that is part of the global shift from competitive to monopoly capitalism.

Business Concentration
Research on the rise of press conglomerates, director interlocks, and the financial ties of large *newspaper* firms demonstrates why All the News That Fits is a more appropriate logo for *The New York Times* than All the News That's Fit To Print (Dreier, 1982; Bagdikian, 1988; Canada, 1981). According to Bagdikian, twenty-seven business firms control most of the production and distribution of information and entertainment in the United States. These companies serve as a private, unelected Ministry of Information, gatekeepers governed by the sole criterion of maximizing profit.

Janus has detailed business concentration in the *advertising* industry. Though the focus of her research is on the global impact of this industry, she offers important information on the extent of vertical and horizontal integration of these firms and their links to firms in other industries. For example, she shows how the mass media in Latin America are dominated by large, integrated, and mainly US advertising firms. Consequently, these media contain more advertising than anywhere in the developed world. Print and television media devote from 30 to 50 per cent of their space and time to advertising. Moreover, greater than 60 per cent of women's magazine ads and 80 per cent of television commercials feature products promoted by transnational business: soap, drugs, cosmetics, tobacco, processed foods, and alcoholic beverages (Janus, 1984, 1986). She concludes:

> The same firms developing the marketing uses of the new communication technologies control the economies of many Third World countries and dominate their mass media systems (1984: 68-69).

Guback (1982, 1987) and Wasko (1982) analyze corporate concentration in the US film industry. Pendakur (1984) analyzes the impact of this integrated US control on the Canadian film business and identifies the mechanisms by which corporate concentration limits what is available to film audiences across North America. Shore (1983) provides a similar analysis for the political economy of popular music by identifying links among recording, radio and video companies worldwide. Mosco (1987a) and Babe (1979) have identified similar processes at work in the broadcasting area for the US and Canada respectively.

The political economy of corporate concentration and control has expanded to include the newer technologies built on computers, communications satellites, and high capacity cable systems. H. Schiller (1984a), Horowitz (1986), Meehan (1988), and Webster and Robins (1986) situate the major participants in business and military data processing and communication.

Global Expansion and International Division of Labour
The tendency to business concentration makes possible the global expansion of monopoly capitalism and the creation of an international division of labour. Communications research has been particularly extensive on this issue because of the worldwide debate, focussed by several United Nations agencies, on the need to redress the overwhelming domination of Western media and information technology. Critical research has demonstrated the widespread penetration of Western news services (Associated Press, Reuters, Agence-France Press) worldwide. Similar research on advertising and magazines (Janus, 1986), children's literature (Dorfman, 1983), film (Pendakur, 1984), radio (Fejes, 1986; Frederick, 1984), and television (McAnany, 1984, and Atwood and McAnany, 1986) identifies the spread of mass media content, models, and technology from the dominant core to the dependent

periphery.

Global expansion is accomplished in a variety of ways. These include exporting media products, often at well under market costs, setting up Western branch plant companies in lesser developed societies, media education programs (often related to general aid programs), the pressures of international advertisers and financiers, and the generally strong promotion of Western media models. These pressures remain even when a nation, like Brazil or Mexico, sets up its own national public or private media system (Atwood and McAnany, 1986).

The expansion of mass media firms into the Third World advances the general international expansion of business. In addition to the obvious addition of new members to what is now a system of global consumer markets, the mass media provide a vehicle to sell *a way of life* as well as specific products. It is a way of life that includes support for private rather than public enterprise, for competitive individualism over social cooperation, and for applying sophisticated technology to consumption and leisure as well as to production.

Transnational companies, particularly those taking advantage of advanced microelectronics technologies, have begun to build an international division of labour. Global markets for labour parallel global markets for consumers. Computer communications systems give international companies the ability to locate their operations wherever costs are lowest without sacrificing centralized control. As a result, Control Data, or a similar company, can hire workers, mainly women and young girls, to assemble microelectronics components in South Korea or Malaysia at under $1 (US) an hour. American Airlines can take advantage of communications satellite links to hire data entry workers in Barbados for about $2 (US) an hour. Moreover, the same microelectronics technology monitors and measures every bit of work performed, tightening transnational corporate control over its international labour force (Clement, 1988; Nash and Fernandez-Kelly, 1983, and Sussman, 1988).

Information for Sale and for Control

Research in the political economy tradition has tended to describe the mass media/information sector as an industry in its own right and as a major force in the general expansion and centralization of business throughout the capitalist world (Webster and Robins, 1986). On this point, there has not been much fundamental disagreement with mainstream research. More recently, critical research has turned to a major transformation in the product of the new technology: *information*. This is leading critical scholars to question fundamental points of reference within mainstream thinking.

As Chapter One showed, scholars have thought about information in three different ways. Information can be a particular form of *technology*, responsible for processing, e.g. the computer; or distributing, e.g. the communications satellite. One can also think about information as a *system*, comprised of inputs, coding procedures, noise levels, and outputs. Shannon and Weaver's classic description of information theory as a system for understanding the transmission of messages from sender to receiver is a principle example of information as system (Shannon and Weaver, 1959). One can also identify information as a *resource*, not dissimilar from other natural resources like atmosphere, fossil fuels, and metals. The primary difference between the information resource and these other resources is that information is not depletable. In other words, information does not appear to be used up in the process of consumption. Nevertheless, information resource theorists see information, along with raw materials and energy, as fundamental building blocks of social life (Oettinger, 1980).

In contrast to these general ways of thinking about information, critical communications research identifies information as a *commodity* and as a form of social *control*. Though it is still possible to think about information as technology, system, and resource, critical research argues that seeing information as a commodity or a marketable product and as a form of controlling or managing social life, provide a more concrete, historically specific, and accurate conception of information.

Under the shaping influence of business and government, particularly the military, communication and information technology has advanced the ability to *measure* and *monitor* information trasactions more precisely, rapidly, and accurately than ever before. These technologies can do this because advances in electronics make it possible to divide a message (whether a phone call, a batch of bank check numbers, or a set of military codes) into discrete signals or bits. In this electronic bit form, messages can be measured to determine a quantitative value for a component of information. We can literally quantify the amount of information (in kilobits) and the rate at which a particular transmission medium (copper wire, optical fibre, etc) can move the information from one place to another (kilobits per second or kbs, the bit rate). Measurement, as classical theorists as diverse as Marx and Bentham showed, is vital to making something a commodity. Measurement makes possible discrete packaging of a marketable product and the ability to keep track of when it has been consumed. The application of communication and information technology helps us to solve the information resource theorists' problem by enabling us to make this seemingly undepletable resource into a commodity with definable markets subject to a price system (D. Schiller, 1988). Nevertheless, though electronic applications help to solve the problem of making information a commodity, they do not simply *determine* the value of information. Value is also influenced by social forces which identify some information as more valuable than others, irrespective of our ability to measure information bits and the flows of these bits through communication media.

An entire information industry has grown around the ability to package, repackage, buy and sell information. Traditional businesses such as banking, insurance, and retailing have set up subsidiaries and divisions devoted to marketing information produced by the parent company in the course of conducting its established business. Demographic, consumer preference, attitudinal, financial background, and other information can be packaged in forms that make it sufficiently profitable for conglomerates like Citicorp, Sears, and American Express to identify themselves as information businesses. The ability to measure information transactions makes it possible for telephone, computer, interactive cable, or other so-called electronic services companies to charge by the minute or the page of information provided on the screen. Similarly, one can quantify and link to wages, the amount of work an individual information worker performs.

Technology can also keep track of and therefore *monitor* more accurately and effectively than ever before, information transactions. Increasingly, integrated computer, communication and video systems make it easier to observe and act on those observations, whether they be the amount of time it takes for an operator to answer a call, a secretary to type a letter, a mental patient to complete a meal, or the number of loans a bank manager arranges in a week. The technology increases the opportunities for surveillance of all human activity, enhancing the potential to control and manage an increasingly complex society. Bentham's dream of the all-seeing surveillance system, the Panopticon, which Michel Foucault has raised to the level of a central image of our time, can now be realized electronically.

Communication and the State
Traditional research has usually concentrated on the role of government as regulator of communications. The emphasis is on agencies formally

charged with the responsibility to oversee prices, industry structure, media content, etc. Major examples are the Federal Communications Commission and the Canadian Radio-television and Telecommunications Commission.

Critical research identifies the ways this formal regulatory process generally serves the interests of communications companies and large corporate users of communications systems. It also shows how these agencies have been the arenas of major conflicts between these companies and public interest groups. The latter have sought to use the regulatory arena to make the government live up to such promises as universal access to telecommunications at affordable rates and fairness, access, and diversity in the broadcasting system. As well, current research on the regulatory process has shown that the contraction of regulation merely serves to eliminate the potential for opposition just when the public interest lobby was opening up the process to wider intervention. In other words, the government response to some degree of regulatory pluralism was to eliminate regulation. (Mosco, 1987a)

While critical research acknowledges the significance of the regulatory process, it also recognizes that the role of government in the communications system extends to much more than regulation. H. Schiller's early research (1969) identified the significance of communication for government policies that advance the growth of capitalism, the popular legitimacy of the economic system, and the opportunities to use technology for social control. For example, he shows how the US government used its anti-Soviet campaign of the 1950s and 60s to fund a space program whose major benefits went to large private companies like RCA and AT&T. Moreover, he shows how government has retained control over the technology for the development of military communication and surveillance. He further demonstrates how the US government established international agencies such as Intelsat, the global communications satellite consortium, to maintain US government and corporate control of this strategic sector until it could be turned over to more complete private sector control. The government accomplished this by setting up a government-sponsored company, Comsat, to represent US political and corporate interests in Intelsat, much as it did forty years earlier in setting up RCA as its "chosen instrument" to defeat British control of international communication. Despite the participation of over a hundred nations, voting in the Intelsat organization is based on the amount of satellite usage. As a result, control resides with a small bloc of Western nations, led by the United States.

This pattern of Western control in the face of opposition from Third World and socialist states has also been mirrored through research on numerous international bodies such as the International Bureau of Informatics, (Mahoney, 1988), UNESCO, the Organization for Economic Cooperation and Development (H. Schiller, 1976, 1984), the World Bank (Sussman, 1988) and the International Telecommunication Union (Smythe, 1986).

As the modern state is usually the single largest user of media and information technology, consequently, government procurement decisions—particularly those involving the military and policy decisions on industry structure, pricing, and the general extent of regulation—have important economic ramifications (D. Schiller, 1982; Markusen, Hall, and Glasmeier, 1986 point out the American example).

The means of communication can also be direct forms of legitimizing government and corporate activity. Research has examined the many ways the state uses media to mobilize popular consent and to stifle opposition. Demac documents Reagan Administration policies restricting the flow of information that might counter government domestic and foreign policies (1988). Rips (1981) shows how the FBI and other intelligence agencies used alternative media, including campus newspapers, radio stations, newsletters, posters, etc., to undermine and divide opposition social movements in the 1960s and 70s.

Frederick (1984) and Fejes (1986) document the use of government and private radio stations in the US for international propaganda purposes. Frederick's work is particularly interesting because it suggests that propaganda programs are difficult to control and are subject to counterattacks—in this case from Cuba—in an information war. Fejes' research suggests that propaganda and profit are two dimensions of government and corporate communications policy. Historical conditions determine who takes the lead, government or business, and which policy is in the forefront, ideology or profit-making.

In the late 1980s, as state oversight and regulation of electronic media in the United States receded, corporations became more directly involved in the use of media for ideological purposes. Examples range from advertisements that promote the company itself or identify it with "the American way," to direct corporate investment in news programming, such as Biznet, a national news network owned and operated by the US Chamber of Commerce.

Media and information technology have also become integral to police and military activity. Research here has focussed on the connection of media institutions to domestic and foreign intelligence agencies, the use of the media to promote militarism, and the indispensable role of computer/communications systems for advanced weapons systems— including nuclear weapons and the systems that comprise the Strategic Defense Initiative or "Star Wars" project (Chomsky and Herman, 1979, 1988; Bamford, 1982; Mosco, 1987b).

Communication and Opposition Movements

Research into the political economy of communication has concentrated on how business and government, particularly the military, shape and use mass media and information technology mainly for profit and control. There is a smaller though growing body of research on the contradictions inherent in using communication for profit and control, and on outright opposition.

Gitlin's *The Whole World is Watching* (1980), an analysis of media and the student movement, is a good exemplar of research that emphasizes conflicts and contradictions in the communication system. This book shows how a radical student movement acted in such a way as to attract widespread television coverage and thereby spread its message. Gitlin effectively shows how this reliance on established media led movement leaders to bend their strategies to a medium which called for increasing levels of radicalism—particularly of the sort that made entertaining television—to justify coverage. As a result, he suggests, groups such as Students for a Democratic Society (SDS) fell into decline because they made tactical decisions based on media criteria rather than political considerations, and so mistook media attention for popular support.

Demac (1984) offers another version of conflict-oriented communications research in her analysis of Reagan Administration information policies. She examines conflicts within the US government, mainly between the White House and the Congress, and between the government and citizens groups concerned about losing access to information. Under the gloss of budget-cutting and national security concerns, the Reagan Administration curtailed access to government information by closing access completely or by commercializing the information and thereby increasing its price to put it out of the reach of most people. While opposition succeeded in overturning the more egregious cutbacks, such as the attempt to severely curtail service at the chief national library, the Library of Congress, in a more recent work (1988), Demac shows how the Reagan White House effectively manipulated the media, mainly television, so that particularly painful or controversial policy decisions would be received in the best possible gloss. She concludes that the so-called "Teflon President" was able to resist telling attacks more because his Administration mastered the media than because of his unique personality.

There is also a growing body of research on conflicts that result from the influence of US media worldwide and between the often conflicting interests of national and international business. In Europe and Latin America, for example, historical struggles have left a complex mix of commercial and public communications media as the site of conflicts for control (Mosco and Wasko, 1984; Atwood and McAnany, 1986). Also documented are the struggles of workers and organized labour over such things as workers' rights in the media industry, the presentation of workers and trade unions in the mass media, and the efforts of organized labour to use media and new information technologies to expand their power (Mosco and Wasko, 1983). Critical research has also identified the nature of conflicts in the media of English Canada (Smythe, 1981; Hardin, 1985), French Canada (Raboy, 1984), France (Freiberg, 1981), and the Third World (Tran Van Dinh, 1987).

Communication and Culture

Form and Content

An extensive and growing body of research on the form and content of communication follows from three themes in critical analysis, particularly, critical studies influenced by the tradition of Western Marxism.

The first theme relates preeminent or *hegemonic* ideas to the interests of a dominant class. North American research here has flowed from political economists interested in the production of a dominant class ideology, and in the work of structuralism, particularly that of Habermas (1973) and Althusser (1971).

The second major emphasis in critical cultural studies identifies how ruling ideologies oppose movements for social change. This work reflects an interest in broadening the scope of analysis to account for oppositional or *counter-hegemonic* culture.

Finally, some have taken the next step, focussing directly on how movements to oppose and *transform* the established system have used the media and new communication technologies.

The Ruling Ideas

Most work on media content starts from the premise that the ruling ideas are those of a ruling class. Herbert Schiller's *The Mind Managers* (1973) offers an early model of this research for North American scholars. The book is one of the first to address the question of what *kind* of "information society" are we creating. It ranges widely—over advertising and public relations, Disney Productions, *National Geographic* magazine, and other cultural and informational media—to suggest that positive images of private property, free enterprise, individual acquisitiveness, militarism, and the superiority of the white race are spread throughout the world in light, attractive, and easily accessible cultural packages.

Several research projects have followed directly from this perspective. Ewen (1976) describes how advertising and public relations built a mass consumption society based on scientific marketing, matching the application of scientific management in the office. These businesses reshaped family and gender relations and legitimized a culture centered on the home as marketplace (*see also* Leiss, Kline, and Jhally, 1986). Rosenberg has examined the ways business and government joined in spreading these values throughout the world (1982). Her work is unique in that it shows how this took place under the guidance of what she calls the Promotional State, a collection of government agencies and businesses promoting capitalism with the assistance of any new broadcasting and telecommunications technologies such as radio, television, the telephone, undersea cables, and communications satellites.

Similar analyses of ideological production are provided by Mander (1978) for television, Gruneau (1983) for sports, and Allen (1985), Butsch (1985), and Toles (1985) for hobbies and games. These works suggest the need to broaden our conception of media to incorporate the many different means—from hockey to player pianos, from model airplanes to video games—that business uses in assimilating and repackaging authentic human needs into a marketable, if distorted, form.

Considerable research points out the many ways news media content directly reflects a class ideology. Parenti provides an introductory guide on how the media, particularly print journalism, *invent* rather than report on reality (1986). Most of the specific research in this area concentrates on coverage of international events or international media generally. Preeminent examples are Chomsky and Herman (1979) on news coverage of Third World revolutions, Herman on western disinformation campaigns (1982) and demonstration elections in Latin America (1984), Leggett (1978) on how *The New York Times* covered the overthrow of the Allende government in Chile, and Chorbajian (1985) on the media and Olympic Games boycotts. This work is particularly valuable in unmasking the established media's claim to objectivity. Indeed, one concludes that objectivity itself bears little relationship to truth. It is, rather, a set of social practices, even ceremonial rituals, that are used to produce an acceptable gloss on the political ends of media coverage.

North American research has already begun to look explicitly at the relationship of social class to the media (Butsch and Glennon, 1983). This research has critiqued the sheer invisibility of working people and their trade unions in the mass media, whether in an entertainment or informational frame. Invisibility maintains stereotypes as effectively as misrepresentation (Rollings, 1983; Knight, 1982).

A distinct group of works within the ruling ideology perspective is set apart by its concern for uncovering meanings revealed in the form and content of a specific medium. This interest in close textual analyis draws heavily on the work of structuralism and semiotics, emphasizing less the social relations of media production and reception, and more on how form and content structure hegemony. Among the leading work here is Dorfman's (1983) semiotic analysis of children's stories. *The Empire's Old Clothes* starts from the premise that childhood can be regarded as a form of underdevelopment, literally, in the individual sense, and figuratively in the social sense. Popular culture, for example, reflects this idea in form and content. The popular stories of the elephant Babar evoke the problems of growing up as a person *and* as a society under colonial or neo-colonial rule. Similarly, Disney stories and the Lone Ranger succeed in packaging the values of greed, individualism, and the authoritarian state in attractive, comic and dramatic forms. Furthermore, *Readers Digest* extends the infantalization of the reader into adult life, holding out the promise that one need never grow up to become an adult reader. Dorfman sandwiched his stories about stories within a discussion of conflicts—his own included—brought about by the effort to overcome the power of neo-colonial rule in Chile and to build a democratic socialist society.

Comparable research can be found on advertising (Leiss, Kline, and Jhally, 1986), film (Nichols, 1981), and television (Gitlin, 1982). Broadening the definition of media, Winston (1986) presents a structural analysis of technological development in the information society. Arguing that radio, television, the computer, and the communication satellite have all followed the "law of suppression of radical alternatives," he contends that the so-called information society is little more than industrial capitalism in new clothes. Similarly, Slack (1983) contends that policy in technological "innovation" and assessment is culturally channeled to support maintenance of the established system.

Social Conflict and Opposition

Critical communications research on social conflict and opposition continues to emphasize hegemony, but does so by situating the discussion of ideology in struggles led by competing movements and ideologies, most of which are distinctly anti-capitalist.

The Ewens' (1982) work is paradigmatic here. It identifies class struggles over dominant images and modes of expression (such as the official language versus the vernacular or popular mode of speech), historically and in our time. Their essay, "The Bribe of Frankenstein," surveys several of the conflicts that eminate from the overwhelming impact of technology over the last three centuries. The "Official Language" is reflected in both the word, such as the Bible, and the machinery, such as that exhibited in regular celebrations of capitalist power like the Philadelphia Centennial Exposition of 1876. Together, word and machine comprise a "technology of discourse," or "the imperative to develop a means by which the law, knowledge, information, transactions, and priorities of an expanding world market economy could be disseminated and controlled" (1982: 16). In essence, Dr. Frankenstein proposes a machine that will bring freedom, but delivers domination instead. Nevertheless, domination results in growing opposition, reflected in a vernacular print tradition that opposed the official language of the dominant word and machine. People like Gerald Winstanley and Thomas Paine spoke in a vernacular about popular control over the machinery of society. They serve as models for contemporary movements that, awash in a sea of mass commercial media, seek to recapture a democratic, vernacular spirit.

Slack (1984), Meehan (1984), and Webster and Robins (1986) take up the issue of technology and ideology in the modern setting and debate the conflicting cultural constructions of the so-called Information Society. Salter (1980), Gandy (1982) and Haight and Weinstein (1981) consider the role of the media in several contemporary movements to change social policy. Douglas (1986) has assessed the unique efforts of US workers to use established media in organizing a trade union.

The theme of media in social conflict is also exemplified in research that focusses on the contradictions within hegemonic ideology and, as well, within the process of transmission and reception of that ideology. Much of recent research about television, particularly on the presentation of social class on televison, discusses the contradictory themes in this programming that open the possibility for different ways to interpret, react to, and act on this programming according to one's class position. (Kellner, 1982; Newcomb, 1982).

Finally, a growing body of research identifies the relationship between workers in the communications industry and the technology and policies put in place to reshape their work. Bernard's (1982) research on telephone workers in British Columbia is particularly useful because it describes struggles common to workers in most occupations and struggles that are unique to workers in the growing telecommunications and information technology sectors. Her analysis of the successful takeover of the offices of British Columbia Telephone, a subsidiary of the US company General Telephone and Electronics, offers important insights into the problems of trade unions in a business undergoing rapid technological changes that threaten the job security of many workers (See also Mosco and Zureik, 1986). Neilson's (1983) research on unions in the movie industry and Wasko's (1983) on broadcasting unions identify similar conflicts where workers struggle to build some degree of solidarity in the face of new technologies that, as Shaiken has pointed out, are unique because they have been *designed* to destroy jobs (1984).

Alternative Media
Critical research on content and culture has also focussed on the development of distinctly alternative forms, with some growing out of a concern with social conflict. However, it departs from the previous theme in its explicit emphasis on *alternatives* rather than on critiques or conflicts surrounding mainstream media.

Though most of its contributors are not North Americans, Mattelart and Siegelaub's collection (1983) is the starting point for an analysis of alternative media. Downing's work (1984) also gives a detailed analysis of alternative media in the recent experience of the US, Portugal, Italy, and Eastern Europe. Most North American research on the use of the media in social transformation focusses on Latin America, with work on Chile, Cuba, and Nicaragua of particular interest (Bresnahan, 1985; Grinberg, 1986; and Reyes Matta, 1986).

Some research on the media and social transformation addresses especially questions about the extent to which one should use established media, particularly advanced technology, how one should relate to such pervasive and widely accepted values, as formal press freedom, and the opportunities for democratizing the media by turning it over to full popular control (Wasko and Mosco, forthcoming).

Conclusion: A Growing Network and Growing Challenges

Critical communications research has grown considerably over the past ten years. What was once the work of a handful of isolated, individual scholars is now the research agenda of entire groups across North America. Certain institutions, such as Hunter College in New York, the University of California at San Diego, the University of Oregon, the University of Texas, and Simon Fraser University in British Columbia, are clearly identified with collections of critical communications scholars. Most programs now contain individuals that teach courses and conduct research across the range of political economy and critical cultural studies. In addition, the Union for Democratic Communications—a national association of critical teachers, scholars, and media practitioners—provides opportunities, through its newsletter, occasional publications, and annual conferences, for sharing ideas, research and recent developments in alternative media. Even mainstream communications research has taken notice of this work. *The Journal of Communication* devoted a double issue in 1983 to what it called the "Ferment in Field," while the Speech Communication Association launched a journal *Critical Studies in Mass Communication*.

Nevertheless, critical research would benefit from closer collaboration between scholars in political economy and those in cultural studies. This would help us to address more thoroughly such questions as the implications ownership patterns have on the form and content of media products or the ways media texts relate to ongoing social conflicts. Critical research would also benefit from a careful reading of recent developments in neo-Marxist theory, particularly the research on the labour process, the state, and the evolution of imperialism.

In addition to these tasks, we need closer ties between the research community and those directly involved in producing media and information technology, including workers, their trade unions, artists, and activists who make extensive use of media. Some steps have been taken. These include the active involvement of scholars in the National Writers Union in the US, in independent production companies such as Paper Tiger Productions, and the Labor Institute for Public Afairs. In Canada, the federal government Ministry of Labour Technology Impact Reseach Fund has brought together scholars and trade unionists in over fifty projects, to examine the impact of new technologies in the workplace.

Finally, critical thinkers in all disciplines need to pay closer attention to mass media and information technology. Unfortunately for some, the field remains peripheral, hidden somewhere in the superstructure, if not simply a blindspot (Smythe, 1977). Communication is central to our economic, political and social institutions; mass media and information technology are vital to transformations taking place within both capitalist and socialist societies today. To give more attention to research in communication and information technology would help us to clarify the nature of these transformations and their powerful implications.

Chapter Three

Democracy in the Computer Society

What is Democracy?

As pointed out in Chapter Two, the intention of critical communications research to open the media and new technology to full public access and control requires that we understand what access and control mean, and, how our particular ways of relating to technology advance or retard democracy. The most useful way to understand democracy is with a simple expression. *Democracy means the fullest possible public participation in the decisions that affect our lives.* There are three points worth emphasizing about this use of the term.

Participation and Equality

First, as Wolfe (1977) describes it, democracy refers to both the process of *participation* in decisions and the social goal of moving toward *equality*. Participation is critical; in fact, as Held reminds us (1987), the earliest Western society to practice democracy—Greek society from about the sixth to the third century B.C.—was more committed to participation or active involvement in political activity than to equality. Full participation in public life, including service to the community, went to the heart of what it meant to be a citizen. As Pericles, one of the most prominent

Athenian politicians in classical history explained:

> We do not say that a man who takes no interest in politics is a man
> who minds his own business; we say that he has no business here at
> all. (Ibid.: 17)

It was not until the demise of slavery, the system that provided the economic base for classical democracy, that we begin to see the concept of equality broadened to include more than property-owning men.

More Than Politics

Second, as Macpherson (1977) states, true participatory democracy is not limited to the political arena. A fully democratic society is one in which citizens actively create economic, sociocultural, and political participation and equality.

In the *economy*, this means public participation in decisions about what to produce, how to produce it, and using the best means of distribution to realize the spirit of equality. *Sociocultural* democracy expects its citizens to provide the basic necessities of food, shelter, and health care to all. It also includes active participation in producing and transmitting information and culture. Democracy, therefore, means a systematic opposition to knowledge elites, as well as economic elites. Finally, *political* democracy includes active citizen participation in those local, regional and national organizations that provide services, plan, debate, inform, and through various structural and moral means, ensure that leaders and administrators have no incentive to become rulers and elites. (Bowles and Gintis, 1986). A *leader* or administrator reflects the views of constituents and carries them out in an orderly and effective fashion. A *ruler* acts on his or her own desire to maintain power and realize personal or narrow interest group goals.

Democracy is Public

The third dimension of democracy is its *public* character. Democracy is not the sum total of votes taken among isolated individuals, although voting may be one among many democratic actions. In fact, voting can be used as a means to manipulate private individuals by employing a safe, largely passive process to create the impression of democratic participation (Ginsberg, 1986). Computer communications systems can reinforce this largely symbolic version of democracy by making it possible for people to vote without even leaving their living rooms.

However, democracy flourishes when individuals transcend their private selves and meet in public gatherings, in a general community setting in order to discuss, protest, or otherwise establish an alternative view of society. As Lowi and Lytel put it, "a positive relationship between computers and democracy exists ... where there are freely communicating citizens in a political community." (1986: 92)

Perspectives on Computers and Democracy

Why the Concern about Democracy?

With these general thoughts in mind, what is the nature of the relationship of computing to democracy? A response needs to be be prefaced with a word about why we ask the question. More specifically, why is it that today people ask about computers and democracy or technology and democracy, rather than about nationalism and democracy or social class and democracy?

A major reason for the interest in democracy and computers is the common concern about the state of democracy worldwide, a sense that something new is needed to create democracy where it does not exist and expand it where it does. Presently, democracy appears to be suffering from seemingly intractable technical and political problems.

Technology in general—and more recently the computer—is often seen as the "something new" that can offer solutions. More specifically, computer-communications systems create the potential to process vast stores of information rapidly, transmit information to a broad, or narrow, range of people, receive responses, and generally monitor the state of the organization, community, etc. in which one is participating.

According to this view, computers can eliminate what Innis (1972) referred to as the Monopolies of the Word that underlie the concentration of power throughout society. A sense of malaise about democracy and a *deus (ex?) machina* solution—this is the setting for the question: can computers bring democracy?

Moreover, analysts agree that a limited amount of time is available for us to shape computers for democratic purposes. Soon, the computer-society relationship will be so entrenched that it will be difficult to make the changes necessary to use the technology democratically. With this in mind, Kling concludes his introduction to a special issue of *The Information Society*, devoted to the theme democracy and computers, on this note:

There are still many degrees of freedom left on how to computerize. Even those computer systems that are pervasive are less
embedded in social life than we might expect them to be in 40
years. Now is the time to ask hard questions since some social
options remain. (Kling, 1986)

We now turn to three perspectives that have guided research on this
question. Keeping in mind that all category schemes are rough attempts
to make sense of a complex terrain, I find it useful to distinguish among
technological democrats, managerial pluralists, and *critical skeptics.* These
three perspectives provide different ways of seeing the relationship of
computers to society. In what each chooses to emphasize, or not to
emphasize, in what each claims is central, or peripheral, these perspectives offer a unique focus on the computer-society relationship and on
the potential to achieve a democratic information society. Though each
of the perspectives contains useful guidance for understanding computers in society, I find the *critical skeptic* view most useful for assessing the
place of computers in social life and their potential for moving toward
democracy.

Technological democrats tend to identify with the view that the computer, particularly when situated in informatics networks, most likely
advances the development of democracy directly. They assume that
technologies are responsible for social transformation and can achieve
widespread participation and equality, even in the face of social forces
that would preserve the entrenched positions of dominant elites.

The other two groups of theorists take a more mediated approach to
technological development. Both take a path, best laid out in Raymond
Williams' work (1975), that situates technology within a *social* setting
that shapes the design, production, distribution, and use of the technology.

Managerial pluralists start from the view that social complexity and
the uneven distribution of abilities in society limit the development of
democracy. In their pessimism about democracy, they claim that, at
best, we can achieve popular representation in the political domain and
in a plurality of participatory associations. They argue that society needs
stronger management to achieve what little democracy is possible.
Managerial pluralists worry that computers will raise democratic hopes
in an increasingly complex society which actually requires less, not
more, democracy. Pessimistic about the social potential for widespread
democracy and fearful that computers may raise unwarranted expecta-

tions, managerial pluralists would put the technology to work doing what they feel it can do best: help elites to manage social complexity.

Critical skeptics, agreeing that the social setting is vital for understanding the use of technology, still assess the social setting differently. They see power concentrated in economic and political organizations that advance commercial over public interests. In this setting, computers further the unequal distribution of power and, despite countervailing political action, undermine the very limited democracy that some now enjoy. Critical skeptics conclude that computers do not democratize society. To them, at best, computers can ony serve as one of the tools that a democratic social movement would use to achieve widespread participation and equality.

Technological Democracy
Using this perspective, particularly when they are integrated into telecommunications networks, computers overcome major boundaries to democracy. Although most analysts who accept this perspective point out how, historically, social forces constrain technological development; technological democrats view the social impact of computer systems as so overwhelmingly powerful that traditional constraints are less formidable today than they were in previous eras of technological development.

Since technological democracy has the obvious popular appeal of the machine utopia, much of the writing in this area sets out to *popularize* computing and promote its widespread acceptance in the transition to an information society. Toffler (1980) and Naisbitt (1982) offer good examples of this. Toffler in particular sees computer communications systems advancing widespread public participation and equality in social life by allowing both easy access to information and, more importantly, the opportunity for citizens to respond instantly to questions of public significance. The interactive capacity of telematics systems, in this view, facilitates public airing of issues and public decision-making on a far more regular basis than previously possible. Moreover, such systems aid the general shift to decentralized political decision-making and management of public institutions.

In the economy, the new information technology advances what Toffler and others call the "electronic cottage." Here, the model is one or more individuals working at home, largely controlling their own work life. Once again, combining information processing with communications power allows individuals, even though part of a large business, to work from their own homes or in small, relatively home-like, neigh-bourhood work centers. Much of this vision is based on the premise that, as Naisbitt puts it, "One of networking's great attractions is that it is an easy way to get information." (Naisbitt: 217)

Technology, they contend, by making access to information easier, cuts short any efforts, public or private, to build monopolies of knowl-edge. Furthermore, modern methods of distribution enable any individ-ual to disseminate ideas with relative ease. Every receiver is simulta-neously a potential transmitter; every reader, a writer; every writer, a publisher. Computers thus contribute directly to the widespread demo-cratization of socio-cultural life.

More scholarly analysts, working within the paradigm of technologi-cal democracy, generally come up with the same conclusions, but with more reservations and a keener eye for the obstacles. A prominent example, Pool's *Technologies of Freedom* recognizes the new technology's ability to overcome the barriers to democratization of information and, consequently, social life. Nevertheless, in spite of their technological power, in Pool's view, computers are prone to more obstacles than the popularizers would admit. For him the chief constraining forces are national governments that apply outmoded regulatory control to the new technologies that, in themselves, make government regulation impossible to implement or unnecessary. However, Pool does justify some form of government regulation when technology makes possible large, centralized networks that can easily restrict the flow of information.

Pool's more modest version of technological determinism concludes that the spread of inexpensive processing and distribution systems undermines the ability of governments to regulate computer commu-nications systems. More importantly, because the technology fosters widespread access and control, (communication that is "dispersed, decentralized, and easily available,") such regulation is unnecessary. Nevertheless, the restrictions persist, he argues, because it is bureau-cratically or politically difficult to dismantle old institutional solutions. Regulatory bureaucracies develop strong techniques for self-preservation, while governments find it politically useful to screen information and limit access to the means of communication, for fear that expanded access might upset entrenched power. Though technol-ogy, likely, advances democracy, he maintains that realizing the demo-cratic potential of the new electronic information technology is likely to be a politically stormy process. Pool suggests that this storm looms in the present efforts of Western industrialized nations to diminish or eliminate regulation of electronic communications. It is also evident in attempts by advanced industrial nations to convince lesser-developed countries that restrictions on the free flow of information and data across borders, however understandable in the interest of maintaining national sovereignty, are impossible to achieve or unnecessary.

Pool's perspective can also be found in numerous political and policy analyses such as the work of Dizard (1982), Cleveland (1985) and the Ganleys (1981). These, particularly the Ganleys, emphasize the international dimensions of technological potential and political barriers.

Turing's Man reflects the perspective of technological democracy in the cultural domain. In this book, Bolter considers the computer one of a small number of "defining technologies"—the clock and the steam engine are other major examples—in the development of Western societies. Like Pool, Bolter points out what he believes to be the technology's anti-democratic potential because " computers make hierarchical communication and control far easier." Nevertheless:

> ... they also work against the fundamental sense of purpose, the absolute dedication to the party line, which is the core of the autocratic state. The computer programmer is always aware of other options. If anything, the great political danger of the computer age is a new definition of anarchy. (Bolter, 1984: 225)

Technological democracy appeals in part because it places the burden of social change on the technology itself rather than in social institutions. Moreover, it offers an attractive optimism about the potential of the new electronic technology to bring about widespread participation and equality. Finally, it echoes deep-seated cultural values of technological utopianism and opposition to government control.

However, this perspective is burdened with a fundamental flaw. By emphasizing the determining influence of technology, even in Pool's and others' "soft" versions, technological democracy misses an important historical lesson: technologies embody, in their production, distribution, and use, existing political and social relationships; technologies are thus little more than congealed *social* relationships.

Hence, as Williams has perceptively noted, there was nothing inherent in the technology of radio that led it to the highly centralized (one transmitter to many receivers) model that characterized its use in broadcasting (1975). In fact, as Brecht pointed out, at the beginning of broadcasting radio could be used as a highly decentralized device, one that would make every radio receiver a potential transmitter. However, actual radio use embodied centralized economic and political values that developed the technology towards building mass audiences for profit and for one-way political discourse. Computers and other information technologies are still not used in ways fundamentally different.

Moreover, technological democrats tend to see democracy individualistically—the individual working at home or expressing an electronic opinion or vote are common examples. For the technological democrat, Democracy, like Technology, like the Economy is a *thing*, that can be maximized or minimized. The danger in this view is that it fails to recognize that democracy is a *social process*, propelled by social movements and public gatherings much less susceptible to centralized manipulation than the isolated tele-worker or tele-voter.

Two alternative perspectives that address these shortcomings start from an explicit social science, rather than a technological, perspective.

Managerial Pluralism

Managerial pluralism starts from the view that contemporary society is a complex of cross-cutting organizations, strata and interests arising from a highly defined division of labour and a diversity of socio-cultural experiences. According to this view, these social forces guarantee some measure of democracy because it is particularly difficult for any one organization, stratum, or interest to dominate. Furthermore, groups moderate their demands and participate in a constantly shifting process of forming and reforming interest alliances in order to achieve some measure of success in the political marketplace.

A fundamental social challenge, in this view, is the *proper* management of complexity, especially when the goal is to preserve diversity without sacrificing the ability to reach decisions. Managerial pluralists such as Daniel Bell (1973) see computers as a mixed blessing. Much of their research shows how computers and information technology contribute efficiently and effectively to economic organization, thus extending long term productivity growth. Beniger's (1986) work, in particular, provides detailed historical evidence for showing that electronic technology extends a "control revolution" that machine technology initiated in the eighteenth century, thereby making it possible for economic structures and markets to perform more efficiently.

Even though control advances economic success, it does so at the expense of a narrowing scope for economic democracy. Presently, democracy in the economic arena includes widening participation in the fruits of a productive economy but *not* widespread distribution of economic decision-making *power*. Managerial pluralists limit decision-making in the economic arena to managerial and technical experts.

For the managerial pluralist, however, this economic success creates problems for the political realm. One problem is captured in the expression "information overload"—or an excess of data, accelerating beyond our capacity to manage, absorb, and use it. More fundamental to the pluralists is "political overload." They fear that technological and economic success will raise popular expectations for technical solutions to what pluralists believe are essentially value questions, not readily (if at all) subject to remedy In spite of serious difficulties in satisfying the demands for equity, fairness, distributive justice, popular access and control, all of these values enter the political domain. These values are often seen in the concrete demands of the many interest organizations whose members are convinced should be met and, armed with computer communications technologies themselves, convinced that technology makes their demands easier to meet.

"Political overload" is compounded in the socio-cultural realm where deeply-rooted pluralist, egalitarian values add to the pressures on the political sphere. According to Bell (1976), though the work of Lasch is also relevant here (1978), a culture propelled by boundless hedonism overloads the political system with demands to solve the many problems that a pleasure-seeking culture creates. In essence, the political realm is where the economy, operating according to efficiency principles, and the culture, seeking constantly for immediate satisfaction, clash.

One finds this view expressed by numerous writers, in addition to Lasch and Bell (Crozier, Huntington, and Watanuki, 1975; Brittan, 1977; Committee on the Constitutional System, 1987). One even finds it, presented in a more discrete and implicit form, in government policy reports on the new technology. Major reports from France (Nora and Minc, 1980), Canada (Canada, 1982 and 1987), and Australia (Telecom Australia, 1980) emphasize the difficulty of developing policies, particularly with the additional burden imposed by dependency on the United States. The concern here is the ability of US business and government to shape the policy agenda—for standards, market structure, etc.—and thereby constrain the agenda of solutions for the rest of the industrialized world.

As a result, managerial pluralists conclude, we are confronted with unreasonable and unrealizable expectations, with, in Huntington's expression, an "excess of democracy." Or, as Crozier concludes, "the more decisions the modern state has to handle, the more helpless it becomes." These writers call for diminished expectations, for "some measure of apathy and noninvolvement," and "balance." Huntington is fairly critical of former US governor and Democratic party presidential nominee Alfred Smith for once remarking that "the only cure for the evils of democracy is more democracy." According to Huntington:

> A value system which is normally good in itself is not necessarily optimized when it is maximized. We have come to recognize that there are potentially desirable limits to economic growth. There are also potentially desirable limits to the extension of political democracy. Democracy will have a longer life if it has a more balanced existence. (Crozier, Huntington, and Watanuki, 1975: 115)

Managerial pluralists fear that, though computers and information technology may enhance control over the economy and advance sociocultural democracy, they will stifle political decision-making. As a result, some have called for limiting access to government and to information about government operations (Demac, 1984). Research on the global control of information, and specifically, on US government policies, has described how this is being achieved through a variety of strategies, including: deregulation, privatization, cutbacks in funding education and information programs, disinformation campaigns, and the development of state and corporate public relations apparatuses to manage, channel and filter information (Mosco and Wasko, 1988).

The managerial pluralist view, useful for rooting technology in social structure, recognizes that societal conditions can give rise to serious conflicts over technology. The fundamental problem with this perspective is in equating political pluralism with democracy; it seals off the economic realm from contestation, which results in an excessively mechanistic view of economic relations and an overly conflict-ridden view of the political domain. In fact, Poulantzas (1978) has suggested that this mechanistic view of the economy, that it is separated from social conflict—what he calls "the isolation effect"—is a central *myth* serving capitalist society.

As Bluestone and Harrison (1982), Shaiken (1984), and Howard (1985) have shown, control and efficiency are only one side of the computer-assisted economy. The other side contains social conflict, the misuse of resources (human and technical), deepening insecurity that affects social as well as work life, and numerous other problems.

Furthermore, the political system often shows a powerful ability to take decisive action. Consider, for example, the ability of modern industrial states to take strong, coherent, action to promote generally conservative economic policies and strengthen military forces. The United States government alone has spent over one trillion dollars on the military in the 1980s. Moreover, with the general support of its allies, the United States has taken on one of the most complex projects in history, the Strategic Defense Initiative or "Star Wars."

The evidence of both economic conflict and political strength suggests problems for those who contend that we are experiencing a "governability crisis" resulting from "political overload." If anything, as developed societies promote policies of deregulation, privatization, and a general sense of "return to the marketplace," they pile added responsibility onto an already over-burdened market system. Consequently, a greater danger may be *economic crisis resulting from market overload*. Indeed, there have already been suggestions that the volatility in financial markets that started in 1987 was initiated by too great a reliance on unrestricted market forces for economic activity.

One can learn an important lesson from pluralist thinking, though to learn it we must go outside the pluralist domain to a point on the boundary where pluralism meets a more critical view. The work of Offe (1984) and Habermas (1973) situates this "crisis of democracy" in a fundamental problem—what may be a fundamental contradiction—confronting Western societies. Over the past century, Western governments have maintained a rough balance between the pressures that advance capital *accumulation* and those that aim to advance democracy and achieve popular *legitimacy*. Recent developments, including the growth of an international division of labour and the rise of Asia as a major force in the global economy, have put added pressure on Western governments to promote accumulation, to "unleash" industries, and otherwise eliminate barriers to technological growth.

Offe and Habermas remind us that this drive to capital accumulation, however well-founded, bears a cost in the legitimatacy of the belief that Western governments are committed to democracy and merit widespread popular support and active participation. According to these theorists, managerial pluralism reflects well-founded worries about Western economics, but solving fundamental problems by removing the "excesses of democracy" are as unlikely to succeed as the visions of the more optimistic technological democrats. Unlikely, because eliminating democratic mechanisms does *not* eliminate the interests that these mechanisms served. Rather, these interests tend to go after other means, including economic institutions, that may not be well equipped to absorb democratic demands.

There is evidence that established governments recognize the problem of legitimacy and are making use of information technology to redefine the very notion of democratic legitimation. This can be seen in the Thatcher Government attempts to redefine unemployment constantly, so that the official figures can be less than the actual number of people who register. The government defines this as being more "realistic." Thatcher has also redefined union democracy by enforcing postal ballots for union elections. This "reform" makes it easier for workers who would not normally participate actively in union affairs, to influence union policy from their homes, where they are more susceptible to government and corporate media influence.

Critical Skepticism
Technological democracy starts from the direct impact of computers and information technology, managerial pluralism from conceptions of the state. A *critical* perspective begins with an analysis of the economic or political economic context of computers. Critical *skepticism* arises from the view that analysis of the contemporary political economy indicates little direct potential for using computers to advance democratic ends. Forces at work in the economies of those nations that lead in computer development make it difficult to identify or foresee democratic tendencies. Among these forces are the tendency to centralized industrial planning and control, centralized monitoring and information control, and the tendency to treat the products of computer communications systems—namely data and information—as marketable commodities.

There is nothing inherent in computer technology that would inevitably lead to corporate centralization; technological democrats have even argued that the opposite is more likely. Yet the research of Mowshowitz (1985), H. Schiller (1984), Clement (1988) and Webster and Robins (1986) points in another direction. These critical skeptics concentrate on the rise of large, transnational, vertically- and horizontally-integrated companies that use electronic technologies to centralize planning and, particularly, fiscal control, while decentralizing or deconcentrating operations over an increasingly global sphere of production and markets.

The goal is to build a relatively stable international division of labour, in part with a technology that overcomes those time and space constraints that made global expansion difficult in the past (Nash and Fernandez-Kelly,1983; US Congress, 1987a). Developments in computer communications networks such as the Integrated Services Digital Network, or, what D. Schiller calls "the global grid" (1985), facilitate this development because they provide the communications highways central to the circulation of data and information.

Critical skeptics also identify the ways in which computers that centralize managerial control, tighten control at the point of production, chiefly through the ability of computers to measure and monitor workplace performance. Noble's research suggests that labour control considerations are integral to the design, production and use of numerical control systems (1984). Shaiken describes their use to monitor, if not replace, the work of skilled machinists (1984). G. Marx (1986), Howard (1985), and Clement (1984) examine the ways computer systems are used to monitor the keystrokes of typists and the answering rate and performance of telephone operators and related workers in the insurance, banking, airline and other service industries. These analysts contend that such information provides management with impersonal and seemingly objective grounds for extending workplace control.

Sterling (1986), K. Wilson (1988) and Webster and Robins (1986) see these same applications growing on the consumer side as information on electronic transactions is used for "social management"—large-scale marketing of products and services based on detailed monitoring of consumer choices.

In addition to the impetus to use computers for corporate workplace and consumer control, critical skeptics point to the growing importance of information as a marketable commodity. Where technological democrats view information as the product of *technology*, and managerial pluralists view information as a *resource*, critical research sees information as a *commodity*. (D. Schiller, 1988)

In a world where raw material and manufacturing commodities are no longer the centerpieces of economic growth and profit, information takes on growing significance. Demac (1984), the Schillers (1988) and Roszak (1986), consider how the growing market value of information leads to a general shift away from the idea that information is a public good. The result is the decline of public institutions such as schools, libraries, and government information services, in favour of private corporate control of information commodities.

These developments hold important political and sociocultural implications for democratic participation and equality. Numerous studies in North America (Gandy, 1988) Europe (Bjorn-Andersen, et al., 1982), Latin America (Rada, 1981) and Australia (Reinecke, 1985) have raised the possibility that commercial control of computers and information technology will deepen social class divisions nationally and internationally, as people now divide into those who can afford the technology, services and content—the *information rich*—and those who cannot—the *information poor.*

Critical research does raise concerns about the political uses of computer information, with particular attention paid to government intrusion into individual and family privacy (Burnham, 1980), to the use of public opinion and electronic interactive systems in manipulating the electorate (Roszak, 1986), and to the use of computers to extend military power (see Chapter Six).

Critical research also focusses on what propels society to shape technology for specific uses, rather than on what technology makes possible. While technological democrats see the potential for *decentralized* decision-making and a broader base of control, critics see little decentralization or delegation of *power* to lower levels of authority. Rather, they see the *deconcentration* of operational decision-making or routine administration over a broader organizational and geographical expanse, without a concomitant distribution of power over strategic decisions.

The decentralization of power is usually thwarted by the economic and political interests of those who have the social power to apply computer and information technology. With the absence of economic democracy limiting the ability to achieve political and sociocultural democracy, economic concentration and the growing value of information commodities shrink the public sphere of decision-making and also those processes vital for carrying out democratic rule.

Critical skeptics, having successfully charted much of the political economy of computing and information technology, show good cause for concern about the lack of potential for democracy. If there is a deficiency in their critical view, it is in insufficient attention given to the problems that political and corporate elites experience in attempting to control the technology and its uses. As the 1987 stock market crash and a general financial instability indicate, there is no certainty that the drive to global centralization guarantees its flawless realization.

Moreover, there is both opposition to these control efforts and growing alternative use of computing and information technology that suggest a potential for democracy. Let us conclude this chapter with a look at this potential. However, as we do so, keep in mind a lesson of critical skepticism: that it is not technology that creates democracy; rather, democracy grows out of economic, political, and social forces that use a variety of tools, including advanced technology, to achieve democratic ends.

Toward Democracy

Research from the critical skeptic view already considers how we can think about computers and democracy. The goal is to do this, avoiding, on the one hand, the determinism that gives technological democracy a false optimism; and, on the other, the fatalism that leads managerial pluralists to promote oligarchy as inevitable and, in fact, preferable to full democracy. Research on the economic, socio-cultural, and political dimensions of computing can suggest paths to further democracy.

The telecommunications industry is among the leaders in using computer technology to control workers and the work process. Computers that could assist telephone operators and technical workers with information to support their work and give them a greater sense of control are, more typically, used to measure and monitor most every activity and present that information to management who then use it for control purposes (Mosco and Zureik, 1987).

Nevertheless, or perhaps because computers are used in this way, telephone workers led efforts to advance the goal of extending democracy to the workplace. Their activities are a significant example of how *democracy grows from movements committed to its realization, not from the application of technology.*

The research and development director of the Communication Workers of America identifies the union's goal as "complete and effective Union involvement in all aspects of technological change, including veto power over the introduction of new equipment." (Howard, 1985: 192) Some telephone workers have even put this commitment into practice. In the early 1980s, Australian telephone workers responded to their industry's plan to computerize and automate their work by proposing an alternative to the US model of centralized control: a system of local, worker-run offices. Moreover, workers opposed centralization rather creatively; instead of striking, they switched off computers that collected customer information on long distance calls. This free long distance service helped win public support for the union's demands (Reinecke, 1985). In Canada, the British Columbia telephone workers responded to similar use of the technology in stronger fashion; the Telecommunications Workers Union took over the offices of BC Tel and used their knowledge of the new technology to run the phone company for a week (Bernard, 1982). Such activities make all the more stark the differences between management use of technology to increase control and its potential to advance workplace democracy.

The International Association of Machinists and Aerospace Workers acknowledges this directly in its "Technology Bill of Rights":

> The new automation technologies and the sciences that underlie them are the product of a world wide, centuries-long accumulation of knowledge. Accordingly, working people and their communities have a right to share in the decisions about, and the gains from new technology. (IAM, 1981: 1)

The IAM declaration is important particularly because it acknowledges the wider economic forces that must be addressed by efforts to democratize the workplace:

> The narrow economic criteria of transnational companies are causing an erosion of the nation's manufacturing base and the collapse of many communities that are dependent on it. While other countries in the world have a pressing need and a legitimate right to develop new industry, it is nonetheless vital that corporations not be allowed to play workers, unions, and countries against each other, seeking the lowest bidder for wages and working conditions. (IAM, 1981: 2)

Experiments and models for putting workplace democracy into practice are being developed in numerous places, with leading work from Sweden and Norway, where computer scientists and engineers have worked to advance workplace democracy with the labour force in the insurance, chemical, metal, print and other industries. (Swedish Center for Working Life, 1985)

In reaction to Western control of mass media, telecommunication, and information technology, Third World countries have taken the lead in calls for a New World Information and Communication Order. This has brought before the United Nations, and other international fora, the demand that the world's poorer nations participate equally and fully in decisions over the global production and distribution of electronic technology and information. UNESCO's International Commission for the Study of Communication Problems (the McBride Commission) made democracy a centerpiece of its report:

> The inherent nature of communication means that its fullest possible exercise and potential depend on the surrounding political, social, and economic conditions, the most vital of these being democracy within countries and equal, democratic relations between them. It is in this context that the democratization of communication at national and international levels, as well as the larger role of communication in democratizing society, acquires utmost importance. (UNESCO, 1979: 440)

This thought and action about economic democracy develops alongside serious critical thinking about social and cultural dimensions of the problem. Winner's work (1977) is particularly instructive here. Acknowledging the difficulty, as many critical thinkers do, of thinking about democracy in an age of computer-assisted elite rule, he nevertheless suggests fundamental changes in our way of seeing technology that are starting points for thinking about democracy.

First, Winner calls for "new technological forms" that require a "new sort of inventiveness and innovation" to overcome "the often wrongheaded and oppressive character of existing configurations of technology." Such inventiveness might come if we plan for "the direct participation of those concerned with their everyday employment and effects." Our guiding principles for technological development should lead to systems that are immediately intelligible to nonexperts, highly flexible and mutable, and that minimize human dependence. In essence, he argues, we produce better systems when we produce them democratically. Finally, development should be guided by a deep sense of the "appropriate." For, "here, the ancients knew, was the meeting point at which ethics, politics, and technics came together." (Winner, 1977: 326-327) There is nothing automatic about the choice of an appropriate technology. Unlike such technological democrats as Bolter, Turing's man (or woman) is not necessarily more aware of limits, more democratic, or anarchic. Working in a nanosecond world is as likely to produce what the ancients called *hubris,* or destructive pride, as it is humility.

In some circumstances, such as teaching peasants to read, the appropriate technology is masses of people carrying lesson books to the village, as has been the case, with widely acknowledged success, in Nicaragua. (Kozol, 1985) In other cases, it means experimenting with bringing electronic communication and information systems directly to local communities, as in the San Francisco-based Community Memory Project. (Siegel and Markoff, 1985) In all cases, it means constant watchfulness, not to monitor for social control, but to ensure that basic rights—to equal access and control, in essence to democracy—are not violated.

Conclusion: The Will to Democracy

I conclude by returning to the political realm where democracy is created by a society committed, *not* to the narrow technicist goal of computer literacy, but, as Siegel and Markoff put it, to "computer citizenship":

> Computer citizenship means knowing enough about the social, political, environmental, and military implications of computer technology to make personal and public choices. Even if we never learn how to "boot a disk," or haven't even heard that terminology, we must learn to be good citizens in the information age. In fact, the vast resources now dedicated to teaching computer use may simply be diverting us from a more important learning process. (Siegel and Markoff, 1985)

Societies committed to widespread citizen participation in the decisions that affect people's lives understand the necessity of openly discussing the potential for computer use to centralize power, violate human rights, deepen class divisions, and contribute to military devastation. At the same time, such societies must plan to overcome these problems by advancing the widest possible involvement of the very people whose lives they touch in decisions regarding use of technologies like the computer. The computer may or may not be an instrument for democracy, but it certainly represents one test of our will to achieve it.

Chapter Four

Perspectives on the State and the

Telecommunications System

> The crisis consists precisely in the fact that the old is dying and the
> new cannot be born; in the interregnum a great variety of morbid
> symptoms appear.—Antonio Gramsci (in Offe, 1984: 276).

In Chapter One, it was shown how *telecommunications systems* provide
the pathways for the production, distribution, and reception of messages, whether voice, data, or images. As these systems have grown in
importance, so too, have the stakes—*who* will control their operation
and profit from their use. As a result, the field of telecommunications
policy and regulation has expanded from a largely technical domain to a
source of enormous economic and political contention.

This chapter shows how research in *telecommunications policy and regulation* would benefit from using recent work in political theory, particularly theories of the *state* in developed capitalist societies. In essence, it
offers a distinctly *political* view of the political economy of telecommunications. This political view is also applied directly in Part II of the book,
in chapters that examine the military influence on information technology, the American policy process, and the influence of that process on
Canadian policy-making.

Such a political view is often necessary as policy research in telecommunications, especially on deregulation, tends to be more descriptive than analytical. It identifies the major participants in the policy arena, such as equipment manufacturers, service providers, regulators, and users; and describes the major issues over which they contend such as industry structure, pricing, and the extent of regulation. While descriptive research is useful to keep us abreast of developments in technology, services, and changes in the "players" and their relationships, the lack of analytic focus leads to simplistic conclusions. Will the arena be technology, market, or regulation driven? How can we adjust to *inevitable* deregulation and privatization? Will there be more government intervention through regulation, or less, with a deregulatory strategy?

The political scientist Robert Reich, a supporter of private markets, has argued that this approach leads more to myth-building than analysis:

> Posing the issue as a struggle between free enterprise and stifling government control, the conservative parable has obscured the central issue of how we organize and maintain that set of rules and constraints which we call the market. The conservative's idyllic "free market," unencumbered by government meddling, is a logical impossibility. The important question ... is whether these "rules of the game" ease and encourage economic change, or forestall it. (Reich, 1987: 48-49)

In this view, deregulation does not lessen government action but may actually increase it, because deregulation is "only a shift in the nature of government action, from commanding specific outcomes to creating and maintaining new markets." (Ibid.: 224) For example, in the United States, deregulation and the divestiture of AT&T has meant that a federal judge determines the decision-making structure and screens fundamental decisions about how firms can behave in the telecommunications marketplace. In Canada, deregulation of telecommunications equipment and specialty service markets, such as private line services for business, has meant more work for the regulatory agency, the CRTC. Under deregulation, it must see to it that Bell Canada is not competing unfairly by using revenues earned in regulated monopoly markets (public telephone service) to subsidize and thereby drive out competition in open markets (private line and other customized services). As a result, under deregulatory policies, there remains extensive government intervention with no decrease in bureaucracy.

Where policy research is more analytical than descriptive, it sees technology as the determining factor, or else, concentrates on economic concepts divorced from their political context. In other words it tends to be *technicist* and *economistic*. As Canadian political scientists Woodrow and Woodside (1986: 101) put it:

> It is striking, however, that "political factors" have *not* always been acknowledged and taken seriously within the telecommunications field which has traditionally tended to emphasize technology, economics and law as more significant factors shaping society.

They cite major Canadian policy documents such as *Instant World* (Canada, 1971) and *Telecommunications for Canada* (English, 1973) as examples of reports driven by technological and economic, typically neoclassical economic, factors to the exclusion of political ones.

This narrow view states that natural monopoly regulation of companies such as AT&T, Bell Canada or the British Post Office, may have been the appropriate policy for an industry characterized by a narrow range of technologies and widespread economies of scale and scope. The rise of a technologically driven service economy, a complex array of buyers and sellers, erosions in nearly every justification for natural monopoly status, and the development of markets—if not fully competitive then at least "contestable"—make deregulation and privatization both necessary and inevitable. (Bruce, et al., 1986; Shepherd, 1983)

Where analysis has departed from the technological or economic, it has either been through attempts to apply neoclassical economic models to the political domain, in so-called public choice theory; or, through detailed investigation of the micropolitical domain, in studies of how regulatory and public policy bodies are captured by their staffs (Woodrow and Woodside, 1986; Posner, 1974; J.Q. Wilson, 1980; Noll, 1987).

Drawing on recent developments in political and social theory, this chapter takes a step toward developing a distinctly *political* perspective on telecommunication policy and regulation. Part One examines how forms of governance in developed capitalist societies are related to means selected to address social demands. This frames a broad perspective within which to situate current developments, assess their significance and consider the prospects for the future structure of telecommunications policy and regulation.

Part Two outlines three models for understanding the state in developed capitalist societies. Furthermore, it shows how these models present different ways of explaining both the *functional* and *political* importance of recent developments in telecommunications policy, particularly the turn to deregulation and privatization.

The goal of the chapter is to broaden our understanding of the state's relationship to telecommunications through models that suggest alternative ways of seeing that relationship. With other work on this subject sparse, I use the chapter to suggest and explore, rather than offer definitive conclusions or detailed criticism.

Part One. Beyond Regulation and Deregulation

Drawing on recent work in sociological and political theory, this section identifies some mechanisms that developed capitalist societies use to process social claims or demands, and suggests how these mechanisms are organized into forms of governance. The goal here is to broaden the range of available concepts that explain the relationship of the state to telecommunications beyond the simplistic dualism of regulation/deregulation. How might we begin to organize these concepts into a coherent theory of telecommunications policy?

Processing Social Claims in Developed Capitalist Society

Drawing on the work of Luhmann (1982), we can identify four modes of processing social claims in developed capitalist societies: *representation* or political power, the *market* or monetary and exchange power, *social control* or power derived from socialization, values, norms, etc., and *expertise* or power based on the possession of information, what Bell has called the codification of theoretical knowledge (1976). These ways of processing claims are also present in less advanced and non-capitalist societies. However, these societies rely on other forms for settling claims and also tend to structure the relationship among forms differently. The specific configuration identified here applies to the developed capitalist world.

Each of these modes possesses strengths and weaknesses which serve, or fail, specific needs of developed capitalist societies at particular historical junctures.

Representation incorporates a wide range of social claims, but, because of this, subjects the system to regular bouts of demand overload. The result of too many claims for the society's institutions to handle, the society experiences a decline in its ability to govern or manage the range of demands.

The *market* is based on assigning monetary values to social claims, making a more manageable system, but at the cost of restricting claims to those that can be reduced to financial measurement. Furthermore, over time, market-based societies favour institutions whose concentrated economic and political power can structure the market to process social claims. Finally, the market is subject to rigidities in the exercise of claims, what Hirschman calls a bias in favor of *exit* over *voice* (1970). According to Hirschman, the primary means of expressing disagreement with a market choice is to leave the market. There is little legitimate opportunity to succeed in changing a market structure by using voice, i.e., persuasion and protest.

Expertise has the value of drawing on socially sanctioned views of what constitutes correct information, knowledge and, ultimately, truth. The twentieth century has defined scientific and technical knowledge as privileged sources of truth which carry the power of inevitability. Consequently, expert based decision-making is particularly valuable in a system with leaders eager to reduce the claims being made on its resources. However, success in reducing claims depends crucially on the sustainable ability of experts to convince that expertise achieves satisfactory results and that only a select few, all highly-trained individuals, can claim expert status. Given the lack of a natural power base for this technocratic class, these tasks become even more essential (Gouldner, 1979). Technological failures such as Three Mile Island, Chernobyl, or the space shuttle program undermine the widespread social acceptance of expertise as a legitimate mode of settling social claims. Moreover, theorists such as Winner (1977) argue that, by definition, expertise fails to consider the diversity of possible information, something he considers essential for making judgements that work over the wide range of people affected.

Finally, *social control* over cultural values and norms exhibits a powerful mechanism for settling claims because it is rooted in the daily lived experience of people, the structure, and the rhythms of life. Social control becomes a more powerful means to settle claims than expertise because it is rooted more firmly in the emotional experience of people. One disaster can undermine belief in science; values and norms are less easily shaken.

Nevertheless, the successful inculcation of values presupposes a massive and complex institutional apparatus—including the family, schools, churches, law enforcement, etc.—for socializing people to agree sufficiently on what values are appropriate and how they are to be realized.

There are different ways to configure these modes of settling claims. The organization in Figure 4-1 is based on two basic conclusions:

1. Representation and expertise are fundamentally different modes. In principle, representation incorporates the widest range of claims; expertise only those that meet strict truths tests.

2. The market and social control are also fundamentally different; the market is an indirect and opaque means of settling claims, social control is direct and explicit.

Figure 4.1
Forms of Governance for Processing Social Claims in Developed Capitalist Societies

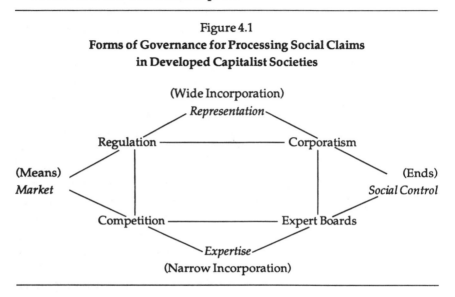

(Wide Incorporation)

Representation

Regulation ———————— Corporatism

(Means)   (Ends)

Market   *Social Control*

Competition ———————— Expert Boards

Expertise

(Narrow Incorporation)

Forms of Governance in Developed Capitalist Societies

These four ways of settling social claims combine to produce four basic forms of governance in developed capitalist societies: regulation, competition, expert boards and corporatism. Forms of governance vary depending on which of the settlement modes is emphasized. For example, in advanced capitalist societies, nationalized enterprises such as Air Canada or the BBC would represent regulation with a bias toward the representation side of the spectrum. On the other hand, regulatory bodies such as the FCC or the CRTC, whose purpose is limited to setting market rules for private companies, would constitute regulation with a bias to the market.

Understanding that there is a range of governance forms that can be plotted along the axes described in Figure 4.1, the following discussion focuses on four ideal types. However, a fundamental premise is that state intervention is present in every form used in developed capitalism, including the private marketplace. One can acknowledge degrees of state intervention within each mode, from a minor facilitative role to a powerful directive capacity.

Regulation offers representativeness within a private market structure. For example, the US Federal Communications Commission is responsible for representing the public interest by taking into account the views of those whose lack of market power would give them little voice in a pure market structure. Nevertheless, the Commission, like its Canadian counterpart, the CRTC, is responsible for maintaining a private market in communications.

Private competition is a form of governance that relies on the market to clear social claims and privileges the ability of experts to decide on how to make the best use of the market mechanism. In principle, technical, management and investment experts are those most appropriate to decide what to produce and how markets should be structured for distribution. Contrary to popular myths about the market, fostered in part by systems theories that reify component parts, the market is not self-creating and self-sustaining. The market is a form of governance that relies, generally, on public bodies, for setting rules about creating and sustaining markets.

Regulation and competition are familiar modes of governance in North America. Two others forms, *expert boards* and *corporatism*, are less familiar, though both have been used and are attracting increasing attention, particularly among those concerned about the shortcomings of regulatory and competitive market solutions. Prominent among these shortcomings is the perception that the political system suffers from an excess of claims, what have been characterized as the "excesses of democracy" or "excessive expectations ... generated by democratic aspects of the system." (Crozier, et al., 1975; Brittan, 1977)

Following Offe (1984), one can identify two ways of dealing with the perception that the political system suffers from demand overload. First, *reduce the number of social claims*. The market does this by limiting the ability to make claims to those who have sufficient financial resources. This develops a bias to short-run gains and an unstable arena that makes overall management difficult, particularly for long term planning.

Expert boards, or groups of people whose authority is vested in socially defined expertise, offer an alternative means of reducing demands. Such bodies proliferate in an advisory capacity throughout government and some have suggested the need to make them more powerful. In the United States for example, George Kennan, a former US ambassador and a major influence in creating a containment policy against the Soviet Union in the late 1940s, has called for legislation to meet what he perceives to be excessive demands on the political system. He has in mind an

> advisory body, advisory both to president and to Congress, but standing outside them, and made up of persons remote from participation in partisan political activity but qualified by training, experience and temperament to look deeply into present trends and possible remedies and to tell both the legislative and executive branches of the government of the things they *must* do, whether they like it or not, to head off some of the worst eventualities that seem now to be, almost unhindered, in the making. (Kennan, 1986: 6)

Such an advisory body would tighten social control by reducing the legitimacy of social claims conflicting with its own definition of expert-based authority. The growth of expert based panels and task forces at both the federal and provincial levels of government in Canada are similarly limiting.

An alternative to reducing social claims is to *increase the steering capacity of the state.* In principle, regulation provides some managerial control by concentrating the power to define the public interest in a small group of individuals. Recent proposals depart from the regulatory model by calling for strengthening executive control and introducing explicit corporatist principles into governance. In the United States, the three hundred member Committee on the Constitutional System (1987), led by Senator Nancy Kassenbaum, Republican of Kansas, C. Douglas Dillon, Secretary of the Treasury under President Kennedy, and Lloyd Cutler, former counsel to President Carter, has identified "chronic deadlock" as the fundamental problem of the US constitutional system. To overcome "governmental gridlock," they call for constitutional amendments that would strengthen executive power and party discipline.

A more explicit form of representation increases the control powers of the state through *corporatism.* This form of governance gives authority to individuals who represent specific sectors in the economic division of labour, particularly different sectors of business. Labour and consumer interests may play a role, typically secondary or peripheral, depending on their political power. Rather than reducing social claims, this form of governance brings social claims to the fore and gives them voice through economic representation.

To its proponents, corporatism better manages and controls social claims because it vests authority directly in a body that reflects what the state defines as legitimate and forces all claimants to channel demands through this body. Moreover, corporatist powers are rarely as clearly defined as traditional constitutional ones. This leads to what Offe calls the benefits of "organized formlessness"—an informality and extra-legal operation that permits informal discussion, consensus building, personal agreements and a capacity to deal rapidly with changing conditions while shielded from publicity.

Corporatism has been more prominent in European than North American history (Schmitter, 1977). James Weinstein (1968) gives an account of an early US effort at a corporatist solution, the National Civic Federation, which, from 1900 to 1918, created and implemented a social reform agenda put together by leaders in industry and finance with the support of the American Federation of Labour and the United Mine Workers. In so doing, the Civic Federation was able to gain recognition for collective bargaining, the minimum wage and other reforms. According to Weinstein, this undermined both the growing power of independent trade unions and explicitly socialist political organizations. Corporatism has been practiced in Canadian politics as well, particularly in instances where a social democratic party like the NDP has held the balance of power in a minority government.

A recent example of a corporatist governing body is the Municipal Assistance Corporation which brought together government, business and labour to produce the financing package and governance reforms to steer New York City out of bankruptcy. In fact, MAC's architect, investment banker Felix Rohatyn, proposes to build on this model with a national corporatist strategy.

Rohatyn premises his call on the failure of market-based deregulation. In an article published in July of 1987, Rohatyn starts with a premise made more auspicious by the crash of the stock markets three months later: "the United States today is headed for a financial and economic crisis." Rohatyn goes on to decry "a climate of deregulation pushed to dangerous extremes":

For the sake of competition, we have broken up AT&T, and the result has been both bad service and higher prices. We have deregulated the airlines and the resulting price wars did, indeed, lower fares. However, one airline after another is on its way to bankruptcy or to being acquired by another. The result will be a few huge airlines, with questionable financial structures, poor service with possibly higher prices, and worrisome safety factors. Deregulation of the financial markets has resulted in an explosion of private debt, unprecedented market speculation, and the sordid abuses in the financial industry that have been coming to light in recent months. Deregulation, as with most things in life, has to be done in moderation; it has been carried too far. The free market is not always right; it surely is not always fair. It should not be turned into a religion. (Rohatyn, 1987: 3)

To bring the US back from where Rohatyn sees it, "on the brink," he calls for a commission that would include members of both political parties, people in business, labour and academic experts who would at best, propose solutions, and at least "provide a coherent frame for debate of the economic alternatives."

The US and, to a lesser degree, Canada, lack the militant trade union activity and socialist politics that have made corporatism a more prominent feature of the European political landscape. This helps both governments avoid the danger of corporatism, which, according to Jessop (1982), is to risk introducing problems of fundamental class conflict into the heart of the state apparatus. Nevertheless, there are those such as Rohatyn and Reich, who propose a narrow form of corporatism, restricted to the political center or right of center. This form, which Reich dubs "collective entrepreneurialism," would overcome the danger of unmanageable anarchy. In Reich's (1987) terms, "opportunistic individualism ... induces collective gridlock." Reich's remedy is corporatism, based on a new spirit of "collective trust" among business, government, and labour.

Part Two. Thinking About the State and Telecommunications Policy

The overview presented here of the relationship between modes of settling social claims and forms of governance broadens our conceptual powers and helps move us toward a theory of the state and telecommunications policy. From there, we consider how major perspectives in political theory make use of these concepts to explain the role of the state in telecommunications policy.

Alford and Friedland (1985), among others, identify pluralist, managerial and class perspectives as the major ways of seeing the role of the state in developed capitalist societies. One can also distinguish between the major focus or *function* of state activity in each perspective and the primary social tension or *political* conflict that arises out of state activity. Each perspective acknowledges several functions of state activity and numerous sources of conflict, but concentrates on the one principle function and source of conflict which, each claims, offers the most explanatory value.

Figure 4.2
Perspectives on the State and Telecommunications Policy

Perspective	Domain of Explanation	
	Functional	Political
Pluralist	Realize Values	Clash of Interests
Managerial	Manage Complexity	Clash of Elites
Class	Accumulate Capital	Hegemony/Struggle

Pluralist Theory

The *pluralist* perspective develops from the view that power is situational, that it operates in specific circumstances over specific issues. The pluralist sees the state as only one among numerous organizations, including business, unions, voluntary associations, churches, etc., around which sets of interest coalitions focus their attention to meet their needs. The state itself is held together by a legal structure and an organizational culture that reflect widely held values and acts on these values to structure impartially the preferences of competing interests (Dahl, 1956).

Pluralist analyses of deregulation begin with the noticeable shift in political values from a concern with detailed regulation in the public interest to a commitment to general policies which facilitate operation of private, competitive markets (Derthick and Quirk, 1985). According to pluralists, this shift represented a groundswell in the form of public support for private marketplace solutions over government intervention. It also resulted from pressure led by intellectuals and policy makers as they coalesced in their agreement on the need to minimize regulation.

Referring to Figure 4.1, there is a general shift from representative- to market- and expert- based solutions. This value shift forces the state to assess the pressures of competing interests in a different fashion. Those who claim the state should intervene directly to support public concerns

of fairness and equity lose influence to those who would have the state
expand competition through private markets.

In essence, according to pluralists, the state oversees a marketplace of
competing interests, with no particular interest capable of exercising a
shaping influence on decision-making. The range of competing participants marshal their resources to back the claims they feel the state
should meet. An interest succeeds to the extent that it can convince the
state of its substantial political clout *and* that it conforms to the dominant
value preferences of the day better than competitors do. Pluralists offer
the functionalist view that deregulation and privatization grow from a
value shift that prompts restructuring the interest arena in favour of
those relying more on private markets for settling claims.

When pressed to identify the source of these changing values, pluralists in the United States and Canada tend to emphasize developments in
technology which, in this case, have broadened the range of telecommunications services (Noam, 1987; Janisch, 1986). Furthermore, they
point to the difficulty of managing the wide range of claims accepted out
of legal and political necessity under the public interest standard. An
"overloaded government" cannot manage change successfully (Easton,
1965). This problem is often deepened by the tendency of regulators to
use the rules to their own benefit, what J.Q. Wilson (Wilson, 1980) calls
"staff capture" of the agency.

The shift to a market principle streamlines the process of settling
claims, eliminates many as illegitimate, and undermines the organizational power of regulatory bureaucrats (Nozick, 1974; Janisch, 1986).
Finally, pluralists point to changes in policy analysis which, over time,
created a critical mass of experts who supported the shift in
government's role from direct regulation to overseeing markets (Derthick and Quirk, 1985).

From a policy point of view, pluralist theory sees two problems with
the turn to deregulation. First, some would suggest that by replacing the
public interest principle with a marketplace standard, we replace a
societal value, however murky, with a purely instrumental solution
which begs the question of values. However, analysts such as Reich contend, one cannot hope to solve fundamental problems of governance by
turning to the competitive marketplace. This is because the market
works against building *trust* among businesses and between business
and government, something pluralists feel is essential for achieving *collective* solutions to the complex problems posed by the contemporary
world economy.

According to Reich, regulation fails not because regulatory bodies are populated by a class of anti-capitalist civil servants and social engineers, as Kristol and other neo-conservatives maintain. Rather, it is because businesses lack trust or a commitment to the spirit of the law. As a result, rather than comply, businesses deepen "the miasma of regulation" through seemingly endless contention and litigation. Reich concludes that

> The ploy may be rational from the standpoint of the lawyer and his client, but it is often irrational for American business as a whole. Each maneuver generates a countermaneuver from within the regulatory bureaucracy and Congress; every feint a dodge, a more complicated prophylactic for the next encounter. The result, over time, is a profusion of legislative and regulatory detail that confounds American business (Reich, 1987: 219)

As pluralists see it, reliance on the marketplace may free up resources that have been stifled by monopolistic and regulatory constraints, but it is also likely to exacerbate the failure of North American business to join with government and other interests in arriving at collective solutions to global economic problems. Consequently, pluralists call for a fundamental reorientation of socialization practices so that we begin to emphasize mutual trust and collective responses to problems. It has also led Reich and others to move toward corporatist and expert-based forms of governance.

The present turn to deregulation worries pluralists, like Dahl and Lindblom, who have moved from their now classic statements in support of pluralist explanation to what Held calls "neo-pluralism" (Dahl, 1956, 1982; Lindblom, 1977; Held, 1987). They fear that pluralism no longer explains the politics in the US situation because the balance of interest forces has become distorted by the growth of corporate power. In contrast to his 1956 *A Preface to Democratic Theory*, Dahl now argues that "corporate capitalism" tends "to produce inequalities in social and economic resources so great as to bring about severe violations of political equality and hence of the democratic process." (p.60) For Dahl and others, the turn to the marketplace will only aggravate this problem. Instead, they call for greater representativeness, for explicit state measures ensuring fuller equality and participation from groups that would otherwise be submerged beneath the marketplace power of business. For them, the problem is not building trust, but rather building democratic structures that would provide the basis for it. To the extent that emphasis moves from situations and values to structures and management, neo-pluralism takes on more of the look of managerial theory.

Managerial Theory

Where the pluralist views power as situational, tied to specific events and circumstances, the managerial theorist sees it as structural, embedded in the rules governing the operation of organizations and institutions. A pluralist looks for power in the constellation of interests whose differing pressures result in a key decision such as the break-up of AT&T, or the reorganization of the Bell company into Bell Canada Enterprises (BCE). Managerial theory sees power in elites that conflict over the policy *agenda* that frames a series of discrete decisions, such as the general shift in the framework of regulation from public interest to private marketplace. The pluralist asks who won and lost in this decision; the managerial theorist asks who controls the policy agenda.

For managerial theorists, the fundamental driving force in both developed capitalist and socialist societies is the need to manage the growing complexity wrought by technological change and the increased division of labour. Managerial perspectives draw their inspiration from several streams of thought, prominently the work of Weber (1978) and Schumpeter (1943). Their focus on bureaucratic rationalization and control over the means of administration marked a managerial departure from the pluralist view of Durkheim and the class analysis of Marx.

For Weber and Schumpeter, bureaucratic elites take a central role in the twentieth century arena of power as a result of the critical role they play in technological and political management. Consequently, pluralism is strictly circumscribed by managerial necessity. The substance of democracy is limited to conflicts among elites; though the rituals and symbols of democracy proliferate, chiefly as forms of social control. An ill-informed citizenry is unable to distinguish between substance and symbol.

According to Skocpol (1979) and other "state-centered" theorists, the international arena is increasingly characterized by both competition and cooperation among centralized states. State policies now tend to reflect the outcomes of internal elite conflicts over whether to pursue nationalist or internationalist strategies.

Managerial theorists explain deregulation as a response to the growing complexity of the telecommunications industry and the failures of representative regulation to manage the industry successfully. One source of complexity is the quantitative increase in available services made possible by the growth of technology. More importantly, according to the managerial view, the quantitative increase in services has led to qualitative changes in the structure of the industry. Old regulatory approaches based on distinct technologies and discrete services and industries do not work in an era of integrated technologies, services and markets.

For example, the distinction between communication and data processing initially had its roots in both technology—the difference beween a telephone and a computer—and in industry structure, AT&T and Bell Canada, which were regulated and IBM, which was not. Microelectronics diminishes the functional distinctions between technologies: telephones contain microprocessors, computers communicate. Industry structures blur as computer firms enter telecommunications and vice versa. The growing stakes in computer communications leads many large information users to enter the market so that, now, banks, insurance firms, retailers, and others become information providers. In essence, several discrete, manageable technologies and industry sectors merge into an increasingly integrated, and far less manageable *electronic services arena*. (Bruce, et al., 1986) Managerial theory maintains that the experience of the FCC in the United States, the CRTC in Canada, and state authorities in Europe has shown that it is difficult, if not impossible, to apply traditional regulatory categories to this new arena, or even to develop new ones that might improve regulation and management.

Managerial theory also maintains that in the absence of fundamental structural change, i.e. a new policy agenda, more powerful interests in the industry resist challenges from competitors by using the regulatory apparatus to maintain their power. One example of this managerial version of the familiar "capture" thesis sees major telephone companies and private broadcasters, building alliances with regulators and their governmental overseers to shape whatever changes take place in the arena to their advantage. The control these established interests achieve is worth the costs of a fragmented system whose rules bear little relationship to reality.

Deregulation, according to this view, stems from the development of a coalition powerful enough to undermine the old line established powers. In telecommunications this would include, chiefly, new conservative governments and large corporate users. Functionally, deregulation is still state intervention used to extend rationalization and managerial efficiency by overcoming the fragmentation caused by dominant interest capture of state agencies. Politically, a new power bloc seizes the policy agenda from a bloc linked to the traditional regulatory agenda. The new group wins out because it is able to apply its economic, political and informational resources more effectively; although, as the restructuring of AT&T and Bell Canada would indicate, not without significant compromises with the established powers. Much of the cost of the conflict shifts to those groups in society least able to oppose successfully (Aufderheide, 1987).

The major policy concern within the managerial view is that the market may not be the best long term vehicle for effective management of the sector. Deregulation and privatization provided the jolt that was needed for an industry characterized by both rapid technological change and stagnating regulation. But the initial result is excessively fragmented markets that fail to provide necessary coordination, guidance, or planning for the new arena, and eventually, power reconcentrates in the hands of industry leaders while calls increase for a return to regulation. Managerial perspectives on deregulation dread a return to what they perceive to be a cycle of regulatory stagnation.

We already observe these concerns being raised about the telecommunications industry. Weinhaus and Oettinger cite the value of a monopoly controlled public switched network to the military and the concerns of the Pentagon about how divestiture and deregulation can erode network efficiency and integrity (Weinhaus and Oettinger, 1987: 89-90). A Brookings Institution report argues that the US needs a National Technology Office, a government agency which would underwrite basic research in information technology and support creation of what are increasingly called "precompetitive" joint commercial ventures in order to strengthen the US position by overcoming the fragmentation inherent in open competition. (Flamm, 1987) Similar calls have come from Canadian policy makers. (Canada, 1987) Others worry about the rapid reassertion of monopoly power in the post-divestiture period, following the pattern of reconcentration established in the airline industry (Guyon, 1987; Kilman, 1987).

As a result of these concerns, managerial theory leads us to anticipate growing discussion of non-regulatory alternatives to private markets. Possible candidates include forms of corporatism, particularly where oppositional forces are strong enough to require co-optation and expert panels or boards, where opposition is not strong.

Class Theory
Class theory sees power as systemic, and consequently, calls on the analyst to comprehend more than its manifestation in situation and structure. In general, situational and structural power are the realization of systemic power relations. To understand telecommunications policy, we need to expand the focus beyond the divestiture case or the agenda of decision-making which has come to be called deregulation. Class theory sees control over decisions and agendas as expressions of dynamic processes and power relations that exist in the system at large—in this case, developed capitalist societies.

Two major strands of class theory encompass the perspective's functional and political dimensions. Each grows out of and responds critically to earlier class theories of state monopoly capitalism (Jessop, 1982).

The State as Ideal Collective Capitalist
The first, or *state derivationist*, view derives the state from the fundamentals of capitalism, particularly from the need to overcome systemic contradictions. According to this perspective, the state functions as the "ideal collective capitalist," serving the interests of capital in general, not just the monopoly sector, as state monopoly capitalist theory would contend.

These interests include, first and foremost, advancing capital accumulation by providing and maintaining a productive infrastructure, creating and enforcing a legal order that makes markets and commodity exchange possible, regulating conflicts between capital and labour, and promoting the total national capital in world markets (Jessop, 1982).

As the state works to meet these goals, it faces problems that develop from a fundamental contradiction. The state is called on to perform a wide range of managerial activities but is denied entry to the private productive core to generate the necessary surplus to perform these activities. Consequently, the state's activities on behalf of capital depend on its abilities to secure revenues from the privately generated surplus. The state is faced with the challenge of promoting accumulation as it seeks to withdraw revenues from the accumulation process. The globalization of capital adds to pressures on the state because it is also responsible for achieving a sufficient degree of global capitalist coordination, necessary for markets to work without advancing the creation of a global state (Barker, 1978). Though day-to-day relationships between the state and capital are characterized by bargaining and compromise, capital retains the ultimate discipline, the institutionalized right of capital withdrawal.

State Power
Responding to the view that state derivationist theory is too functional, too focussed on legitimate, integrative state activities, a second, or *state power*, variant of class analysis, addresses political conflict in capitalist society. Drawing on the work of Gramsci, state power theorists see the state in developed capitalist societies as a vehicle for building hegemony and maintaining class power, without appearing to do so. Though force and coercion remain means of control, developed capitalist states increasingly work hegemonically, that is, by mobilizing and reproducing the active consent of non-dominant classes through moral, political and ideological means.

In this view, the state faces systemic conflicts that spring from class antagonisms woven into a labour process that maintains the division between managerial control and wage labour. The state, responsible for controlling these antagonisms before they become systemic conflicts, uses two complementary means of hegemonic control that are particularly important. Combining Poulantzas (1978) and Jessop, we can call these the *isolation-unification effects*.

The *isolation* effect is the process whereby the state identifies the agents of production, not as members of antagonistic classes, capital and labour, but as individual legal subjects. As a result, economic agents tend to experience capitalism, not as a system of class relations, but as relations of competition among mutually isolated individuals and/or fragmented groups of workers and capitalists.

Complementary to this, in the *unifying effect*, the state presents itself as the strictly political public unity of the people as nation, the abstract sum of formally free and equal legal subjects. As the sole representative of the nation, the state is the central source of dispute resolution, aiming to turn class, gender and national conflict into individual instances for state mediation.

To achieve these ends, the state employs a variety of tactics. From time to time, the state shifts the locus of actual power from one part of the state apparatus to another, depending on the balance of pressures on different parts of the state. In essence, the state presents itself as the sole agent for solving the problems of individual juridical citizens until such time as pressures threaten to aggregate into a major organized or class-based threat. At that point, the state can introduce *direct coercion* or *reform* itself to eliminate the major source conflict.

These tactics do not always succeed. They sometimes fail because the more limited and structured sets of interests that form in each particular sector of the state, clash with the long-term needs of capital. As Benda (1979) has shown, state managers do not necessarily operate out of a sense of long term systemic interests. Rather, they advance bureaucratic rationalization—a combination of self- and group interest—which does not always correspond to the systemic interest. Tactics also fail because they clash with people's lived experience and with the organizing efforts of non-dominant class members.

To the extent that they fail, there is movement away from what Poulantzas calls the "normal" to the "exceptional" form of the state, one which elliminates democratic institutions and the autonomous organization of non-dominant classes such as has taken place in Chile under Pinochet. Corporatism is a form between normal and exceptional which is looked on favourably because it allows for formulation of policy outside the normal voting, party, or regional apparatus. It also allows for more of the necessary *ad hoc* decision-making that permits incorporation of supportive groups from the non-dominant classes and the complete exclusion of any radical elements.

Deregulation and the Information Commodity
From a class perspective, deregulation responds to the recognition that telecommunications, and its related informatics and communications sectors, have come to occupy a central place in the capital accumulation process. Under the shaping influence of capital, with considerable state (particularly military) assistance, technology has deepened and extended the ability to make the products of computer communications, such as data and information, marketable commodities. The data/information commodity, a value in its own right, also enhances the value of more traditional commodities.

In general terms, information, and the technology that produces and circulates it, overcome the space and time constraints that have previously inhibited capital from expanding territory and function, while retaining centralized control (Castells, 1985). The application of communication and information technology is vital for building an international division of labour that permits capital to take profitable advantage of the most stable markets for financing, raw materials, and labour. As a 1987 report from the US Congress, Office of Technology Assessment notes, this increases the power of large transnational corporations:

New transportation and communications technologies, including high-speed air travel, bulk shipping facilities, flexible manufacturing and automation, distributed data processing and communications capabilities, and high-speed transmission of information, have allowed transnational corporations to shift operations between countries, depending on contingencies such as labor costs, availability of resources, and the political and economic climate of their host nation. These developments have increased the power of the transnational corporation, as economies of scale have allowed the internationalization and vertical integration of their markets. (US Congress, 1987a)

The process of deregulation and privatization accelerates the commodification of information by rupturing the traditional relationships of business, the state, and labour. These relationships provided a workable regulatory solution during an era of continuous economic growth, national market focus, and a strong labour movement. In the United States, the relationship that linked the old AT&T, the Congress and the FCC, the Communications Workers of America, and individual phone users is a prime example of the earlier solution. In Canada, this solution linked Bell and other monopoly telephone companies, the government, regulators, unions such as the Communications Workers of Canada and the Telecommunications Workers Union of British Columbia, and local customers. In return for providing secure employment and near universal phone service, AT&T was guaranteed an effective monopoly and a steady and secure return to shareholders.

According to a class perspective, this relationship is called into question by increasing reliance on telecommunications for economic growth, the centrality of global markets, and weakened trade unionism. Deregulation and its corollaries, divestment, privatization, etc., are instruments that forge the global expansion of telecommunication and information, as industries, and as sources of transnational capital expansion generally. One reason for this is that deregulation eliminates such alternatives to narrow market values as a commitment to employment security and low cost local service. AT&T has eliminated thousands of mostly union jobs since divestiture. Bell Canada has also eliminated thousands since the company was reorganized. (Chapter Five examines the employment consequences). New telecommunications companies, like their counterparts in the deregulated airline industry, are lower-wage, less unionized firms. Even proponents of deregulation (Noam, 1987) admit that phone bills have increased for individual households and are likely to increase further as deregulation advances. From a class perspective, in the absence of a counter political movement, this is just the begining of a process that will transform almost all electronic communication, telecommunication, and information products and transactions into marketable commodities.

Deregulation and Social Control

This stress on capital accumulation risks an overly economistic view. Deregulation is additionally a political instrument, one that "unleashes" new instruments of social control. As Robins and Webster put it:

> There is a sphere in which capital seeks to influence, not ideas or profits, but the very rhythms, patterns, pace, texture and discipline of everyday life. Within our wider focus upon power relations in society, this represents—to use Foucault's term—the terrain upon which operate the 'systems of micro-power.' For us, the 'communications revolution' is socially significant insofar as it represents a recomposition of the microstructures—and of the experience—of everyday life. (1988: 46-47)

The capacity of telecommunications and information technologies to measure and monitor every transaction amplifies the potential for workplace and consumer surveillance, producing a substantial increase in opportunities for social management and control. According to the Office of Technology Assessment (US Congress, 1987b) "Now, there are nearly unlimited means of electronic surveillance, some from great distances (even from satellites) and with almost no risk of detection by those being watched." (p. 13) According to a class perspective, analyses that concentrate solely on the economic potential, the financial winners and losers, miss what is most significant about the technology. It holds the potential to be, at the same time and in all aspects of social life, an instrument for capital accumulation *and* social control.

The stakes in social management and control add significance to the struggle over eliminating regulation. Indeed, when non-dominant groups began achieving success applying pressure on the regulatory apparatus to implement their values more forcefully, the movement to deregulate undermined this success. It was not until 1969 that a US court made the FCC, acknowledging what the court termed "a profound hostility to the participation of Public Intervenors and their efforts," grant standing to public interest groups in Commission proceedings (Head and Sterling, 1982: 499-501) This resulted in a decade of strong public pressure on the FCC, particularly regarding mass electronic media. According to a class analysis, deregulation is a response to the pressure of mounting social claims on the communications system; it is a means of eliminating social claims that the courts decided could not be cut off by FCC administrative action. Deregulation thus becomes one way the state re-forms itself to eliminate an arena of potential class conflict.

However, one result of deregulation is to increase pressure on the market to realize those universal service, fairness, and other values that regulation sought to achieve as well as putting increased pressure on the social welfare apparatus of the state (Lifeline services, Link-up America, Phone Stamps, etc.) to offset the anticipated failure of the market to meet non-market goals. As Keane puts it, this is asking the system to do the impossible:

> The implication is that the overall survival of the 'unregulated' sphere of capitalist exchange depends upon the continuous application of forms of 'collective regulation.' ... In a word, welfare state policies are required to do the impossible: they are forced to reorganize and restrict the mechanisms of capitalist accumulation in order to allow those mechanisms to spontaneously take care of themselves. (In Offe, 1984: 15-16)

Opposition to Deregulation
Politically speaking, none of these solutions is likely to satisfy non-dominant groups, particularly the beneficiaries of earlier regulatory arrangements such as trade unions, individual customers, small business, and voluntary associations. We already see evidence of coalition-building in opposition to deregulation.

However, the strength of those—particularly transnational users—who support deregulation, divestiture of AT&T, privatization of British Telecom, and reorganization of Bell Canada, as well as the movement toward deregulation and privatization on the European continent, make a return to the old form unlikely. The balance created by opposing forces, particularly the ability of trade unions and the public interest lobby to recover from a decade of decline, will influence the mix of regulatory, corporatist, or expert-based alternatives that are introduced.

Offe, and other class analysts, would deny the possibility of a satisfactory long-term solution. Reich is correct, they would contend, arguing that some form of collective solidarity or trust is necessary to buffer the uneven distributional consequences of globalization. But given the fundamental conflict of interests in developed capitalist societies, such trust is possible only *within* certain classes or a particular social movement. No broad-based society-wide solidarity seems possible.

Moreover, the tendency to deregulation and privatization is only likely to make it more difficult to develop a sense of common purpose. Class theorists maintain that the private market is an economic and technical instrument for settling claims. It is rooted in individualistic self-interest. It cannot be expected to succeed at this *and* support collective actions for which meaningful and norm-oriented behaviour is essential.

The private market will more likely than not lead to *market-overload,* the class theory counterpart to government-overload in managerial theory. Class theory argues that the pressures to open competitive markets, domestically and internationally, for a range of commodity, near-commodity, and even non-commodity goods and services (social services is a good example of the latter), likely lead to market breakdowns. The "governability crisis" is most likely a symptom of a deeper crisis of the marketplace.

Class theories of the state have flourished over the past two decades. There is considerable debate within the perspective and with pluralist and managerial theories. A major concern within class analysis weighs the significance of non-class factors in creating the conditions for effective opposition. Though class is a dimension of the politics of deregulation, particularly in the debate on universal service and employment, much of the organized opposition in the US, Canada, and other developed capitalist societies is based on groups whose cohesion is indirectly tied to social class. Gender, age, religion, the environment, and nationality are the usual bases of solidarity in opposition. Class analysts have begun to incorporate non-class factors in their understanding of opposition and the formation of social movements, though most are simply catalogues of non-class forces. To my knowledge, Haight and Weinstein (1981) have offered the only analytic argument that seeks to understand, in the tradition of Piven and Cloward's work on social welfare movements, the relationship of movement activity to the policy process in communications.

Conclusion

In 1400 A.D., 1300 years after the death of Ptolemy and 70 years before the birth of Copernicus, astronomers persisted in stretching the model of an earth-centered universe to fit what their observations told them was not so. Today, neo-classical economists persist in stretching the model of an open, competitive marketplace to fit a world of oligopoly and monopoly. They argue that we can eliminate telephone price regulation even though markets are not competitive because they are *contestable*.* Moreover, we can support government subsidized corporate cartels in the computer industry because these are now *precompetitive arrangements*.

The descendants of Ptolemy believed that by adding a few more cycles to their diagrams, they could avoid a paradigm shift. The descendants of Adam Smith believe they can do it with euphemisms. This chapter has been a modest effort, by no means Copernican, to suggest ways of accentuating the *political* in the political economy of telecommunication; specifically, by drawing on contemporary political and social theory, the chapter has pointed to concepts and conceptual schemes for viewing the political dimension of telecommunications policy and regulation. Concretely, it has offered ways of expanding the discussion of policy issues beyond dichotomous thinking (to regulate or not to regulate), and ways of seeing the politics of policy which do justice to the central role of telecommunications in contemporary social life.

---

* This is of more than conceptual interest. According to *The Wall Street Journal*, AT&T, not the consumer is "the bigger winner" in those American states that have lifted profit regulation. In Maryland, "which AT&T considers a model of how price—rather than profit regulation—should work" the company earned a 125% return on investment for the year ending March 31, 1987. In Pennsylvania it is earning a 20% return, and in South Carolina, AT&T has gone from an operating loss to a rate-of-return on investment of 43.6%. (Guyon, 1987)

Chapter Five

Labour in the Information Age:

A Critical Sociological Perspective

Introduction: The Sociological Imagination

To be aware of the idea of social structure and to use it with sensibility is to be capable of tracing linkages among a variety of milieux. To be able to do that is to possess the sociological imagination. (Mills, 1959: 11)

Chapter Four touched on the impact of deregulation and privatization on labour and trade unions. This chapter uses a critical sociological perspective to address in more detail the role of work and working people within the rapidly changing computer and communication industries. To do this, we need to begin with a particular vision of social science, what C. Wright Mills referred to as *the sociological imagination.*

The sociological imagination is a way of thinking about society that starts with the connections between history and biography. What are the links between the major political, economic, and social upheavals taking place around us and the day-to-day activities of our lives? In Mills' more graphic terms, it means making the link between the personal feeling of experiencing life as "a series of traps" and the "seemingly impersonal structures in continent wide societies." (Ibid.: 3) Social scientists keep their eyes open to these connections because, as Mills puts it:

> What we experience in various and specific milieux ... is often caused by structural changes. Accordingly, to understand the changes of many personal milieux we are required to look beyond them. And the number and variety of such structural changes increase as the institutions within which we live become more embracing and more intricately connected with one another. (Ibid.: 10)

A Critical Perspective

The sociological imagination is a broad vision about the need to comprehend the relationship between historical change and individual experience. A critical sociological perspective, one means of applying this imagination to social life, begins by examining how social relationships are formed and change due to the very process of *producing* what we need to *reproduce* ourselves. In other words, how are people organized to fulfill the basic functions necessary to keep the society going over the generations? Though admittedly an oversimplification, Figure 5.1 summarizes this process by linking processes of production, or a primary economic strategy, to specific social forms. These forms are then linked to the major cultural bonds such as kinship, custom, and contract. Cultural bonds integrate social forms and permit them to develop into a larger community structure. At the same time, each level of social production and reproduction is subjected to disintegrative processes, chiefly emerging out of experimentation with new forms of production.

Figure 5.1 is historical in two senses. It identifies an early and a late period within a particular social formation, such as the transition from commercial to industrial capitalism. It also distinguishes successive social formations such as feudalism and capitalism. The result is a framework, admittedly more suggestive than definitive, for understanding social change. The framework does not indicate any *necessary* set of stages through which a society must pass as there is still extensive debate among sociologists about the specific elements described here (Giddens, 1983).

Nevertheless, the diagram offers a useful way of seeing the results of the drive to produce what we need to reproduce ourselves and thereby maintain social life over the generations. Moreover, it sets a historical context for understanding changes taking place today. Specifically, it

Figure 5.1
A Way of Seeing the Development of Social Forms

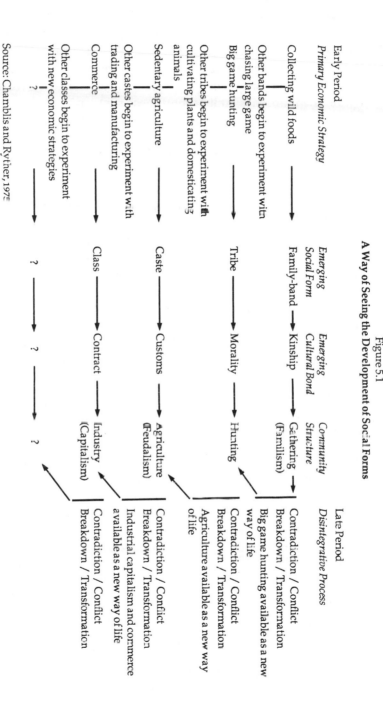

Source: Chambliss and Ryther, 1975

leads us to consider whether the growing implementation of computer communications systems suggest the development of a new "primary economic strategy." Or does the proliferation of these technological systems simply reflect the deepening and extension of industrial capitalism? More specifically, what is the place of labour and the working class within the industries built around these systems?

These issues are inextricably connected. We need to have some idea of the form of society in order to comprehend labour's role within it. This is an exercise in the sociological imagination.

Deepening and Extending Control

Mills used the sociological imagination to criticize established perspectives that he felt were not especially useful for understanding the vital link between the historical process and individual development. Chiefly, he singled out "grand theorizing," which builds mountains of concepts and models that, however elegant, lack social rootedness. He also criticized "abstracted empiricism," which, according to Mills, worshipped at the alter of data or isolated facts without a defined theoretical or historical context that would help us make sense out of empirical observations. A similar exercise of the sociological imagination leads us to question just what kind of society are changes in communication and information technology purportedly bringing about.

Most leading perspectives in this area see the technology pushing beyond capitalism, particularly industrial capitalism, toward a new form of society. These perspectives, largely variants of Bell's postindustrial society thesis, see computer communications systems as, in Pool's expression, "technologies of freedom" (Pool, 1983). At best such technologies will serve as instruments to rid society of fundamental antagonisms endemic to capitalism (Toffler, 1980). But, if not this beneficent, according to these theorists, technology will provide the instruments to manage and contain social conflict in a manner not possible under industrial capitalism (Bell, 1973).

In either case, society develops beyond industrial capitalism to a more prosperous (as productivity rises), less regimented (because technology permits decentralization), and more cooperative system (since work is redefined to mean people providing services for each other).

The primary economic strategy shifts to services from making and distributing goods. Class differences change into status groups based on consumption tastes, particularly the consumption of information and entertainment. Contractually-based networks give way to networks

The question marks in Figure 5-1 are replaced with:

Strategy	Form		Bond	Structure
Service	Status	/ Information	Electronic	Information
		Groups	Communication	Society

linked by computer communication systems. Industrial capitalism gives way to an information society.

Alternatively, there are good arguments to be made that rather than leading to a new social form, developments in communication and information technology are deepening and extending major characteristics of the capitalist system.

The conceptual roots of computer communication systems are embedded in problems of controlling factors of production, particularly labour. As Braverman has described, Charles Babbage developed the principles of computer technology in the 1830s in order to lower the costs of production, chiefly labour costs, and to extend managerial control:

> One great advantage which we may derive from machinery is from the check which it affords against the inattention, the idleness, or the dishonesty of human agents. (Babbage, 1832, cited in Braverman, 1974: 195)

Capitalism has applied this principle of control throughout the history of information technology applications. As Canadian sociologist Graham Lowe (1987) has demonstrated in his history of office mechanization, the principles of control which Babbage identified, but could not apply because he lacked the technology, were put into practice over the next century through three major successive developments.

The *typewriter* was used to mechanize, cheapen, and feminize clerical work. Next, managers used *mechanical accounting* and calculating devices, e.g. adding machines, to further routinize and deskill office work. Finally, *Hollerith* machines, mechanical punch-card calculators developed at the turn of the century, adapted these single purpose devices to create complex multi-function control systems, paving the way for the computer and today's automated office.

With this in mind, it is hard to disagree with Giddens' comments on the postindustrial society thesis:

> But there is a much more integral and continuous connection

between information control and processing and the rise of capitalist society than such a view would suggest. (Giddens, 1983: 175)

The historical development of information control networks is deepened and extended today with the development of integrated systems comprised of digital computers for processing information, fibre optic cable and communication satellite systems for distributing it, and high-definition screens for display. These make up computer communication networks that measure and monitor information transactions and permit the packaging and repackaging of information into a marketable commodity. There is nothing fundamentally new about a society in which information and labour are commodities produced and sold for profit.

With this in mind, as Chapter One noted, the term I find most useful to think about a society marked by the use of computer communications systems for control and profit is not post-industrial society, information age or any of the others. Rather, I call it the *Pay-per Society*. First, the term captures the essence of what computer communication systems are used to do—measuring and monitoring information transactions for control and profit. Second, we hear more and more reference to pay-per in a variety of areas. For example, there is pay-per telephone call, pay-per view in video, pay-per bit, minute, screenful, or page in the information business. Advertisers refer to pay-per body in marketing audiences. In the office it's pay-per keystroke, per customer, per phone call, etc. The Pay-per Society, including the commodification of information, is a detailed version of what Giddens refers to as a fundamental process in contemporary capitalism, the commodification of time and space. (Giddens, 1983) Computer communication systems that significantly reduce the constraints which time and space imposed on production, distribution and consumption of commodities deepen and extend capitalist society.

Labour in the Pay-per Society

A critically informed sociological perspective identifies four processes that help us map out the place of labour in the Pay-per Society. These are domination/hegemony, contradiction, opposition, and transformation.

Domination

Domination / hegemony is a dual process by which a powerful class exercises its social control, including control over labour. Domination is the direct exercise of coercive power, typically through physical control or the threat of that control. Hegemony, following Gramsci (1971) and Williams (1980), is power exercised by controlling the values that people use to define themselves and their place in everyday life.

(Un)employment

Both domination and hegemony are enhanced by the application of computer communication systems. Domination is achieved by using these systems to eliminate jobs or deskill them and thereby cheapen their value. Research in the North American telecommunications industry (Mosco and Zureik, 1987), where state of the art communications systems are used, indicates significant employment impacts. In 1950, there were 244,190 telephone operators in the United States handling 175,721,148 long distance calls. By 1980, the number of such calls increased to 2,641,713,000, a 15-fold increase. Yet, the number of phone operators employed actually dropped to 128,214. Kohl estimates that, without technological change, operator employment would have reached over 3.5 million by 1980. Management was able to cut its wage bill by introducing computerized switching systems that performed the work of telephone operators. Employment declines have not been as precipitous in Canada, chiefly because of stronger union resistance to job cuts and more widespread social resistance to policies of deregulation and privatization which make job cutbacks easier to carry out.

Computer communications systems are now being employed throughout the telephone system. In addition to a declining need for operators, telephone companies use new technologies to eliminate the jobs of craft workers, who perform such technical work as installation and repair, and clerical workers, who do record keeping, billing, and related jobs. (Mosco and Zureik, 1987) Deregulation and the breakup of AT&T has made it easier to eliminate jobs because telephone companies are no longer under pressure to moderate development of job-destroying new technologies. Rather, they feel the intense pressure of heightened national and international competition, which leads them to find new ways to cut employment. It is not encouraging to see significant job declines in an industry at the forefront of technological innovation. (Table 5.1).

Automated systems have been, or are now being applied throughout the communications industries to eliminate jobs in printing (Zimbalist, 1979: 103-126), broadcasting (Wasko, 1983: 85-113), film (Neilson, 1983: 47-83), and the computer industry itself (Kraft and Dubnoff, 1986). Indeed,

Table 5.1
U.S. Telephone Companies Since Divestiture:
Income Up, Employment Down

Company	Revenue ($ billions)		Income ($ billions)		Employees (as of Dec 31)	
	'84	'87	'84	'87	'84	'87
AT&T	33.19	33.60	1.37	2.04	365,200	303,000
Ameritech	8.35	9.54	.99	1.19	77,514	78,510
Bell Atlantic	8.09	10.30	.97	1.24	79,500	80,950
Bell South	9.63	12.27	1.26	1.67	96,000	98,664
NYNEX	9.57	12.08	.99	1.28	94,900	90,000
Pacific Telesis	7.82	9.13	.83	.95	76,881	71,877
Southwestern Bell	7.19	8.00	.88	1.05	71,900	67,085
US West	7.28	8.44	.89	1.01	70,765	68,523

Source: *The Wall Street Journal*, March 9, 1988: 16.

as Shaiken and Scott, two experts in automation technology, indicate: what distinguishes this period of technological development from others, such as the industrial revolution, is that new technologies are specifically *built*, not to increase the productivity of workers, but to eliminate them. (Draper, 1985: 49)

The Redistribution of Work
In addition to using technology to diminish the number of jobs, business is directing a massive redistribution of work activity to lower costs and extend control over the workplace. Three major redistributional activities are the shift of jobs from unionized to non-unionized occupations within the communication industries, the shift of work activity, once performed by wage labourers, to consumers, and the development of an international division of labour.

The areas of greatest job growth in the information sector are largely non-unionized. This reflects a shift, noted by Oettinger (1980), in the general structure of the information industries. Traditionally, the information sector was mainly comprised of companies that produced information products (paper) or conduits (telephone cable) and information services(mail delivery) or content (broadcast programming). Over the years, strong unions have been organized in Canada and the US to represent workers in these industries. However, in the past decade or so, the largest area of industry growth is outside of these sectors, in computer service bureaus, software design companies, and computer time-sharing firms, among others, where the line between products and services, conduits and content is blurred.

This shift of activity results, in part, from the recognition by investors that it is more appealing and profitable to invest in sectors where the workforce is unorganized. The shift also conforms to general societal employment shifts. Extrapolating to the future, the US Bureau of Labour statistics identify these five as the largest job growth occupations to 1995: building custodian, cashier, secretary, office clerk, and sales clerk—largely non-union, low-paying jobs. The last four are part of what is known, too politely, as the pink-collar ghetto—jobs that large numbers of women have moved into over the last twenty years. They pay low wages and offer little or no mobility potential. (Rumberger and Levin, 1985)

In addition to jobs shifting from sectors where workers have wielded some power to areas where they have not, we can observe a shift in work activity from well-paid wage labour to consumers.

The telecommunications industry leads this development. The proliferation of retail phone stores gives consumers choice in the selection of equipment; but it also means that consumers now purchase and install equipment that the telephone company once paid workers a middle-range income to deliver and install. More and more of the directory assistance and dialing work is now the consumer's responsibility. Specific charges for each individual phone service permit companies to use financial incentives to get consumers to perform more of the work. This is similarly the case for repair, disconnect and reinstallation services. This shift diminishes the need for hard-fought and well-paid craft work and thereby increases managerial domination over the labour force.

One can find some examples that run counter to this trend as many consumers now have workers do jobs once assumed to be outside of the labor marketplace. However, when one looks to the major areas where this growth is taking place—the fast food industry and day care are prime examples—it is clear that these areas are among the lowest-paying occupations in the labour force.

A third shift is the development of an international division of labour. Computer communications technology allows a company to centralize key finance, marketing, research and planning decisions in a First World head office by delivering a regular stream of information brought in by its global information network. This frees a company to use the world—increasingly the Third World—as its source of raw materials, production sites and labour. Companies now routinely take advantage of cost differentials, anti-union policies and generally favorable political conditions. (Bluestone and Harrison, 1982; Siegel and Markoff, 1985; Nash and Fernandez-Kelly, 1983).

The international division of labour also gives enormous flexibility to a company that can respond to changing political or economic conditions by shifting parts of its activities to a more stable or cheaper location. Companies have pursued this in a number of ways, including operating twin plants that permit shifting work from one to the other in the event of labour trouble, contracting with multiple vendors for materials to address the same problem, and opening up so-called off-shore information-processing activities that make use of communication facilities to take advantage of low-cost Third World clerical workers. (Fuentes and Ehrenreich, 1983; Nash and Fernandez-Kelly, 1983) Computer communications systems that can centralize decision-making and deconcentrate operations extend control over labour.

Deskilling
Such control is also achieved through changes in the nature of work. New communication and information technology deepen and extend the process that started with the rise of industrial capitalism: *deskilling*, separating conception from execution in the workplace and concentrating conceptual power in management. Deskilling removes the fundamental distinction between human and animal labour. As Marx put it:

> A spider conducts operations that resemble those of a weaver, and a bee puts to shame many an architect in the construction of her cells. But what distinguishes the worst architect from the best of bees is this, that the architect raises his structure in imagination before he erects it in reality. At the end of every labour-process, we get a result that already existed in the imagination of the labourer at its commencement. (Marx, in Braverman, 1974: 45-46)

Deskilling takes the power of conception away from the individual worker and vests it in machines and management. As early as 1832, Babbage recognized that such a process could be applied "to mental as to mechanical operations." (Babbage, 1832: 191) A modern day Babbage, Harvey Brooks, professor of technology and public policy at Harvard and a member of both the National Academy of Sciences and of Engineering identifies the "further subdivision of jobs, deskilling," as a means of controlling costs and labor (Brooks, 1983: 122). Recent research has applied and refined the deskilling thesis in factory (Shaiken, 1984), office (Howard, 1985), and service (Reiter, 1986) settings.

Deskilling is pronounced in the telephone industry, where skilled craft and semi-skilled operator service workers once predominated. Today, management continues the process of deskilling craft workers that began with the shift from mechanical to electro-mechanical switching systems. Fully electronic digital systems now organize and direct the work of craft employees, such as repair workers, who once controlled the process by "trouble shooting" for problems, determining the timing, the pace, and the precise means of doing repair work. Today, craft workers are found behind the same video display terminals (VDT) confronting operators and clerical workers, and in similar fashion, respond to direct and detailed orders from the screen.

For telephone operators, deskilling shifts plugging into and out of a cord board to responding to instructions that appear on a VDT. Under the former system, operators were limited to working at the board. Nevertheless operators had some control over the types of calls, the pace of work, and could share the work burden among a group of operators. Today, computer controlled systems determine who takes what calls and how often. Work stations are individuated so that there is no work sharing; once one customer is off the line, another is automatically fed on.

Finally, clerical workers who once controlled service order, record, and billing systems for individual customers, now have their work completely structured by computerized filing systems. The machines now embody managerial control over conception: the work force is reduced to machine tending.

Hegemony

These processes of domination are reinforced through *hegemony*, a more subtle process of achieving managerial control. Hegemony insinuates control into workers' expectations, attitudes, and thought processes. It is the process of making managerial control part of the taken-for-granted culture of the workplace. (Zuboff, 1988)

Hegemony differs from domination in that it works at the *microsocial* level by changing attitudes, values, modes of expression and, in essence, principle *ways of seeing, ways of talking* and *ways of thinking* about social life. Foucault sees it as a form of power that has accelerated in use since the eighteenth century:

> But in thinking of the mechanisms of power, I am thinking rather of its capillary form of existence, the point where power reaches into the very grain of individuals, touches their bodies and inserts itself into their actions and attitudes, their discourses, learning processes and everyday lives. The eighteenth century invented, so to speak, a synaptic regime of power, a regime of its exercise *within* the social body, rather than *from above* it. (Foucault, 1980: 39)

According to Foucault, beginning in the eighteenth century, people came to realize the value of surveillance as an economical means of social control. This gave rise, initially, to changes in forms of incarceration, such as the Panopticon, a prison structure developed by English social philosopher Jeremy Bentham. The Panopticon, a circular prison with a central tower, permitted guards to observe constantly the behaviour of inmates. For Foucault, the image of the Panopticon, a society under constant surveillance, has been greatly magnified in the twentieth century as those in power realize it is "more efficient and profitable in terms of the economy of power to place people under surveillance than to subject them to some exemplary penalty." (Ibid.: 38)

In Mills terms, surveillance is a key point where history touches biography in the twentieth century. The historical development of technologies that centralize and extend military and civilian government, and, also, corporate power are being used to manage and control large numbers of people *at the individual level*.

Computer communications systems now advance workplace hegemony by making possible the detailed monitoring of work activity. Heretofore, technological limitations made managerial control less certain. Management had, by today's standards, blunt instruments to realize in practice its principles of workplace control. Much uncertainty about control is being eliminated by computer systems that measure and monitor in detail the work of each individual (Figure 5.2).

In the telephone industry, electronic switching systems that feed calls to operators also monitor how long it takes to process each call, how many calls an operator handles each day, the length of breaks, etc. Operators are subjected to sixty to seventy measures in all. The major index, Average Work Time (AWT), measures how long it takes for an operator

---

Figure 5.2
Some Office Jobs Currently Subject to Electronic Monitoring

Word processors

Data-entry clerks:
    Monitor speed, errors, time working
    By keystrokes counted by computer

Telephone operators
    Monitor average time per call
    By automatic call distribution and timing system

Customer service workers
    Monitor time per customer, number and type of transaction
    By automatic call distribution and timing system and computerized
       transaction counting

Telemarketing/other sales
    Monitor time per customer and sales volume
    By call and transactions timing and computerized sales tabulation

Insurance claims clerks
    Monitor number of cases per unit of time
    By computerized measurement of time spent on each form

Mail clerks
    Monitor letters or packages processed per unit of time
    By computerized sorting machines

Bank proof clerks
    Monitor checks processed per unit of time
    By computerized proof machine

Source: US Congress, 1987b: 29.

---

to handle a call. This measure is updated regularly so that workers are frequently reminded if their time exceeds a norm of about thirty seconds per call.

Here, hegemony inserts managerial control into the rhythms, or better, the microrhythms, of day-to-day, second-by-second work. In broader cultural terms, hegemony works through company sponsored competitions that link rewards to those among rival groups of workers who achieve the lowest AWT.

The same computer controlled systems can monitor the performance of telephone craft workers by counting things like the number and speed of repair orders handled over a day or week. Here is how a repair worker in Canada explained the problems of detailed surveillance:

> Managers know everything you do from morning to night. There are analysts who demand to know where you have gone. The fact that you have gone is known since you must turn off your board. The computer keeps track of everything you do. (Mosco and Zureik, 1987: 78)

Another craft worker talks about managerial review of detailed surveillance reports:

> Department heads, etc. take the print-outs and sit down together to review the units per hour, minutes per visit per repair, sales per month, etc. of each worker. (Ibid.)

For now, computerized performance monitoring is concentrated among less skilled clerical and sales jobs. This alone makes it a particularly significant development for women, who have swelled the ranks of these occupations in the last twenty years. Nevertheless, such systems are expanding into more skilled craft work and, according to the US Office of Technology Assessment, are likely to expand further:

> Even the most complex work has its routine elements, and given sufficient analysis, those elements can be identified, grouped together, and counted. The jobs of commodities broker, computer programmer, and bank loan officer, for example, could lend themselves to monitoring. (US, Congress, 1987b)

Contradictions

A critical sociological perspective extends beyond domination and hegemony to identify *contradictions,* or fundamental social problems that emanate from the very practice of domination and hegemony. Two primary contradictions mark the contemporary workplace: between work and productivity and between work and consumption.

Research has questioned the efficiency of transferring the skills of trained machinists to computer controlled systems (Noble, 1984; Shaiken, 1984). Such a shift accomplishes increased managerial control, but often at the price of increased malfunctions and lost flexibility. Others have studied the office and identified the, often hidden, costs in expert personnel, software, and, most importantly, organizational dependency on a complex and poorly understood system, that can make the actual costs of office automation systems considerably higher than anticipated. (Kling and Kraemer, 1985)

Telephone workers put this contradiction best when they say that phone work has lost "the personal touch." Average Work Time quotas pressure operators to cut off subscribers prematurely, craft people "follow orders" rather than risk reprimand for questioning a computer order that they know to be incorrect, or cut corners in repair work to meet job quotas. For clerical workers it means comments like the following one Gregory (1982) reports in her research on office automation, "... when a person makes a mistake with a computer, to try and get that mistake corrected is so much red tape. So you tend to let it go. Maybe when they see how bad the information is, they'll give us back our jobs."

Telephone workers generally indicate that, though they are handling more calls or doing more repairs, the quality of service has not kept pace. In essence, the managerial control of computer communications draws management into adopting a narrow, quantitative measure of productivity which, while meeting short-run competitive pressures, can lead to long-run problems. After recognizing the cost savings and control possibilities in such rigid systems, Harvey Brooks cautions that they can force companies to adapt

> very slowly and incompletely to the rapidly changing technology and markets we face today in many industries. It is urgent that as a society we move toward a different philosophy of the division of labour, one that pays more attention to the continuous upgrading of human resources. (Brooks, 1983: 122)

The difficulty, which Brooks does not address, is that highly skilled workers are less willing to accept complete managerial control. It is also considerably more difficult for management to achieve widespread control over skilled workers who can, if inclined, use their skills to undermine centralized decision-making. Computer programmers, disgruntled by attempts to automate or otherwise deskill their work, have been known to use their skills to monitor company plans and undermine those that work against the interests of skilled workers.

The productivity contradiction is sharpened by the contradiction between work and consumption. If unemployment and deskilling lower the cost of labour, they also diminish the potential for mass consumption that the system relies on for expansion.

North American society has addressed this problem by increasing government and consumer debt. In the US, Reagan Administration policies supported this growing debt burden as a means of financing the modest economic expansion of the 1980s. As the financial crisis reached a critical state in late 1987, more and more analysts came to recognize that this can only provide a short-term solution. The continuation of such practices risks a fiscal crisis or even a more general economic one.

A long-run solution of sorts, is to restructure the class system, particularly by lowering the living standard of the middle class. The attack on trade unions, led by conservative governments in the US, Canada, and Great Britain, and the subsequent decline in the real wages of working people have been part of an effort to implement a new system of social classes. This effort has been partially masked by the increasing number of two-income families, which have maintained living standards in some households, but at the expense of an increase in the amount of wage labour performed by household members. However, if the short-run solution invited a fiscal crisis, the latter invites a crisis in political legitimacy. As more people question the social commitment to equality and fairness in the society (Offe, 1985), systemic contradictions become more transparent, systemic solutions, such as the redistribution of power and resources, become more obvious.

Opposition

Contradictions that mark labour's role in the communications industries help to create *opposition* that can constrain the forces of domination/hegemony and, in some cases, advance efforts to transform the social relations of the workplace. The Pay-per Society is a far from stable world. There is an accelerating gap, increasingly clear to more and more of the workforce, between the potential of the technology to democratize power and distribute economic gains more equitably, and the current drive to use the technology merely to centralize control and profit.

This gap is particularly pronounced for women, who have filled 80 per cent of the new jobs created in the US economy and are filling most of the new jobs opening up in the communication and information technology fields (Hacker, 1986: 26). Entering the job market out of economic necessity, or because they have incorporated values from the women's movement, women are finding that their pay and working conditions belie the promise of the new technology (Hacker, 1986; Hartmann, 1985).

The newspaper, broadcasting, and film industries have used the increasing flexibility of technology to package and repackage material, and increase profit by redistributing it to databases, videotex systems, cable television, and the videocassette market. To workers in these industries, this is a transparent attempt to wrest control and economic value from their labour. As a result, these industries have experienced numerous "new technology" strikes, fought over who will control production and reproduction of media, not only over traditional salary and wage issues.

There is considerable concern about technological change in the telephone industry where there is a strong feeling that systems which were supposed to improve workers' lives are instead being used to eliminate jobs, deskill work, lower wages, and intensify already stressful work. Labour has responded to this use of technology against its interest, a use accelerated by deregulation and the breakup of AT&T, with unprecedented opposition and unrest.

The gap between potential and reality has also become evident to many workers drawn into the growing microelectronics industry in the Third World. Companies have moved to Southeast Asia, Mexico, and other regions of the Third World, to save on labour costs and to exercise the sort of managerial control that is prohibited by law or contract in the developed world. However, the growth of trade unions and outright attacks on these companies have led microelectronics firms to intensify automation, return work to the developed world and otherwise curtail Third World operations. Company managements fear that their operations will be caught up in the sort of social uprising that overwhelmed the Marcos government in the Philippines. (Fuentes and Ehrenreich, 1983; Sussman, 1984; Siegel and Markoff, 1985)

Transformation

C. Wright Mills recognized that the sociological imagination could not stop at describing social life. It must live up to what he called "the Promise: its chance to make a difference in the quality of human life in our time." (Mills, 1959: 226) More concretely, Flacks and Turkel have called on sociology to "take as its goal human emancipation ... a condition in which each person has the chance to participate consciously in the formulation and direction of the social organization affecting him or her." (Flacks and Turkel, 1978: 193)

This commitment to social *transformation* seeks out social practices that push forward fundamental changes in the nature of labour in communication and information activities. A good example from the developed world is the activity of the Swedish Center for Working Life. The Center works with graphic and computer employees, and their trade unions, to advance worker control of printing and publishing (Swedish Center for Working Life, 1985). Other examples of popular control of technology include the worker plan to reorganize the Lucas Aerospace Company in Britain, GLC Enterprise Boards, and the Dutch Science Shops. In the Third World, Nicaragua has organized a nationwide literacy work campaign that raised the communications competence of its people to the highest levels in Latin America (Kozol, 1985). These examples aim to *transform* social and informational inequalities by changing the fundamental information production and distribution processes of their respective societies. However, it is important to guard against overemphasizing the significance of these efforts at social transformation. The forces using the new technology to advance elite rule are prodigious. Nevertheless, they are still subject to contradictions and conflicts that open the way to opposition. Such opposition provides clues to what labour will look like under a different system of production.

One should not look to technology to provide a sense of what replaces the question marks in Figure 5.1. Rather, we need to consider the work of people committed to alternative ways of producing what we need to reproduce ourselves *with or without the new technology*.

There is very little of this transformational thinking from which to draw today. Broad policy proposals provide some help. The Machinist union "Technology Bill of Rights" (Chapter Three) is a good example of the broad approach. It offers the type of alternative way of seeing new technology that is required to shake people's thinking. There has not even been widespread discussion of proposals that are one step below this broad visionary approach.

One set worth reflecting on is offered in Goldhaber's *Reinventing Technology* (1986), a study sponsored by the Washington, DC Institute for Policy Studies. One may find the book overly reliant on technological solutions that would come from a reconstituted federal bureaucracy. In an era marked by the ascendancy of conservative politics, it is easy to be cynical about proposed government agencies that include the Agency for Heightened Democratic Involvement and the Agency for Technology for Improving Childhood. But such understandable cynicism should not lead us to lose sight of a fundamental lesson. We need to think about the appropriate policy structure that developed societies would use to take the necessary first steps implementing a transformational strategy.

Goldhaber's thoughts are important first steps in this direction, particularly in the area of labour and new technology. He describes several agencies that would be responsible for implementing changes in the workplace. These include offices to use technology for full employment, and offices for job design that would promote gender equality, reskilling, and worker self-management. These agencies would provide the opportunity to raise issues of worker control to the center of the employment agenda and rectify the gross imbalance in government funded workplace research on anything other than technological fixes to boost productivity.

Conclusion

This chapter has applied a critical sociological paradigm to understand labour in communication and information industries. It started from Mills' vision of the sociological imagination and proceeded to situate contemporary developments in communication and information technology within a wider social structural setting.

The chapter demonstrated how communication and information technology is used to control labour. At the same it deepens contradictions and conflicts that open opportunities for social transformation, and for concrete alternatives to the Pay-per Society based on popular control over technology.

Contrary to mainstream theoretical perspectives and popular conceptions of the so-called information age, new information technology deepens and extends the social relations long dominant in capitalist society. We are more likely moving toward a "Pay-per" Society than a "free" society.

PART II

PUBLIC POLICY
IN THE PAY-PER SOCIETY

Chapter Six

The Military Information Society
and "Star Wars"

The second half of this book contains three chapters that address public policy issues in the development and application of computer communication systems. This chapter addresses the role of the military. We start with the military because, over the years, it has exerted the most substantial influence on the development of computer and communications systems. Chapters Seven and Eight, respectively, examine the civilian policy process in the United States and the impact of that process on public policy in Canada.

Military priorities have increasingly shaped the development of technology in the United States, particularly the development of communication and information technologies. This chapter examines the nature of military influence over the information society and focusses on "Star Wars" as the major contemporary manifestation of this influence.

The Military and New Technology

As the historian of technology Merritt Roe Smith has shown, the US military has exerted strong influence on the design, dissemination, and management of new technologies. It has influenced design "by establishing standards and specifications for various goods and contracting with private manufacturers for their production." (Smith, 1985: 6) Eventually, these technologies, from dehydrated foods to nuclear power plants, enter the civilian economy. Military support, including the financial backing of government funded research and development as well as the legitimacy of a government seal of approval, ease the process of technological dissemination. In some cases, such as "instant" foods, the consequences are arguably benign. In others, such as nuclear power, the impact is quite different.

The military, particularly the US Navy, was a major force in the application of nuclear energy to civilian uses. In fact, in 1953, the Navy received the backing of the US Atomic Energy Commission to oversee the design and construction of the first civilian nuclear power plant built in the United States. According to Hewlett and Duncan (1974), the Navy won out because nuclear power, particularly systems based on light water reactors, worked well on naval vessels. This success helped to inflate the hopes of reactor manufacturers, including such major defense contractors as General Electric and Westinghouse, and power companies. These interests used the US Navy's success to argue that energy costs would be reduced to a negligible fraction of a user's budget, if not "too cheap to meter." However, applying the relatively small scale naval use of nuclear energy to widespread commercial power generation raised enormous technical, managerial and political problems that continue to cause widespread negative social consequences. In a similar fashion and at around this same time, as Noble describes (1984), the US Air Force promoted the dissemination of numerical control tools by going as far as paying prime contractors to learn how to use the new technology. This action was not only far out of line with cost effectiveness, it contributed to the deskilling of the American machine tool workforce.

This military influence on design and dissemination extends to Canada. For example, over the past several years the US Pentagon has worked on the development of a microwave-powered aircraft for low-altitude surveillance. In 1988, the Canadian Ministry of Communication, with considerable fanfare, including a public test overseen by the Minister, boasted about its own SHARP (Stationary High Altitude Relay Platform) aircraft, a version of the one the Pentagon has developed. The boasting did not place surveillance at the center of SHARP's activities. In fact the Canadian government's draft request for development proposals (Canada, 1988) from industry describes the project as one that "could be used to provide services such as communications and broadcasting over an area on the ground up to 1000 km in diameter." (p. 1) Since the range of existing means to disseminate telecommunications and broadcasting material are quite extensive, including ground microwave, coaxial, copper and fibre optic cable, and communications satellites, it is hard to comprehend the additional value of an aircraft operating in a continuous circle at an altitude of 21 km. The Ministry's request for proposals does acknowledge the surveillance function, though it is presented in a rather benign fashion:

> The round-the-clock surveillance capability, combined with communications, could be effective in enhancing the safety and efficiency of fishing in Canadian territorial waters, as well as providing enhanced surveillance to control illegal activities. (Canada, 1988: 2)

Nevertheless, it is hard to resist concluding that the technology has little more than surveillance to recommend it.

In addition to its influence on the design and dissemination of technology, the military has set the pattern for the structure and style of corporate management. According to M.R. Smith (1985), the centralized and hierarchical structure of the military arms industry was applied to the management of the railroad industry. In fact, he contends that

> the history of every important metalworking industry in nineteenth century America—machine tools, sewing machines watches, typewriters, agricultural implements, bicycles, locomotives—reveals the pervasive influence of military management techniques. (p. 11)

This influence deepened in the twentieth century with the application of military regimentation to Henry Ford's automotive plants and the development and application of scientific management practices best identified with the work of Frederick W. Taylor. Taylor was steeped in the management of the firearms and machine tool industries. He drew on this experience for the development of time and motion studies and other techniques for measuring and monitoring work, deskilling craft workers, and concentrating skills in management. It is not coincidental that Taylor would refer to worker efforts to retain control by restricting output as "soldiering." In recent times, military practice has funded and legitimized the use of survey research on large populations and the application of computer-assisted management systems.

Military Chosen Instruments

The influence of the military on the design, dissemination and management of technology counters the myth that technology is a product of private marketplace development. This applies particularly to communication and information technology. These technologies are in large measure the product of direct military intervention in the private marketplace. This intervention has taken many forms including research and development by the military as well as Pentagon contracts with private companies. The military has also used the vehicle of identifying its "chosen instrument" to develop technology in the interests of what the state defines as national security.

Broadcasting

The creation of the American broadcasting system was a direct response to a concern raised by American military and diplomatic interests that the US could not challenge British imperialism as long as Britain controlled the undersea cable system, then the dominant means of international telecommunication. This control enabled the British military and industry, from wool traders to news wire services, to overwhelm competitors.

To combat British domination, the US government and major businesses, including AT&T, General Electric, Westinghouse, and United Fruit (which operated its own plantation system throughout Latin America), agreed to establish what the government called its "chosen instrument" in communications, the Radio Corporation of America. Backed by major US companies and the federal government, RCA would build the radio alternative to cable transmission and use its dominant position in radio to open new means of US control in communication. To accomplish this, the company would operate as a cartel owned by the corporate participants. The US Navy, which had pioneered in ship to ship and ship to shore radio communication, was able to appoint an admiral to serve as government representative to the RCA board. In this way, US military as well as corporate industrial interests were maintained.

Even after the cartel broke up and RCA, with its NBC broadcast subsidiary, went on to establish dominance in the radio and television industry, the military continued to influence corporate policy. RCA has consistently been a major defense contractor, generally within the top twenty or so firms receiving Pentagon money. In the corporate merger binge of the 1980s, General Electric recreated part of the initial chosen instrument by buying RCA. GE is an even more significant defense contractor than RCA. It is in the top ten in both overall and "Star Wars" contracts. More importantly, GE's purchase of RCA further concentrates power in the already tightly oligopolistic defense industry and provides opportunities for direct Pentagon influence over a major mass medium.

Communications Satellites
Forty years after the advent of broadcasting, the US military was faced with what it saw as another challenge to its global hegemony. This time the challenge was not British, but Soviet, and the technology was the communication satellite. The response of the US government was much the same as with RCA.

In 1962, the US government established another "chosen instrument," the Communications Satellite Corporation (Comsat), to advance the military and corporate applications of satellite technology in the US. Moreover, Comsat was to organize an international body, Intelsat, comprised of non-Communist countries, to promote and manage the development of communications satellites worldwide.

Like RCA, Comsat was organized as a cartel, half of whose shares rested with the major US international telecommunications corporations: AT&T, RCA, International Telephone and Telegraph (ITT), and Western Union International (WUI). Again, even after the cartel sold its shares, the military maintained a substantial role in the operation and oversight of Comsat. One analyst dubbed it "the old soldier's home," a reference to the prominence of retired military officers working for the company (Kinsley, 1976).

.Comsat carried out its international mandate by creating Intelsat, an international satellite network that provides communications services, including telephone, data transmission, and television. Though the chief beneficiaries of the Intelsat network are business customers (e.g., the television networks), in the developed world, the system serves over one hundred countries, excluding the Soviet Union and many of its allies. Furthermore, Comsat was able to construct the global system in such a way that policy-making power rests with member nations based on the amount of their satellite use. Consequently, though its voting strength has diminished in recent years, the United States has consistently held over 20 per cent of Comsat's votes. The combined voting strength of the US and Western Europe is enough to ensure control by advanced capitalist societies.

Computers: MCC and Sematech

It is commonly accepted that US markets are driven by private firms competing openly. However, there are enough exceptions to this view to question this conclusion, particularly as it pertains to the information society. The US government is the single, largest user of information systems in the United States. In the 1988 fiscal year, the federal information systems budget was $17 billion or one-tenth of the entire market for computers, software and services.

The relationship between the Pentagon and the US computer industry has always been strong (Flamm, 1987). In the 1940s and 1950s, the US government, led by the Pentagon, provided most of the funding for computer research. Furthermore, the Pentagon gave big contracts to commercial firms to build the production equipment needed to create the microchips that have revolutionized the industry. The US military is also largely responsible for underwriting the development of computer software systems such as COBOL. To complete this cycle, the Pentagon has been the major consumer of computer products. It even funded the transition from large, unreliable vacuum tubes to transistors, and eventually, semiconductor integrated circuits. So dependent was the electronics industry on military contracts that one 1957 business analyst worried that " 'Peace' if it came suddenly, would hit the industry very hard ..." though the analyst concludes that "military electronics is a good business despite the 'risk' of peace." (Harris, 1957: 216) Between 1958 and 1974, the military bought 35 per cent to 50 per cent of integrated circuits produced in the United States. The Pentagon continues to consume about 15 per cent of the value of all integrated circuits produced in the US. (US, Congressional Budget Office, 1987)

In 1958 the US created DARPA, the Defense Advanced Research Projects Agency, to organize military research and development efforts in computers. DARPA, born in the furor raised by initial US failures to launch a space satellite, and Soviet success with its Sputnik program, worked with MIT to build time-sharing computers and with MIT, Stanford, and UCLA to create packet switching, a system that packages bits of information for efficient and economical distribution over a communications network. (See Table 6.1) These developments led in turn to the creation of Arpanet, a prototype computer communications network. The military used these evolving computer communications systems for a wide range of applications including the development of the Intercontinental Ballistics Missile (ICBM), worldwide intelligence gathering by the National Security Agency, and in battlefield sensing, used as part of the "automated" war in Vietnam.

Table 6.2 reports on a study by the Congressional Budget Office (CBO) on federal government spending on semiconductor research. As the table documents, and the study concludes, most of the US government's semiconductor research budget goes to military ends. In fact, the table underrepresents military spending. The $55 million that the Sandia National Lab spends is budgeted to the Department of Energy, but most of the spending is for military missions. Furthermore, the table does not include projects indirectly funded by the government, such as DOD's Independent Research and Development Program or research supported by the Incremental R&D Tax Credit.

Table 6.1
Defense Department Funding of Mathematics and Computer Science Research, 1967-1986

Year	Total Federal Spending (in millions of 1982 dollars)	Percent funded by DOD
1967	357	70%
1968	313	67%
1969	271	69%
1970	226	64%
1971	241	60%
1972	260	59%
1973	232	61%
1974	211	61%
1975	211	57%
1976	250	58%
1977	291	48%
1978	299	47%
1979	267	54%
1980	281	57%
1981	297	53%
1982	350	54%
1983	403	53%
1984	408	49%
1985	519	53%
1986	555	58%

Source: Flamm, 1987: 46.

Table 6.2
Federal Semiconductor Research in 1987

Department / Program	Funding ($ millions)
Department of Defense	
Very High Speed Integrated Circuits	122
Strategic Defense Inititive Organization	60
Air Force	60
Navy	28
Army	25
DARPA	16
Manufacturing Technology	14
Microwave and Millimeter-Wave Monolithic	10
Integrated Circuits (Mimic)	
Defense Nuclear Agency	7
Department of Energy	
Sandia National Laboratories	55
Photovoltaic research	15
Other National Laboratories	8
National Science Foundation	30
National Bureau of Standards	4
	Total: 454

Source: US, Congressional Budget Office (1987).

The Congressional Budget Office is concerned that Pentagon control of semiconductor research lessens the production of chips of commercial value, particularly in the short-run, a reflection of the highly focussed approach of DOD research. For example, extensive research on producing radiation-hardened chips, which increases their survivability in a nuclear war, increases their cost with very little increase in commercial value. The "Star Wars" program calls for producing high speed gallium arsenide (rather than silicon) chips. These particular customized chips, required by the demands of the SDI project, would cost $1200 each in 1988. A commercial version of this chip is already available today, less the ability to survive in a nuclear war environment, for about $20. Thus does Pentagon funding lead computer research in the United

States to pursue technologically demanding, but commercially irrelevant, directions.

It is expected that barring a significant change in political direction, the Pentagon will continue its influence over US computer and information policy. A study by the International Data Corporation identifies the major US government computer users and charts their computer needs from 1987 to 1992 (Table 6.3). The Department of Defense is expected to consume at twice the level of its closest competitor, the General Services Administration.

Table 6.3
Projections of US Government Computer Procurement

Agency/Department	1987-92 Procurement ($billions)
Department of Defense	Total 14.6
Army	(5.0)
Navy	(3.9)
Air Force	(3.7)
Office of the Secretary	(2.0)
General Services Administration	7.3
Treasury Department	6.1
NASA	5.2
Department of Agriculture	3.4
Department of Justice	2.0
Department of Commerce	1.8

Source: International Data Corporation reported
in *Business Week*, November 23, 1987.

It is, therefore, hard to disagree with the Science Adviser to President Reagan, when, in testimony before a Senate committee, he identified the significance of the computer for US military activity:

It has been the incredible leaps in data processing, as much as any single area, which has fueled this explosion. .... It was data processing which overcame John von Neuman's skepticism of ever making the ICBM work in the first place. It was data processing at the heart of the move to MIRVing. It was data processing which tied ICBM fleets together for coordinated execution. It was data processing which has provided the ICBM accuracy necessary for preemptive strikes. And it is data processing which will be at the heart of any defense against ballistic missiles. (US, Congress, Senate, 1984: 8)

The US computer industry received its first government blessed chosen instrument in 1984. Microelectronics and Computer Technology Corp. (MCC) is a company made up of leading data processing companies, who agreed to pool certain research and development activities. This time the external threat is Japan, whose microelectronics industry is a threat to American business and to Pentagon planners who do not want to see the US dependent on foreign, even if allied, sources for strategic components such as advanced semiconductors.

The ten founding companies include the seemingly ever-present RCA, Advanced MicroDevices, Control Data, Digital Equipment, Harris, Honeywell, Motorola, NCR, National Semiconductor, and Sperry Univac. IBM's lack of cooperation and the preference of firms to pursue individual growth over patriotic cooperation have made MCC's record, according to one assessment "spotty." (*The New York Times,* March 8, 1987) Nevertheless, according to a Brookings Institute study (Flamm, 1987), MCC has grown from its ten founding members to twenty-one companies, with an annual research budget between 60 and 70 $million. Its October 1984 staff, of 120, grew to 400 by early 1986. Moreover, the absence of short-term technical achievements should not lead us to lose sight of the important political achievement that MCC represents for those who want to maintain strong military influence over the evolution of the information society.

MCC is not merely a Justice Department approved cartel of leading computer firms. The company was founded by Bobby Inman, former Deputy Director of the CIA and the former director of the National Security Agency. The NSA is a top secret agency that operates a global computer/communications satellite system that routinely monitors international telex, telegraph, telephone, radio and other transmissions, emanating from or directed to the United States. MCC is one instrument the military, its associated intelligence agencies, and the US computer and telecommunications industries use to direct and coordinate international strategy.

The creation of Sematech, the Semiconductor Manufacturing Technology Institute, represents another such instrument. Sematech is a company funded by both government and private capital to do microchip research and development. The Congress has approved an appropriation of about $100 million a year while private sector members plan to match the government contribution, for an average annual budget of over $200 million over the next six years. Sematech is made up of the major US industry competitors in the field: IBM, Hewlett-Packard, Harris, National Semiconductor, Motorola, Texas Instruments, Intel, and others.

Sematech has resulted from concerns that the US is lagging behind in chip research. A report of the Defense Science Board Task Force on Semiconductor Dependency states that the U.S faces an "an unacceptable threat—the erosion of the US semiconductor industry and the consequent decline of the high technology base on which both the US defense and economy rely." (*Wall Street Journal*, December 10, 1986) The report is particularly fearful of Japanese dominance of the field because "the Japanese cannot be relied upon to transfer leadership semiconductor technology to US systems suppliers for military uses." (Ibid.) The Pentagon appears equally fearful, though it expresses the fear in more measured language, that US companies do not respond to US security needs. Rather, companies make their research plans based on expectations about the civilian commercial market, which has not grown as rapidly, particularly in areas where the military forsees major needs. Consequently, the Pentagon called for the development of a company that would receive federal appropriations of from $250 to $335 million to conduct research in areas of military need. Even with this government money, which could be put to more profitable corporate use, industry people are skeptical. The vice chairman of Intel concludes that Sematech will not succeed "if the industry won't provide substantial support, and that's questionable." (Ibid.) On the other hand, the President of Harris Semiconductor sees that "our only choice as an industry is to try (Sematech) or die." (*Wall Street Journal*, November 17, 1987)

Nevertheless, those outside the industry see "a lot of truth" in the view that "Sematech is merely an elaborate bailout for aging semiconductor companies that can't keep up." (Ibid.) A principal researcher in a National Science Foundation study of the chip industry concluded that the "The problem is wildly overstated." (*Wall Steet Journal*, January 8, 1988). Sematech *is* a bailout, but it is more than just this. Sematech bails out these companies, but at the price of guaranteeing that they respond directly to US military priorities. In this respect Sematech is just the latest in a history of chosen instruments for US government, and particularly, US military, policy.

Worldwide Military Command and Control
In addition to shaping the commercial broadcasting, satellite, computer and related industries, the Pentagon controls a vast computer/communications system of its own.

The Pentagon and intelligence agencies control about 25 per cent of all radio frequencies used in the United States. Government agencies with primarily civilian responsibilities control another quarter and the remaining half of the total frequencies available are in private hands. This is roughly equivalent to saying that one out of every four radio channels in the United States is under military control. Along with this, the Pentagon is the single largest user of telecommunications in the United States. Its yearly budget for communication and intelligence exceeds the total annual revenues of all the commercial radio and television stations in the United States. Through the Defense Communication Agency and the Defense Telecommunication and Command Control System, the Pentagon deploys a global system of communications satellites, submarine cables, computers and terrestrial telecommunications systems to operate perhaps the most powerful communications and data processing system in the world.

According to a US Army Deputy Chief of Staff, "Literally every weapons system that we are planning and bringing into development in some way employs minicomputers and microelectronics." Battlefield computers are used primarily for remote sensing of enemy troop movements, precise targeting and firing, and damage assessment. Miniaturization has even taken the portable computer to the modern battlefield. GRiDSE.T is a powerful briefcase-sized computer, including a built-in modem for telecommunications. It has been tested in action in Lebanon and Grenada, on the Space Shuttle, and in a nuclear weapon retargeting exercise aboard an airborne command post.

Computers are also used extensively in naval forces. A typical guided missile cruiser carrying nuclear warheads, antisubmarine rocket torpedos and attack helicopters is managed by sixteen on-board mainframe computers and twelve mini's. These computer data banks are organized into a system like Aegis which is driven by eighteen tactical software programs that provide instructions on what weapons to fire, at what targets, and when.

Military computers are integrated into systems of Command, Control, Communication, and Intelligence (C^3I). These systems are integrated globally into the US Worldwide Military Command and Control System. Thus, it is easy to conclude that computers have expanded the range, speed and accuracy of weapons systems. Linked to communication technologies, particularly satellites, computers have expanded intelligence gathering, surveillance, and reconnaissance. As the real size of the battlefield increases over the earth and into space, C^3I systems requirements to process, communicate, and issue commands grow more vital.

The Military Information Society Includes Outer Space

The pervasive influence of the military in US technological development seriously undermines the view that private enterprise is the chief engine of growth in America. The close relationship of government, particularly the military, to US business—including the use of cartels and chosen instruments—constantly challenges the view that private, competitive markets have been the best means for realizing national economic and political goals. The military control of the space program alone belies the view that the US has been committed to the peaceful uses of outer space. Indeed, the "Star Wars" project is just the latest in a long series of space-warfare projects that began even before the US was technically capable of launching a space satellite.

In fact, the US military interest in space predates the launch of Sputnik, the first Soviet space satellite, by over a decade. In 1946, the Air Force sponsored a study, *Preliminary Design for a World-Circling Spaceship* which contained material on the military application of space satellites, including reconnaissance and communication (Rand Corporation, 1946). Subsequent Air Force projects on pilotless spacecraft for communications, early warning, navigation, and reconnaissance grew out of this research. In the early 1950s, studies stressed the need to develop an accurate and reliable Intercontinental Ballistic Missile (ICBM). These expanded, in 1956, to fully funded programs for satellite reconnaissance, and subsequently for climate assessment and, of particular importance, military communication.

The growth of US military forces worldwide created enormous problems of coordination and integration that only a very sophisticated communication system would be able to manage. Established systems for C^3I were not sufficient, particularly in the event of a nuclear war. Space communications systems anchored in satellites would meet this pressing need. Consequently, the Pentagon began a major program to promote the development of communications satellites.

Though it was the Republican Eisenhower Administration that proposed these programs, military satellites received enthusiastic backing from the Democrats as well. A 1957 Democratic policy statement, signed by former President Truman, Senators Adlai Stevenson and Hubert Humphrey, and New York Governor Averell Harriman reads:

> Let us not fail to understand that control of outer space would be a military fact of the highest importance ... the air war of yesterday becomes the space war of tomorrow. We must do more than merely catch up. The all-out effort of the Soviets to establish them-selves as masters of space around us must be met by all-out efforts of our own. (Manno, 1983: 39)

And from Senator Lyndon Johnson, who would go on to become the President most deeply committed and closely identified with the space program:

> control of space means control of the world, far more certainly, far more totally than any control that has been achieved by weapons or by troops of occupation. Space is the ultimate position, the posi-tion of total control over Earth. (Ibid.)

In 1958 Eisenhower gave primary responsibility for manned space exploration to an ostensibly civilian agency, the National Aeronautics and Space Administration (NASA). Amendments to the NASA act sub-sequently subordinated the civilian programs to military requirements. In this way, the military was able to influence program decisions on the Mercury and Gemini flights that culminated in the Project Apollo lunar landings. In fact, the Air Force Systems Command won direct control over experiments on Project Gemini.

The Air Force co-ordinated testing of how to conduct maneuver and rendezvous operations in Project Gemini with its own program to develop military space vehicles. The major early projects: SAINT (for SAtellite INTercept)—the first anti-satellite spacecraft; Dyna-Soar—a rocket-launched space glider developed for the Air Force by two former advisers to Adolph Hitler, Walter Dornberger and Kraft Ehricke; and BAMBI (for ballistic missile boost intercept)—the earliest version of the "Star Wars" defense, BAMBI would deploy hundreds of satellites armed with heat-seeking missiles and fire at Soviet ICBMs during their assent period; were cancelled in 1963 because of mounting budget con-straints and the growing military commitment in Indochina. Later on in the decade, a proposed Manned Orbiting Laboratory met a similar fate after $1.3 billion was spent on the project.

In the 1970s, US military and intelligence agencies built satellite systems to enhance ground based military forces. These systems were used principally for reconnaissance, early warning, communication, and navigation. In 1972, supporters of a strong military space program applauded President Nixon's approval of the Space Shuttle project. They did so because the Shuttle program was designed and managed according to military specifications. Its major characteristics—reusability, maneuverability, large carrying capacity—grew out of military objectives. Flight details are covered in greater secrecy than for other NASA space projects. Moreover, the military uses half the shuttle flights, and, will likely require a greater percentage in the aftermath of the Challenger disaster. Most analysts agree that NASA had to pay the price of military control in order to keep the Shuttle under its formal aegis or, put more simply, to remain in existence.

According to a 1987 study by the Federation of American Scientists, the military accounts for 49 per cent of the 337 operational satellites worldwide; 53.5 per cent of US satellites are military, including 26 satellites for intelligence alone. The Defense Department budget for satellites, which, historically, has lagged behind that of NASA, is now twice the NASA amount. The Pentagon now spends between 15 and 20 $billion a year on military space activities, compared with only $8.9 billion for NASA.

It is hard to disagree with Air Force General Bernard Schriever, who was put in charge of Air Force space programs in 1954 and whose ideas have propelled the United States along its "Star Wars" track:

> Space for peaceful purposes—what a bunch of goddamned bullshit that was!

The Place of "Star Wars" in the Military Information Society

The "Star Wars" program or so-called Strategic Defense Initiative (SDI) takes a major step toward the further militarization of outer space. There has been a great deal written about SDI, but almost all of the analysis addresses a single technical question: Can SDI provide a defense against a nuclear missile attack? This question is often subdivided into such components as: Can SDI stop all or only a percentage of incoming missiles? Can it protect population centers or is it limited to a defense of

Table 6.4
Worldwide Operational Satellites, 1987

Type	Number	%
Military	165	49%
Civil communictions	108	32%
Civil mainly earth resources	31	9.2%
Scientific	27	8%
Manned	6	1.8%
	Total: 337	

Source: Federation of American Scientists, 1987.

Western nuclear facilities, the heart of the deterrent?

These are important questions. Critics make a good case that "Star Wars", particularly as a total defense, is technically unfeasible, would cost astronomical sums, and would likely increase international instability because it will undermine existing arms limitation agreements.

Moreover, critics point out that SDI requires computing capabilities that can only be found in science fiction. "Star Wars" supporters acknowledge these computing limitations and have mounted a five-year $600 million Strategic Computing Initiative (SCI), that aims to develop so-called fifth generation computer systems capable of solving complex reasoning problems, understanding natural language, seeing with precise acuity, and commanding other intelligent processes. DARPA, responsible for SCI, claims this will take computer systems an order of magnitude further in capability, with storage capacity and speed of execution beyond the earlier generations—vacuum-tube, transistor, integrated circuit, and very-large-scale integrated circuit technologies (U.S., DARPA, 1983). Critics, including computer scientists who have worked on the "Star Wars" project, maintain that DARPA's view is based on overly optimistic assessments of the computer's ability to mimic and expand on human intelligence. They contend that such optimism is insensitive to the dangers of machine error, with potentially cataclysmic consequences (Parnas, 1985).

The "Star Wars" project has sparked one of the most significant debates of our time. Nevertheless, it suffers from the myopic view that SDI is *only* about what it says it is about. The failure to reflect on the wider military, economic, political, and ideological significance of "Star

Wars" means that we have failed to come to grips with its place in a militarized information society. In essence, "Star Wars" may not work in the narrow technical sense of providing a shield against incoming missiles, even as it does work in the wider sense of deepening and extending a military definition of the information society.

Specifically, despite its title, SDI can also work as an *offensive* military system, either as part of a first strike nuclear attack or, more likely, to attack specific targets such as recalcitrant Third World nations. Moreover, SDI pumps massive amounts of money into the high tech sector and, concretely, SDI provides the state with the means to pressure the transnational microelectronics industry to harmonize its objectives with what the US government perceives to be the national interest. The latter includes winning international competition with Japan and drawing the Soviet Union into a military spending race that many believe the Soviet Union cannot survive. Finally, Star Wars and the Strategic Computing Initiative are powerful ideological weapons. "Star Wars" holds out the vision of a *defense* against nuclear weapons and an end to the principle of Mutually Assured Destruction. Strategic Computing assures Americans that all this can be done and their standard of living protected, without the need to rely on Vietnam style troop commitments and the often faulty judgements of military commanders.

Will "Star Wars" Work?
William Broad, a science reporter for *The New York Times* claims that "Star Wars" has become "both impossible and inevitable." He is clearer about explaining the "impossible" side of this paradox. According to Broad, and apparently also the experts with whom he is co-authoring a book on the subject:

> The best evidence indicates that, given the current size of the Soviet arsenal of long-range ballistic missiles aimed at the United States, some 10,000 warheads strong, a space-based defense has no chance of working as envisioned by President Reagan. For the foreseeable future, man and his technology, however great, cannot reasonably hope to create a shield that would save the nation's cities and citizens. (Broad, 1987: 80)

Broad simply echoes an argument that much of the scientific community has been making since President Reagan announced the commitment to "Star Wars" in March 1983. The Strategic Defense Initiative cannot work to provide a protective shield against nuclear attack. As the Congressional Office of Technology Assessment (1986) has argued, "Star Wars" systems are subject to countermeasures which are much cheaper to build. Just one example of an inexpensive countermeasure is a system of decoys that would overwhelm surveillance response systems and make penetration of the shield inevitable. Conservatively speaking, SDI would have to provide a defense against 1,500 incoming missiles. If a missile is not destroyed within the first few minutes of launching, it will discharge 10 warheads and 100 decoys that are indistinguishable from missiles. Hence, within minutes of a launch, SDI would have to track 100,000 or so objects, distinguish the missiles from the decoys, and destroy the missiles. Eliminating the missiles before they discharge their warheads is the most demanding and the least feasible part of SDI.

To understand how unfeasible this is, consider the US Navy's Aegis system, the current "state of the art" in making complex software systems work. The goal of Aegis was to provide near automatic protection for naval vessels, a far more modest goal than protecting the US land mass. Aegis was designed to track several hundred missiles, allocate the correct counter-weaponry, and fire at up to twenty targets simultaneously. In its first operational test, the system could only call up three targets at a time and could hit only ten of sixteen. In its first major battlefield experience aboard the cruiser USS Vincennes, Aegis mistook an Airbus (175 feet long) for an F-14 (62 feet long), miscalculated the plane's altitude by 3000 feet, and concluded that the Airbus was descending when it was actually ascending. As a result, the Vincennes downed a passenger plane killing 290 people. Since it is far easier to devise inexpensive countermeasures, the only result of pursuing SDI is the familiar one of spiraling actions and counteractions that would result in an expensive escalation of the arms race that is likely to, if anything, increase global insecurity.

Moreover, technical critics have concluded that SDI systems will require extraordinary developments in technology, in software even more than hardware, which we are unlikely, if ever, to see. The software in SDI would have to work with flawless precision without the opportunity of a test under realistic conditions. *No software system has ever worked properly under these conditions* and SDI would contain the most complex software ever designed, anywhere from ten million to twenty-five million instructions. Even early versions of SDI software have contained between 10,000 and 100,000 errors. As a result, according to a computer scientist who worked for the Strategic Defense Initiative Organization on the software requirements of "Star Wars" systems, even massive spending will not provide the software necessary to deploy the "Star Wars" defense with confidence. (Parnas, 1985) Most computer experts would agree with Robert Taylor, the former head of computer research at the Pentagon:

> I think it is pretty clear that it can't be done; SDI puts demands on software that are just absurd in terms of the state of our knowledge. (Horwood and Grogono, 1987)

Or, accoring to Nobel prize recipient Andrei Sakharov:

> I am strongly against the creation of SDI by either the United States or the USSR. Such a system cannot be effective. It would be destroyed very early in a war, even before the thermonuclear stage is reached. Moreover, the destruction of SDI early in a war could provoke a thermonuclear response.
>
> Destroying SDI is technically much simpler than creating it. The system will depend on a relatively small number of observation stations that will be very vulnerable. As for systems that seek to destroy missiles after they have been launched—X-ray lasers and so on—they can be rendered ineffective simply by shortening the missile's boost phase time. Studies show that by cutting the boost-phase time in half, defensive missiles would not be able to respond in time. (*Harper's Magazine*, October, 1987: 20)

As military planners' reliance on electronic systems grows, nuclear policy comes to be based increasingly on a "launch on warning" strategy, a policy of using nuclear retaliation against an enemy attack indicated solely by computer-satellite-radar tracking systems. This policy of relying on machines to launch a nuclear war is, in the minds of some, the logical response to a decision-making time frame now reduced to minutes and seconds. Specifically, the nuclear missile distance between the US and the Soviet Union is about thirty minutes, less than ten if you include the nuclear equipped submarines waiting off each other's coast.

Concern is also growing that launch on warning widens the potential for simple mechanical error to lead to nuclear war. This has even been expressed by some at the command posts of the US military-industrial complex. In an interview on the subject, the then head of IBM initially denied the likelihood of nuclear war resulting from computer malfunction, but appeared to change his mind in the middle of his answer:

> the more the whole philosophy of launch-on-warning becomes attractive, the greater the danger. And as machines of war and missiles become more prey to preemptive strike, the more temptation there is to put more and more of the data in the hands of a computer and take the human being out of the equation. To the extent that you do that, you are indeed putting the US into a position where a computer could trip us up pretty badly. (*Computerworld,* June 15, 1983, p. 15)

General Richard Ellis, who was once responsible for the US major nuclear force, including bombers, tankers, reconnaissance aircraft, and ICBMs, expressed a similar concern about the reliance on machines in situations of enormous time pressure. He described to a Harvard seminar the "iffy business" of relying on processed information to make judgments about a possible attack:

> All the information comes in to NORAD (North American Air Defense Command). It's ground up in their computer programs and presented to them in a matter of minutes, in some cases seconds, as fused information, which indicates to the commander out there that such-and-such is happening. All one can do is hope that the software isn't faulty, or the hardware isn't spooky, and the person is not making a hasty judgment. Things can go wrong. (Harvard University, 1982: 5)

And things *have* gone wrong, as they are likely to in complex environments. The NORAD system was once fooled by radar reflections off the rising moon to conclude erroneously that the US was under attack. Moons were simply not among the building blocks that the program used to categorize the world. It had no way of assessing: This looks more like a rising moon than an enemy attack; since a program can only sort every event into a prespecified set of categories, the presence of the rising moon was simply sorted, this time into the *wrong* category. Catastrophe was averted because the system contained enough human control to detect the error in time. Future systems are less likely to contain as much opportunity for human intervention. In the future, it is more likely that, as Galtung (1987) has put it, launch on warning will be replaced by *launch on suspicion.*

Yet, this concern about malfunctions takes an overly mechanical view of responsibility. There are series of very direct human decisions that enter the chain leading to a decision to launch missiles. Simply because a step in the decision process went awry because of a mechanical error is not sufficient reason to assign responsibility for nuclear war to the machines.

The Vietnam War offers a good lesson here. In Vietnam, computers in the field were specifically programmed to tell Pentagon computers that raids over neutral Cambodia were actually raids over Vietnam. Highly placed elected officials, permitted to see the summaries produced by Pentagon computers, wrongly believed that they were receiving a privileged view of the battlefield. Of particular interest is the response of then chairman of the Joint Chiefs of Staff, Admiral Moorer, to a congressional committee investigating the matter. Here is how Moorer, whose position placed him among the top people who decide whether the US would engage in nuclear war, responded to the committee:

> It is unfortunate that we had to become slaves to those damned computers. (Weizenbaum, 1981: 560)

Launch on warning or, for that matter, suspicion, is a far more ominous matter, when we consider that sitting at the very top of the nuclear chain of command is someone who programs computers to mask a war and then claims to be enslaved by these same computers.

Nevertheless, the new wave of "Star Wars" weaponry—from anti-satellite (ASAT) to ballistic missile defense systems—makes decision-making more complex and more than ever subject to the pressures of split-second timing. For example, in an environment that includes mutually escalating anti-satellite weaponry, if a major early-warning satellite belonging to one side were to cease working because of a meteor strike or electrical failure, the side with the malfunctioning or destroyed satellite might conclude an ASAT had done it and that this is the prelude to an attack. Does it spend precious time checking out the malfunction or does it launch a "retaliatory" strike? As Stares has shown in his Brookings Institution study of anti-satellite technology, such systems will prove increasingly destabilizing as their capabilities increase (Stares, 1987). He contends that the US should respond more positively to Soviet offers to negotiate a ban on such weapons.

Similarly, ballistic missile defense systems require a leap in reliance on machine judgment. It now takes about two minutes to process and verify data from early-warning satellites and an additional three minutes or so to loft an interceptor from a submarine to the firing point. But that is more time than is available to intercept a missile in its boost phase—the critical period before the missile releases warheads and decoys. This complex sequence of computations and decisions potentially can be arrived at in a matter of seconds, *provided that no humans take part in the process.*

It is therefore, not difficult to conclude that "Star Wars" systems are, as Broad puts it, "impossible." But what makes them, again as he puts it, "inevitable?" This is a more important question, because the answer deepens our understanding of the wider social significance of "Star Wars," and its role in an increasingly *military* information society. Broad answers the question with some interesting insights into the military funding system in the US and the wider purposes of SDI systems. Nevertheless, the response is sketchy, couched in a point of view heavily weighted with technological determinism. SDI is inevitable because the government has already committed to funding basic research in SDI technology. Once this is done, he maintains, the attractiveness of technological development in this most technological of societies, makes it almost impossible to turn back.

The remainder of this chapter explores the "inevitability" of SDI from another viewpoint. The momentum for SDI comes from the benefits it delivers to major power centers in the United States. This has little to do with a protective umbrella against a torrent of nuclear weapons, "Star Wars" will likely not work to accomplish that. Rather it is because SDI will work, because SDI *is* working to strengthen the US *offensive* capacity against the Soviet Union and the Third World, to provide an acceptable means of subsidizing the microlectronics industry and assisting US companies to compete globally, to maintain the government's ability to influence US transnational corporate behaviour, and to promote a public belief in the US commitment to automated and defensive military systems. There is so large a gap between the amount of energy devoted to whether "Star Wars" can work as a defense and these others issues that one is tempted to agree with Johan Galtung, founder of the International Peace Federation, when he concludes:

> By shrewdly selling it as a way of "making nuclear weapons obsolete," the Administration has brainwashed the public, including the many who have wasted nearly four years debating the irrele-

vant question of whether a leak-proof shield is achievable. (Galtung, 1987: 249)

"Brainwashing" may be too strong a term. Yet, it is hard to disagree with the view that SDI has been marketed with expert salesmanship. The sales pitch is helped by the arrival of computer graphics on television. In fact, television and SDI appear to be made for each other. As Nelson puts it:

Inevitably, any television news reference to "Star Wars" is accompanied by hyper-realistic animation of rays zapping incoming missiles, videogame-like explosions eliminating enemy blips: seductive imagery that fascinates, makes the product appear tidy and efficient, and also presents the technology as a virtual fait accompli. (Nelson, 1987: 148)

Star Wars is Already Working

The Strategic Offensive Initiative

Galtung concludes that rather than making nuclear arms obsolete, SDI strengthens the nuclear capability, hence he renames the project Strategic *Offensive* Initiative. In essence,

whatever might destroy a Soviet missile right after liftoff might also destroy farmland, a forest, perhaps even a city. A stationary or slowly moving object, such as a human being, would be considerably easier to destroy than a highly mobile, rotating, mirror-coated, hardened object, such as a missile, especially one that has been launched under cloud cover, with decoys and multiple warheads. (Ibid.: 248)

Galtung's view is supported by a study prepared by R&D Associates, a Pentagon consulting firm. According to R&D, a space-based laser system, ostensibly established for defense against nuclear weapons, can "destroy the enemy's major cities by fire. The attack would proceed city by city, the attack time for each city being only a matter of minutes." (*Harpers,* April, 1986: 15) Reporting in the January 1986 issue of the journal *Physics and Society*, Caroline Herzenber, a physicist, argues that lasers "have the potential of initiating massive urban fires and even of destroying the enemy's major cities by fire in a matter of hours."

According to a study prepared by the Library of Congress, Congressional Research Service, the choice of offensive or defensive use for SDI depends on the military purpose. Though there are some limits on offensive uses, the report concludes that:

> Most or all of the weapons concepts that do prove feasible could in principle be used either offensively or defensively. Military objectives would be the driving factors determining their purpose. (*Aviation Week and Space Technology*, November 30, 1987: 23)

At present, the simplest weapon of the SDI arsenal, a homing rocket that destroys targets by smashing into them, is believed to be the most effective offensive force, more so than the lasers, particle beams, and other futuristic weapons that the Pentagon is studying. Such weapons could attack Soviet satellites and battle stations in space. They could also be modified to enter the earth's atmosphere to knock out Soviet planes, radars, and perhaps even missiles in silos. According to physicist Peter D. Zimmerman, "For certain ground targets, it's the best offensive weapon." (*The New York Times*, February 22, 1987) There is still some question about the ability of these kinetic energy weapons to work from space against ground targets. The Congressional Research Service study concludes that atmospheric drag would limit their effectiveness to targets up to about sixty miles in altitude. This would make them mostly effective against satellites rather than ground targets. Nevertheless, even if these weapons are so limited, critics maintain that they will be very useful in fighting an offensive nuclear war. According to Stanford physicist Harvey Lynch, "The most obvious one is to use them in conjunction with a first strike, use them to mop up the weakened response of your adversary." (Ibid.) According to Broad, even some advocates of SDI see it as an offensive system:

> In private, some "Star Wars" advocates say space-based antimissile systems can be viewed as exclusively offensive, given that a leaky shield would work best for fending off a foe's ragged retaliation after a first strike destroyed as many enemy nuclear weapons as possible. (Broad, 1987: 88)

Nevertheless, supporters contend that because the West is "fundamenally pacific," it will not likely use these weapons offensively. State Department consultant Colin Gray is less hopeful. Given what he perceives to be Soviet expansionist tendencies, he concludes his book on nuclear strategy with the ominous view that "It is likely that it will be the United States which first feels moved to threaten and execute a central nuclear strike." (Gray, 1984: 56)

A US first strike would be coordinated by force enhancing systems such as Milstar and IONDS which are hardened to survive a protracted nuclear war. In fact, Milstar is an Air Force communication satellite system whose chief advantage over its predecessor is a greater capacity to operate in a nuclear battle. IONDS is a surveillance satellite system that uses the network of Global Positioning System satellites to provide data instantaneously on the effectiveness of an initial nuclear strike in order to make a second wave attack more productive.

A first strike would be led by anti-satellite weapons to destroy the Soviet early warning and communications capacity. Land-based MX missiles and the submarine-launched Trident II will drop nuclear weapons on Soviet missile silos. An SDI system would be geared to the thousand or so warheads, chiefly from the Soviet submarine fleet, that manage to survive. According to Gray:

> The United States should plan to defeat the Soviet Union and to do so at a cost that would not prohibit US recovery. Washington should identify war aims that in the last resort would contemplate the destruction of the Soviet political authority and the emergence of a postwar world order compatible with Western values. ... A combination of counterforce offensive targeting, civil defense, and ballistic missile and air defense should hold US casualties to approximately 20 million, which should render US strategic threats more credible. (*The Progressive*, June, 1983: 22)

The development of precise surveillance, targeting, and attack systems may not convince Washington officials to attack the Soviet Union, or even to rely on such a system for defense against Soviet attack, but it still strengthens the case for use against recalcitrant Third World nations. A limited "Star Wars" system, one that need not operate flawlessly, could be used effectively as a means of controlling nations or groups labeled as supporting terrorism, the international drug trade, communism, a combination of these, or whatever suitable alternative applies. As Leemans and Luker point out, the threat of a precisely targeted, devastating attack from space to ground or ground to ground weapons, could well serve US policy interests in the Third World:

> The advantages are clear. Recalcitrant third world nations could be intimidated, punished, disarmed, embargoed, silenced, rendered leaderless, or destroyed with little or no risk to American forces and, perhaps, much less protest and political difficulty at home. (*Canadian Dimension,* April, 1986: 44)

Moreover, the Thompsons note, though officials in Washington, including President Reagan, have entertained the idea of sharing SDI technology with the Soviet Union, "no one has offered any shields to the Third World." (Thompson & Thompson, 1985: 144) Analysts already discuss the value of SDI as a weapon against Qaddafi (Broad, 1987: 88). Admittedly, some of this may be just another part of the sales pitch. As critics puncture the argument that SDI will protect against the Soviets, proponents talk about using it against Qaddafi and Khomeini at the same time they talk about beneficial civilian spin-offs like curing cancer or stopping acid rain.

Nevertheless, since the end of World War II, US armed forces have been engaged in a continuing series of wars with Third World countries. One of the foremost American leaders of this offensive, Richard Nixon, has offered important insight on the future combat activity of the United States in his book *No More Vietnams.* In the chapter given the heavy-handed title "The Third World War," Nixon claims that we have likely seen the last of superpower combat for a long time. The world is entering a phase of protracted wars of low- and high-intensity throughout the Third World. He calls on the US to better prepare itself for this version of the Third World War.

In 1988, a Pentagon panel issued the Iklé-Wohlstetter report. (US, Department of Defense, 1988) The panel, comprising military officials and such leading strategists as Henry Kissinger and Zbigniew Brzezinski took up Nixon's view and called on the US to make a major commitment to improve on its ability to fight wars in the Third World. It is necessary to do this even though such wars

> are obviously less threatening than any Soviet-American war would be, yet they have had and will have an adverse cumulative effect on US access to critical regions, on American credibility among allies and friends and on American self-confidence. (Carrington, 1988: 16)

The panel is particularly pleased with technological developments ("By the standards of a decade ago, the accuracies of current weapons are extraordinary") that make it possible to pinpoint Third World targets without risking troops or aircraft. The panel report reflects the significance that the highest US policy circles place on intervention in the Third World.

Sam Cohen, the physicist credited with inventing the neutron bomb, applauded the Iklé-Wohlstetter conclusions and extends them by suggesting specific uses of SDI technology in the Third World because they "hold the potential for considerably more discriminate and effective application in a large-scale Persian Gulf conflict." Moreover, SDI lasers "could eliminate US dependency on overseas bases" and "might have value for counterterrorist operation in the Middle East." (Cohen, 1988)

As the perfect shield to defend against Soviet attack, Star Wars will not work. As a loosely coupled set of weapons systems that would complement a first strike nuclear offensive or attack an enemy in the Third World, SDI can work. In this respect, Star Wars resembles the other major Reagan Administration military buildup, the development of a massive naval force comprised of 600 ships and 15 carriers. As one analyst put it "Aside from the Strategic Defense Initiative ... the maritime strategy represents *the* major change in United States war planning by the Reagan Administration." (Beatty, 1987: 37)

Like SDI, "The Maritime Strategy," as it has been called, is sold as a defense against Soviet attack. Critics, including conservative strategist Edward Luttwak and former CIA Director Admiral Stansfield Turner, say it won't work. Like the many technical critics of SDI, they may be missing the point. According to Beatty, such a force would free the US from reliance on NATO allies, who often try to restrain US intervention in the Third World. No one recognizes this more than Secretary of the Navy James Webb. Speaking before the National Press Club in Washington, Webb singled out a relaxation in the US NATO commitment as the first reason for supporting the Maritime Strategy:

> First, although the NATO alliance is one of the keystones of our military structure, we need to remind ourselves that we are more than a European nation. Moreover, we should bear in mind that no region is better equipped to reassume a great share of the burden of its own defense than Western Europe. (Webb, 1988: 14)

Former Nixon aide William Safire put it more bluntly when he asserted that "For Europe, today's talk is healthy if it leads to regional self-reliance; for America, worldwide action to defend freedom requires a new freedom of action." (*The New York Times,* April 7, 1988: A 27)

The US effort to use SDI and the Maritime Strategy as the means to back out of its NATO commitments contains a powerful irony for Canada. In Canada, social democrats, led by the New Democratic Party, have for a long time called for extricating Canada from the NATO alliance. Such calls did not receive widespread attention in Canada until 1986, when the NDP rose high enough in public opinion polls to be considered a challenger to lead the next government. Since that time, the party's NATO policy has been attacked by Conservative and Liberal Party members and supporters for what the critics believe to be a dangerous anti-American position. In fact, the NDP proposal to remove Canada from the alliance comes at a time when US policy makers at the highest levels promote removing the US from the alliance and replacing it with space and naval high-tech weaponry that they hope will make it unnecesary for the US to rely on NATO support.

Freed from even the admittedly gentle pressures of its NATO allies, "such a Navy would give teeth to what has been called the Reagan doctrine—the US effort to aid guerrilla fighters against revolutionary regimes in the Third World." (Beatty, 1987: 53) The fleet, with a total of 569 vessels by January 1988, has already been used off Nicaragua to frighten the Sandinistas and stands ready to aid US-backed guerillas in Angola. In that sense, the Maritime Strategy is already working "not as a force to fight a conventional war with the Soviet Union but as a force for intervention in the Third World." (Ibid.) Those who suggest that "Star Wars" doesn't compute might learn a lesson from the Maritime Strategy. They might amend their calculations to include what have been the direct targets of US aggression, targets US strategists have sought for ways to hit rapidly, efficiently, and without the use of combat troops.

How "Star Wars" Works Economically

Military projects such as SDI are the primary legitimate means of providing direct government funding for corporate research and development in the United States. The US government has spent billions of dollars on the project already and has budgeted $3.9 billion for 1988. If the object were the provision of non-military services, the contracts with private companies that this funding makes possible would be criticized as improper government intrusion into the free marketplace. In this sense, SDI and its associated information technology programs *work well* for major arms manufacturers such as Rockwell, McDonnell Douglas, Ford Aerospace, Hughes, and major companies with a stake in robotics and artificial intelligence, such as General Motors, Boeing, Martin Marietta and Texas Instruments.

As Table 6.5 suggests, many of the same companies that have benefitted most from Pentagon contracts are the chief beneficiaries of "Star Wars" deals. In this respect, SDI merely deepens and extends long established relationships between government and business in the United States. Business pressures government to maintain a permanent war economy because a war economy channels a stable flow of guaranteed profit.

Table 6.5
Major Private "Star Wars" Contractors, 1983–March, 1987

Organization	Contracts Awarded (millions)
Lockheed *	1,024
General Motors *	734
TRW	567
Lawrence Livermore Lab	552
McDonnell Douglas *	485
Boeing *	475
EG&G	468
Los Alamos Lab	458
General Electric *	420
Rockwell International	369
MIT	353
Raytheon *	248
LTV	227
Fluor	198
Grumman *	193

* indicates top fifteen defense contractor, 1987
Source: *High Technology Business*, December, 1987: 24.
Aviation Week and Space Technology, March 4, 1988.

Aside from the sheer size of the research and development budget that DOD has to dispense, companies benefit in numerous other special ways from the present system of defense contracting. Firms in the military industries are practically free from competition. Ninety-six per cent of all Pentagon contracts are awarded on a non-competitive basis. Pentagon largesse also makes defense companies more profitable than their civilian counterparts. Typically, defense contractors enjoy profit rates twice as high as their non-military counterparts. In addition, defense contractors, more often than not, pay little or no corporate income tax. Of the top twenty-five defense contractors in the 1981-84 period, seven received tax refunds, two paid no taxes, and four paid one per cent or less. General Dynamics, which reported after tax profits of $684 million in 1984, has not paid any US income taxes since 1972. (Shaffer, 1987: 97) When profit rates are recalculated to account for taxes actually paid, return on equity for the years 1981-84 increases from 25 per cent to 35 per cent, almost three times the average for civilian industry. (*Economic Notes*, July/August, 1986) Here is how one engineer in the SDI program assesses "Star Wars":

> No, it won't work, but we need the money for research; and no, it isn't an efficient way to fund research, but it's the only way we've got. (Reed, 1985: 43)

The case of General Motors, the second leading SDI contractor, offers important insights into the wider economic value of "Star Wars." For GM, SDI and other defense contracts provide public money for private investing in computerized design, manufacturing and robotics systems that will modernize the company and thereby contribute to its international profitability.

In 1984, GM spent $2.5 billion to buy EDS, a leading software producer. EDS has substantial government contract experience: its first, a $656 million, ten-year deal to update the computer systems at 47 US Army bases, including a training program for 60,000 US Army personnel; followed by major contracts with the Navy and US Postal Service. (McClellan, 1984: 15-17 and 137-145) In 1985, GM bought Hughes Aircraft, at that time the eighth-largest defense contractor, with $3.6 billion worth of military contracts in 1985 alone.

This form of diversification is particularly attractive to investors because long-term military commitments mitigate cyclical declines in business activity, buttressing a firm from the effects of recession. Furthermore, as a major defense contractor, General Motors is guaranteed a steady flow of government investment that it can apply to the civilian workplace. Admittedly, there has been considerable press attention paid to the difficulties that GM is encountering in meshing its traditional operations with those of EDS and Hughes. Nevertheless, if GM can overcome its organizational problems, the company will soon enjoy the benefits of having bought more than a ticket to an expanded defense sector.

In EDS and Hughes, GM has bought the technical expertise that it will use to automate its automobile assembly plants and expand its international operations. The Strategic Computing component of the SDI is particularly significant here. According to the Pentagon's prospectus on the program, "spinoffs from a successful Strategic Computing Program will surge into our industrial community." Big winners here are "the automotive and aerospace industries as they integrate intelligent CAD (Computer Assisted Design) into the development process and intelligent CAM (Computer Assisted Manufacturing) and robotics into manufacturing." (US, DARPA, 1983: 9) Even allowing for the hyperbole that often fills such documents, SDI is working economically by providing stable funding to major corporations and by subsidizing the efforts of these companies to enter high technology production and thereby contribute to restructuring the American economy.

SDI is still working to benefit specific economic interests powerful enough to propel the program, whether or not it stands a chance of meeting stated defense goals. For example, in the 1986 congressional election campaign, political action committees representing the ten largest US defense contractors contributed almost $3 million to candidates. (*Satellite Week*, September 7, 1987: 10)

Nevertheless, the economic benefits are decidedly uneven. Though military spending certainly sustains a specific sector, the increasingly capital intensive nature of military spending does *not* significantly prop up employment and consumer spending, as it did in the major world wars. Moreover, there are major questions about the ability to adapt to civilian applications technologies designed for esoteric military needs, particularly in a global economy where certain economies, notably the Japanese and West German, are built on applying advanced technologies to the consumer sector. (Shaffer, 1987) Consequently, even though a military-driven high technology sector may not be in the long-run best interest of the US economy, its short-term economic returns—particularly to defense contractors and the states enjoying the political clout to acquire them (California, Massachusetts, New Mexico and Alabama receive the bulk of SDI money)—lead one to conclude that "Star Wars" is already working as planned.

How "Star Wars" is Working Politically

SDI gives the US government the leverage it needs to harmonize corporate activity with what the government perceives to be overall US interests. The need for such leverage increases as the power of transnational business increases because the interests of such companies and the government become increasingly divergent. Government wants business activities that will increase domestic revenues, employment and the security interests of the state. Transnational businesses wishing to exploit a global market, may very well take actions—such as joint ventures with non-US transnationals—that may not be to the advantage of US employment, revenue, or security. Defense spending can send a strong message to suspected corporate recalcitrants.

In the computer industry, the government has been concerned that IBM, the world's largest computer company, has been lukewarm to government-backed joint venture operations, such as MCC, and to research work in artificial intelligence, an area of strong military interest. Joint ventures like MCC and artificial intelligence research may be high on the government's agenda, but not necessarily central to IBM's business plans. Why should IBM share secrets with lesser competitors? Or invest in research whose commercial potential is less than firmly established?

In this case, the Strategic Computing Initiative can work to bring IBM into closer line with US government interests. As the head of DARPA made clear in Congressional hearings on SCI:

> What we expect to happen is that as DARPA stimulates industry research efforts and university efforts in machine intelligence, either IBM will decide that it will be good to do research in this field and to have a capability in it for defense in the 1990s, or it will not.
>
> If it does not, there will be many others who will participate in those research programs and will spin off technology both for defense and commercial applications.
>
> If IBM does not see that, then in my opinion their market share will decline. (*Aviation Week and Space Technology*, February 27, 1984: 27)

The Pentagon's concern with commercial applications and the need to bring IBM into line is prompted to a great degree by Japanese advances in artificial intelligence research. In House hearings, DARPA identified the threat from Japan as a major reason for investing so much in strategic computing. DARPA expected that "the commercial spinoffs will help the US computer industry to meet, and in fact surpass, the Japanese activities." (US, Congress, House, Committee on Science and Technology, 1984: 135)

"Star Wars" supporters are not as vocal about European competition as they are about the feared threat from Japan. Nevertheless, SDI promoters claim that by attracting European participation in "Star Wars" research, they will deter European efforts to develop independent high technology research projects, such as the French Eureka, EEC ESPRIT, and British Alvey. "Star Wars" can work politically against threats from Japan and Europe.

"Star Wars" has also proven a strong vehicle to draw Canada more directly than ever within the US military system. Despite the government's official policy of opposing Canadian government participation in SDI, it does not oppose Canadian private sector involvement in the "Star Wars" project. Moreover, the Canadian government is stepping up its participation in operations that are part of the SDI program in all but official title. One major project is even very close in label. The ADI, or Air Defense Initiative, is a joint US-Canada program to defend against bombers and cruise missiles attacking North America. According to a Pentagon official, ADI augments a "credible complement" to the "Star Wars" Program. As David Kattenburg has reported (1988), Canada has proposed formal Canadian government participation in ADI, even though this is likely to mean Ottawa's involvement in SDI coordination. Despite the semantic games played by policy makers in Washington and Ottawa, in essence SDI and related programs speed up the process of merging Canada and the US into a tighter military linkage. How can Canada resist, in even the slightest way, US militarism when their respective defenses, including air and space defenses, are essentially united?

SDI and strategic computing also provide the state with substantial leverage in directing research and development conducted in the US. Indeed, Pentagon officials state explicitly that this control gives them, according to the undersecretary of defense for research and development, the final authority for awarding military contracts:

I am not enthusiastic about the idea of using defense resources to subsidize the work of people who are outspoken critics of our national defense goals or policies. ... If they want to get out and use their roles as professors to make statements that's fine, it's a free country. (But) freedom works both ways. They're free to keep their mouths shut ... I'm also free not to give money. (*Toronto Globe and Mail*, August 12, 1986: A7)

"Star Wars" can thereby work as an instrument to control the US research agenda and silence criticism of defense policy.

SDI can also work politically against the Soviet Union. Despite the publicity surrounding Soviet advances in ballistic missile research and strategic computing, most analysts see little Soviet achievement in these areas (Gervasi, 1986). But given the consistent pattern of Soviet counter-response to US military expansion (Table 6.6), one would expect that, before too long, the Soviet Union would have to develop its own version of SDI.

Table 6.6
The Nuclear Arms Race

Device	Time of Adoption	
	US	USSR
Atomic bomb	1945	1949
Intercontinental	1948	1955
Thermonuclear bomb	1952	1953
Intercontinental ballistic missile	1955	1957
Submarine-launched ballistic missile	1960	1968
Multiple independently targeted warhead	1970	1975
Long-range cruise missile	1982	1984
Neutron bomb	1983	?
New strategic bomber	1985	1987

However, many people, in and out of the US government, do not believe that the Soviet Union can sustain the spending required to match the US commitment to SDI. "Star Wars" can work against the Soviet Union by drawing it into a spending spiral that will severely strain its economy.

President Reagan appears to believe that this can happen. According to him:

They cannot vastly increase their military productivity because they've already got their people on a starvation diet as far as consumer products are concerned. But they know our potential capacity industrially, and they can't match it. (Cited in Shaffer, 1987: 92)

Writing in the *Atlantic Monthly*, Nicholas Lemann puts the "spend them into the ground" scenario into sharper perspective:

> The other scenario, which can be heard around the Pentagon and elsewhere in the Administration, is this: Of course we are in an arms race with the Soviets. Of course it won't end at the bargaining table. We can win it. Their society is economically weak, and it lacks the wealth, education, and technology to enter the information age. They have thrown everything into military production, and their society is starting to show terrible stress as a result. They can't sustain military production the way we can. Eventually, it will break them, and then there will be just one superpower in a safe world—if, only if, we can keep spending. (Lemann, 1984: 94)

Or, as science writer Isaac Asimov put it, "It's just a device to make the Russians go broke." (Cited in Thompson and Thompson, 1985: 1)

How "Star Wars" Works as Ideology

SDI and the strategic computing program work ideologically by promoting beliefs that resonate strongly with public desires about military activity. Americans would like their standard of living protected, even if it takes military action, but would prefer that it be done in the name of defense and without resorting to large troop commitments. "Star Wars" offers the powerful image of *defense* against nuclear weapons and, particularly with the investment in strategic computing, the prospect of *automated* warfare, of battles in which few soldiers are involved.

Reagan has been able to enunciate this belief system with religious fervor. Here is how he described his SDI discussions with Gorbachev, including God's role in the program, to a group of high school students:

> I told Gorbachev that SDI was a reason to hope, not to fear; that the advance of technology, which originally gave us ballistic missiles, may soon be able to make them obsolete. I told him that with SDI, history had taken a positive turn. I told him that men of good will should be rejoicing that our deliverance from the awful threat of nuclear weapons may be on the horizon, and I suggested to him that I saw the hand of Providence in that. What could be more moral than a system based on protecting human life rather than

destroying it? I could no more negotiate SDI than I could barter with your future. (J. Smith, 1987: 23)

The power of Reagan's view lies very much in his belief in the vision. Indeed, a movie of his, "Murder in the Air," featured the young Ronald Reagan protecting a primitive "Star Wars" device from enemy agents. According to the historian C. Vann Woodward, "the implausible scheme is at one with Reagan politics and personality, a 'nice' weapon's system—defensive, not offensive; killing missiles, not people, another act of American altruism and a bonanza of billions for business." (Woodward, 1987: 29) He likens SDI to the Lone Ranger's silver bullet, used only to knock guns out of bad guys' hands.

The ideology of defense is highly visible among those directly involved in SDI research. For some, a commitment to defense seems to motivate their work. A common statement heard from the physicists working at the center of SDI research, the Lawrence Livermore Labs is that their wish was "to eliminate nuclear weapons." (*The New York Times*, January 31, 1984) Most physicists at Livermore are young men and women (late twenties and early thirties) who can convey a youthful enthusiasm for their work:

> I don't think I fall in that category, of working on weapons of death. We're working on weapons of life, ones that will save people from weapons of death.
>
> There's almost an infinite number of issues to be pursued. The number of new weapon designs is limited only by one's creativity. Most of them have not been developed beyond the stage of thinking one afternoon, "Gee, I suppose you can do so and so." There's a tremendous number of ways one might defend the country. (Ibid.)

Other researchers get caught up in the details of research and simply bracket the politics. Employment in Huntsville, Alabama, fueled with $862 million in "Star Wars" contracts. has grown 23 per cent since the start of SDI. Engineers there leave the politics to others: "It's so easy to get caught up in the details," said one, "you don't think about the wider implications. You just hope that somebody else is doing that. If you're lucky, you wake up someday and realize that nobody's in charge." (Charles, 1987: 750) Engineer George von Tiesenhausen, a scientist brought to work in Huntsville with several hundred German scientists and engineers smuggled out of Europe after World War II, takes a more sober view of SDI. He argues that the program is "money thrown out the window." However, he adds, many engineers "are overwhelmed with the technical challenge as we were during the V-2 (Nazi buzz-bomb) era." (Ibid.)

Supporters of SDI are well aware of the importance of selling "Star Wars" by seizing the language of peace. The influential "Star Wars" lobby, High Frontier, hired consultant John Bosma to organize its public relations effort. Bosma acknowledges the significance of identifying "Star Wars" as "a new approach to arms control":

> A primary objective is to force a drastic reorientation of the arms control debate in such a way as to make it politically risky for BMD (Ballistic Missile Defense) opponents to invoke alleged "arms control agreements" against an early BMD system. In fact, the project should ... seek to recapture the term arms control and all the idealistic images and language attached to it. ... BMD proponents should stress nuclear disarmament as their goal. (*Harpers*, June, 1985: 22-24)

Robert Jastrow, founder of NASA's Goddard Space Institute and professor at Dartmouth College, offers an excellent example of "Star Wars" public relations in action. In an article for the popular magazine *Science Digest*, Jastrow argues that precision-guided weapons will end the nuclear arms race, "It is one of the paradoxes of our time that the remarkable accuracy of the smart warhead, applied to nuclear tipped missiles, may lead to the virtual disappearance of these terrible weapons." (June, 1984: 39)

Few critics of "Star Wars" acknowledge the ideological force contained in the promise, however contrived, of a technologically guaranteed, nuclear-weapon proof world. One who does, however, is the Canadian historian Robert Malcomson:

> "Star Wars" proposes that Americans can, in a sense repeal the nuclear age. It has a powerful nostalgic appeal to the American public, which looks back to the good old days when geography did provide genuine security for the US. ... "Star Wars" is an attempt to escape from the present realities and for many ... this escapist vision is hopeful and comforting. (Malcomson, 1986: 121-122)

Television helps make this vision all the more comforting, present

SDI news stories in what Gitlin calls a "cheerful visual language." The general viewer is presented often with the vivid, colorful, images of animated progress that tells us:

> what can be drawn can be planned, what can be planned can be built, and what can be built can protect. The diagrams helped confer upon SDI the force of the feasible; the opposition looked like progress-bashing grumps. (Gitlin, 1987: 29)

For those who have their doubts that SDI can provide real hope and comfort, there is the ideology of the *spin-off*, or what Canadian computer scientist and former "Star Wars" consultant, David Parnas, calls, "the Jello Theory" of defense spending. Even if the guns don't work, research gets you a better tasting dessert, a common defensive strategy among military supporters. Since the military benefits of SDI await the next century, short term spin-offs remain a particularly important selling point.

Playing on American fears for its educational system and the future of work, Colorado Congressman Ken Kramer boasts that SDI will "lay the foundation for an education-vocational renaissance for the American labour force, particularly the unemployed in the smokestack industries." (Hartung and Nimroody, 1985: 202) A science writer for *The New York Times* holds out the promise for an end to acid rain pollution, improved patient diagnosis, better weather forecasting, improved shop floor production, and an electron beam weapon that will ultimately be used to fight cancer—in financial terms $5-20 *trillion* in private sector sales of spin-off items. (Browne, 1986)

The Strategic Defense Initiative Office even operates its own spin-off programs. One makes available a technology transfer database of unclassified materials that contain some profit potential. SDI officials report on a number of biomedical and industrial uses. These include research by US and Mexican agricultural interests that uses SDI laser technology to track African killer bees, medical company interest in the use of carbon fibre ceramics for prosthetic devices, and tiny cooling devices used for SDI sensors that may be of use in microsurgery. The SDI office is also setting up a classified spin-off program for companies that the Defense Logistics Agency certifies to be acceptable. For access to this database covering technologies in nineteen "militarily critical" areas, companies have to agree not to transfer data to a foreign entity. (*Aviation Week and Space Technology*, November 23, 1987: 84)

The ideology of the "spin-off" is part of a wider process that Boot refers to as *techno-patriotism*. He uses this idea to explain how American mass media could miss the warning signs of an impending Space Shuttle disaster—including engine shutdowns, brake failures, fuel leaks, and cost overruns. Boot argues that, for the news media, the American space program "became a symbol of US technological redemption following an era of American malaise." (Boot, 1986) Wayne Biddle, who covered technology for *The New York Times* until he resigned in frustration in September 1985, claims that "it was always an uphill battle to get articles critical of the shuttle into the paper. There was a great deal of resistance." (Boot, 1986)

It is much easier to understand the resistance when one comprehends the significance of the space program in the minds and spirits of Americans. Consider the startling results of a survey that Peter Hart Research Associates conducted on the attitudes and values of 18-44 year-old Americans for *Rolling Stone* magazine. When asked what event had more effect on them than any other in their lifetime, the most frequent response was the explosion of the space shuttle Challenger. The shuttle disaster was ahead of the Vietnam War, the AIDS epidemic and the taking of the American hostages in Iran, the next most frequently chosen events. (Sheff, 1988)

Popular writers, particularly those who produce science fiction, have their own brand of techno-patriotism. In his analysis of science fiction ideology, Thomas Disch writes that the genre serves "as a debating society, moral support system and cheerleading section for the present and future personnel of space related industries and military services." (Disch, 1986) According to Disch, the enormously popular work of Robert Heinlein is especially significant here because Heinlein considered space, not as the realm of imagination, but as the next frontier "and he was its recruiting sergeant." More recently, people like Jerry Pournelle, a former Rockwell International executive, take up the issue more explicitly, by writing about space-age Rambos piloting "Star Wars" to American supremacy. Pournelle's *There Will Be War* sees the only hope in victory coming from total US mobilization. His non-fiction *Mutually Assured Survival* is a defense of the "Star Wars" program that features a supportive dustcover letter from President Reagan thanking Pournelle for "assisting us in achieving a safer and more stable future for this country."

There are no doubt many examples of journalism and science fiction writing that counter this view. However, the growth of SDI propaganda in journalism and fiction proves that "Star Wars" proponents understand quite well that they have a selling job to do and will do that job in whatever form is available.

Just as the "Star Wars" program is wrapped in the ideology of a world without nuclear weapons, the strategic computing program is packaged by its defenders *as war without American soldiers*, the automated battlefield. However, by giving computers some decision-making power, we take away *responsibility* from human commanders.

It is hard to disagree with Siegel and Markoff who see automated warfare as a major outcome of the Indochina War:

> As the Vietnam War ... demonstrated, Americans—be they soldiers or civilians—are hesitant to support wars of intervention in which the lives of American troops are threatened. (Siegel and Markoff, in Edwards, 1984: 12)

Automated weapons of the sort proposed in the Strategic Computing Initiative make it easier to justify a future Vietnam, Grenada, or Nicaragua. Moreover, whether or not such weapons systems are militarily effective, as Edwards concludes,

> From the history of war after World War II, it seems apparent both that Third World nations will become dumping grounds for intelligent weapons systems they cannot afford, and that machine intelligences may eventually play decisive roles in armed political struggles. (Ibid.: 13)

Conclusion

When one takes into account the technological history, funding, research, development, and applications of advanced communication and information technology, it is not difficult to draw the conclusion that we are moving toward the creation of a military information society, including the militarization of outer space. The leading edge of this military information society is the "Star Wars" project, a system of high technology weaponry managed by complex networks of computer communcications technology. "Star Wars" leads the military information society, not for how it promises to work, but *because it is already working* economically, politically, and ideologically. Moreover, it may not be long before we see SDI systems or their real spin-offs used against some recalcitrant Third World nation or as part of a nuclear offensive.

There is no doubt a price to be paid for making "Star Wars" work in this fashion, since the logic of military technology is a poor substitute for much needed economic and social planning. Patriotism, even techno-patriotism, has its limits. Nevertheless, "Star Wars" critics have been working under the well-meaning, but misguided assumption that by giving the program a sound technical thrashing, it would go away. There is little doubt that such a thrashing has been delivered. Even *The New York Times* Malcolm Browne, who boasts of SDI providing a cure for cancer and acid rain, had to admit to the strength of the opposition, expressed in part by petitions signed by 6,500 scientists and science educators who pledge not to accept SDI funding. More recently, the American Mathematical Society, with 7,000 of the Society's 20,000 members voting, passed a resolution calling on members to refuse SDI research grants. Canadian scientists, particularly in the computing science profession, have been in the forefront of efforts opposing SDI research. In this way, "Star Wars" itself may also be developing an important oppositional force within the scientific community. But one might also wonder how many of these would sign anti-"Star Wars" petitions, if the program were presented, not as a defensive umbrella, but as a set of loosely coupled weapons that would be used selectively against nations or groups that support terrorism, the drug trade, or threaten the security of Western societies. One need not. The scientific community has generally shown far less opposition, and considerable support, for the development of every major weapons system deployed since the end of World War II, many of which have been used in combat against Third World nations.

The point is not to discourage technically-based opposition to SDI, but to acknowledge that it is thin. Technical criticisms are not stopping "Star Wars". The budget has grown substantially in each year since Reagan announced the program in March 1983. Technical criticisms have not even made substantial inroads in the Democratic Party opposition. Though opposition exists, it is mainly applied to differences in how SDI ought to develop, not in whether it should continue at all. The leadership of the Democratic Party approves continued SDI funding and simply does not want to see SDI undermine existing international agreements, such as the ABM treaty. Moreover, it favours funding in line with overall defense growth and a commitment to long-term research rather than early deployment. (Johnston and Proxmire, 1987). This is in keeping with the Democratic Party's longstanding commitment to the militarization of outer space. In addition, some Democratic opposition to SDI stems from a desire to expand US conventional forces to better enable the US to respond unilaterally to global problems. As it is presently constituted, the Democratic Party holds little hope for a decline in the military information society and the military uses of outer space.

Criticism of "Star Wars" would be more useful if it were linked to ways the program is already working to achieve Washington's wider goals. Opposition to it would be more useful if it showed how "Star Wars" is connected to the US effort to restructure its economy, control its labour force and emerge as the most powerful economic force in the international division of labour. "Star Wars" opposition would be strengthened by linking SDI to US government efforts to control the production and distribution of scientific research and information worldwide. Opposition to "Star Wars" would be better off subverting the notion that the world's leading imperial power can even speak of *defense*, let alone provide a technical fix for it and would be further strengthened by pointing to the ways that SDI can work militarily, as offensive weaponry directed against the majority of the world's people living in the Third World.

Chapter Seven

Communication Policy in the United States

The Electronic Communications System

This chapter examines the communications policy process in the United States, which has led other developed capitalist societies in restructuring this process to respond to economic and political pressures. This chapter builds on the theoretical discussion addressed in Part One, particularly Chapter Four, which examined perspectives on the state and telecommunications policy, by analyzing *how* and *why* communications policy is made in the United States. This discussion also serves as background for Chapter Eight which looks at the impact of the US policy process on Canadian communications policy making.

Three major forces propel the communications system in the United States and the rest of the developed capitalist world: providers, users, and regulators. These forces have shaped the growth of computer communication technologies that have increased the value of media and information throughout society.

The *providers* of communication and information services, mainly private transnational companies, have traditionally been the major driving force in the system. These companies have shaped the pattern of technological change in communication and information, taking into account the needs of a largely fragmented collection of users. (Figure 7. 1).

The communication system in the United States has traditionally been led by a group of established providers in print, telecommunications, broadcasting and film—the household names of communications: Time, Inc., AT&T, NBC, ABC, CBS, and Paramount, among others. Over the last decade or so, established providers have been challenged by

Figure 7.1
The Communications Industry in the United States

1. Established Providers
    a. Print: Associated Press, Knight-Ridder, Gannett, Times-Mirror, Newhouse, Tribune, The New York Times Group, Dow Jones, The Washington Post Group
    b. Film: Paramount, Warner, MCA-Universal, Columbia, MGM-United Artists, Fox
    c. Broadcasting: NBC (General Electric), ABC (Capital Cities), CBS
    d. Telecommunications: AT&T/RHCs
    e. Satellites: Comsat-Intelsat

2. Domestic Challengers from Within Communications
    a. Cable television Multi-System Operators (MSOs), e.g. TCI, ATC
    b. Telecommunications: GTE, MCI
    c. Computers: IBM (including Rolm and MCI)
    d. Cable Satellite Distribution Networks: HBO, CNN, "Superstations," Fox
    e. International Satellite Distribution Networks: PanAm Sat, Orion, RCA American (International Cable: Tel-Optik)

3. Domestic Challengers from Outside Communications
    a. Manufacturing: General Motors (including Hughes and EDS)
    b. Banking: Citibank
    c. Retail: Sears
    d. Electronic Services: American Express
    e. User Associations: ICA

4. International Challengers
    a. Developed Capitalist Mixed Enterprises: Japan, Western Europe, Canada
    b. Newly Industrialized Societies (e.g. Brazil)
    c. Less Developed Societies (Particularly East Asia)
    d. User Associations: International User Group (Intug)

companies that have taken advantage of changes in technology and increased user demand. Challenges to established providers have come from companies on the periphery of communications (e.g., IBM), entirely outside the communications system (e.g., General Motors), and from private and public companies based outside the United States. The latter includes a company like Northern Telecom in Canada which has even challenged the lead of AT&T in the design and marketing of advanced telephone switching equipment.

As communications grows in strategic significance for business and government, communications *users*, principally transnational companies and governments, have been able to exert increasing influence on the communications system. National organizations like the US-based ICA (International Communication Association) and global organizations such as INTUG (International Users Group), among others, have been able to use their significant power in the marketplace, to influence both technological development and patterns of regulation. For example, in telecommunications, business users exerted significant pressure on the system to win changes in industry structure (AT&T divestiture) and regulation (significantly diminished) to help create the customized, low cost, private communication and information networks that these large users wanted (H. Schiller, 1981). This has been a politically charged victory because it was won at the expense of individual customers, small businesses, voluntary associations, and other locally-based organizations that have had to pay higher local telephone bills and suffer the disruptions that have come with fast-changing markets.

The role of government in the US communications system differs from that of most other countries. In the US the government is a *regulator* (and a user), but not a major provider. Even in Canada, where the CRTC serves a similar regulatory role to that of the FCC, the government operates as a major provider in broadcasting, primarily through the CBC, and in telephone, through provincially owned companies in the three prairie provinces. Though the communications systems of other industrialized countries are changing, most continue to identify an agency of government as a provider of communications services. In these countries, individual users who may lack market power, have an opportunity to exert political pressure on the communications system. This is more difficult in the United States because the government serves as a relatively weak regulator and a large user. As a weak regulator, the US government role is reduced to that of referee among the major providers and, now, large users.

For example, the Federal Communications Commission (FCC), reacts to concerns by a major interest like AT&T about excessive intrusion into telecommunications markets by IBM or reacts to the demands of a user group that a new service, such as cellular radio or packet switched data transmission is not organized or priced in ways that satisfy large user needs. Moreover, as a large user (the Pentagon is the single, largest user in the United States), the government is more likely to align with the interests of the large user community.

Over the past decade or so, regulators have lessened controls on the private commercial use of communication and information *technologies*. Along with providers and large users, regulators have come to recognize that developments in microelectronics and aerospace technology, chiefly computers, communications satellites, optical fibre cable and high definition display screens, have multiplied the opportunities to take profitable advantage of communication and information technology. Specifically, the major participants in this arena are increasingly aware of the ability to make information a valuable commodity and to use information to add value to many other commodities.

Consider these examples. Most people categorize video as a mass entertainment industry. It is that, but also a great deal more. In 1986, 8,000 companies spent $2 billion to produce 55,000 hours of business video programming. The typical company produced thirty-one programs. Corporate video is expected to be a $7 billion a year industry by 1990. (*Satellite Communications*, October, 1987: 28).

The US government's Paperwork Reduction Act has diminished or eliminated public access to information collected with taxpayer's dollars. Under this legislation, the Reagan Administration has eliminated one-fourth of all government publications. Moreover, it has transferred to the private sector many government information data bases. Government data bases in such fields as agriculture and medicine are now sold in the open market by information service companies. In general, as a result of these changes, end user charges have doubled. (American Library Association, 1988) In some cases, the jump in charges has been startling. A typical Agriculture Department Service has gone from $60 a year plus $42 per hour of use to $1,800 a year plus $96 per hour of use.

This kind of increasing value of information has sharpened the political conflicts over who wins and who loses in the US communication system, as well as influencing the use of information outside the US. In the spring of 1988, five university libraries in Canada announced plans to sell their libraries to private information services companies in a financial arrangement that would raise much-needed money for universities. The universities simply maintained that they would retain control over their holdings. Librarians, and others concerned about private control over information, disagreed, and, in part, from public pressure, the deals were dropped.

The Canadian Association of Research Librarians understood well the spectre of private censorship. In 1987, the Dunn & Bradstreet Corporation, which operates a private data-retrieval service containing basic information on one million companies, cut off more than 200 subscribers, including all labour unions, from access to the service. The company took this action because it did not want unions using the information for collective bargaining and organizing. One is hard pressed to disagree with those who conclude that this "creates a spectre of database purveyors withholding seemingly public information if there is a hint of an adversarial motive." (*Ottawa Citizen*, January 5, 1988, C2.)

Communication and Society

The system of communication and information is unique in that it is central to economic, and socio-political institutions throughout society. This system includes a growing industry that encompasses raw material, manufacturing, service, and information sectors of the economy, including the largest companies and trade unions. Recent developments in technology have led many to conclude that communication and information is *the* central resource in developed capitalist societies and the key to economic growth for the Third World. For the former chairman of Citibank, "Information is capital."

Specifically, as Chapters One and Two stated, businesses can use communication and information technologies to take advantage of what are, more than ever, global markets for capital, labour, and raw materials. This has accentuated the already strong emphasis of regulators on the economic functions of communication and information, enabling businesses to profit from information commodities directly and to use information systems as instruments to carry out cost-effective global expansion.

But the communication system is more than a means to accumulate capital. It is also central to the political process because the widespread distribution of information and the ease of social contact are vital to political democracy. In the past, often after extensive public pressure, regulators have tempered the emphasis on the economic side with a recognition of the political importance of information. For example, regulators have historically protected freedom of speech and of the press, though within the often signficant constraints defined by national security and market considerations. The government has also intervened directly in the marketplace to support diversity of expression by assisting failing newspapers. In broadcasting, regulators have acknowledged the limitations of spectrum scarcity by imposing fairness, equal time, community assessment, and other demands in order to increase the flow of diverse ideas. In telecommunications, regulators imposed universal service requirements to increase the potential for widespread access to the telephone.

In essence, the communication system is unique in that it is an industry whose central purpose is producing both products—mainly information, entertainment and audiences—*and* the images, beliefs, and ways of seeing that comprise social consciousness. This powerful dimension of the communications system makes regulation and policy all the more significant. Though the history of the system in the United States, as in Canada, can be viewed as a clash between economic and socio-political functions, recent developments in industry and technology heighten this historic clash. Those who call for lessening regulation and directing policy initiatives to business use of the technology, see it increasing economic growth, lessening bureaucratic complexity, and heightening social contact (Oettinger, 1980; Beniger, 1986). They point to the problems that regulation posed for speedy decision making and the uncertainty and subjectivity involved in defining regulation "in the public interest." This view is questioned by those who call for greater public control of the technology because they fear the consequences of uncontrolled use on jobs, individual freedom, local community control, and the equitable distribution of information worldwide (Shaiken, 1984; K. Wilson, 1988; Webster and Robins, 1986).

Communication Regulation and Policy

The most dynamic forces in the communications system are large providers and users who take advantage of opportunities offered by new technology and new configurations of old technology. Government agencies with regulatory responsibility have reacted to and overseen this process, but have not been central to fundamental changes happening in the system. As a consequence of this, it is most useful to begin a detailed discussion of regulation and policy by examining the providers, and users, who lead changes in regulation and policy-making, and the technologies which are central stakes in arguments for and against these changes.

Core Providers

The US communications system contains a core of major providers in print, broadcasting, film, and telecommunications. Over the past decade, through mergers and product diversification, ten organizations have steadily increased their control of the print marketplace: Associated Press, Time, Inc., Gannett (USA Today), The Washington Post Group, The New York Times Group, Times-Mirror, Knight Ridder, Newhouse, Dow Jones, and the Chicago Tribune Group. The growing concentration of power among these companies has increased the trend to national and international over local and regional journalism.

The core in broadcasting contains the three major commercial television networks. NBC and its parent RCA are now controlled by General Electric. ABC merged with the broadcasting company Capitol Cities. CBS has been the target of as yet unsuccessful takover efforts as well. The result of mergers and merger threats has been a greater concern for cutting costs, particularly in the relatively expensive area of news gathering.

The core companies in film are six Hollywood firms: Fox, Paramount, Warner, MCA-Universal, Columbia, MGM-United Artists. These companies are highly dependent on the television networks which exert considerable control over production and distribution in video markets.

In telecommunications, as a result of the Modified Final Judgment (MFJ) in the AT&T divestiture case, there is now a basic division between AT&T and its former local companies. AT&T retains control of long distance and international telephone operations, as well as its manufacturing and research arms. The twenty-two Bell Operating Companies (BOCs), regrouped by the Court decision into seven Regional Holding Companies (RHCs) control local service markets. Comsat has traditionally been the core company in domestic satellite distribution and, as part of the global Intelsat network, a power in international satellite markets as well.

Challenges to Core Providers

This set of core powers is increasingly challenged by domestic and international interests. The first type of domestic challenge comes from communication and information technology companies that are taking advantage of technological developments to provide alternative modes of production and distribution. These include alternative television distributors such as large cable television Multi-System Operators (MSOs) (ATC and TCI are the leaders) which between them control close to 20 per cent of cable subscriptions in the US and cable-satellite distribution networks such as Home Box Office, the Cable News Network, and the various "superstations."

Along with these video-based challenges, there is IBM, whose purchase of Rolm and investment in MCI give the computer giant a base for expanding into telecommunications and electronic information service markets. Finally, Comsat's position as the dominant satellite service provider is challenged by companies like Orion and PanAmSat. These companies are following the example of MCI, which opened the door to domestic long distance telephone competition, by trying to cut into the high volume, high profit North Atlantic markets in telecommunications, video, and data.

The second type of challenge comes from US companies whose central business activity is outside the communications/information sector. These companies have recognized the growing value of information as a commodity in its own right and the central importance of information systems for organizing their own, increasingly global, business operations. Major examples here include General Motors, whose acquisition of the aerospace company Hughes Aircraft and the software company Electronic Data Systems, gives the automotive giant two important entry points into the information sector. Finance companies such as Citicorp are establishing national and international business and consumer financial transaction networks that make use of and challenge core networks. Traditional retail companies such as Sears are finding their businesses overlapping with the electronic services provided by telecommunications companies. As a result, like banking, the retail business is undergoing substantial vertical and horizontal integration.

These changes in the communication and information industry are strengthened by a third set of domestic challenges that eminate from the increasingly coordinated activities of the business user community. Business users have acted on their growing awareness that communication and information activities take up more of their costs of operations. One form of action has been the formation of organizations like the International Communication Association and the International Users Group (INTUG) whose purpose is to pressure both providers and regulators to act in the interest of large users. In Canada, the Canadian Business Telecommunications Association (CBTA) has been a major source of user pressure. Users want networks that can handle their high speed data transmission needs with maximum reliability, privacy, and at the lowest possible price. User associations have sought to achieve these ends by supporting competitive entry into telecommunications markets, particularly by companies such as MCI and Orion in the US, (or CNCP in Canada) that would serve specific business interests. User associations have also promoted deregulation and privatization in order to weaken or eliminate the political commitment to social policy goals, like universal access and service, that large users feel encumber regulated networks.

Challenges to the core from domestic providers and users are made all the more significant by the globalization of the communication system. This brings to the fore challenges from international private, public, and mixed enterprises, including challenges from developed industrial societies whose integrated communication / information companies rival those of the US core. Additionally, Third World countries, such as Brazil, are adopting national information technology strategies to establish alternatives to the transnational giants in hardware production and in alternative data networks.

This pattern of challenge and response is propelled by the increasing recognition of the economic potential made possible by shaping the technology to profitable ends. Concretely, this means building networks that incorporate advanced processing, distribution, and display technologies to measure and monitor information transactions precisely and to package and repackage information products. To put it most concisely, companies are concentrating on the information technology sector because they see growing opportunities to shape information resources into information commodities and to configure electronic highways that maximize the production and distribution of these commodities.

The System of Government Regulation and Policy-Making

Government has responded to this changing system of providers, users, and technologies by facilitating corporate concentration and conglomeration, the development of networks responsive to business user needs, and the commodification of information.

Regulators have eased the way for core providers by permitting mergers and acquisitions that have increased concentration of ownership in the core. Regulators have also eliminated several of the content barriers that, in the name of public interest regulation, formerly restricted profitable use of electronic mass media.

Domestic challengers have been given similar government support in decisions to step back from antitrust action (IBM), in legislation (The Cable Communication Policy Act of 1984), and in changing regulations (reduced entry barriers in domestic and international telecommunication). Moreover, government policy has assisted large users by advancing domestic and international networks (e.g., the Integrated Services Digital Network or ISDN) that would benefit large users and by restructuring pricing policies to permit reductions for the business user community. Finally, as was noted earlier, government policies have eliminated or curtailed public and publicly subsidized information programs such as government data bases. This has accelerated the development of private data and information markets.

Because the US regulatory and policy system is propelled by private corporate interests, historically established public goals of the communication system not conforming to these corporate interests have received inadequate attention. There is extensive discussion of how to expand information markets, but little about the implications for universal service and, more fundamentally, about the communication needs of citizens in an information society. There is extensive discussion of communication networks and electronic services, but little about the implications for concentrating the power of social management in fewer and fewer hands. There is extensive discussion about international privatization, but little about the consequences for international bodies such as the International Telecommunication Union, which serve as the meeting ground primarily of public institutions, including Third World nations that see the ITU as one of the few organizations that might redress some of the imbalances between rich and poor countries in international telecommunications.

The following discussion of the structure of regulation and policy in the US communications system needs to be set in the context of fundamental characteristics. This system is shaped by the interests of private providers and users. Instead of actively setting policy, regulators typically react to these interests, permitting private companies to structure the policy agenda. The regulatory and policy apparatus is fragmented among numerous agencies that tend to reflect certain dimensions of these private interests. This fragmentation is often criticized for impeding the government from making policy. The other side of fragmentation, however, is that it eases the ability of private interests to become *de facto* communications policy makers. This has influenced other Western states, including Canada, where, as Chapter 8 describes, private providers and users exert increasing influence on communication policy.

The Federal Communications Commission

The FCC, an independent regulatory agency responsible to the Congress, licenses use of the radio spectrum (e.g. radio and television stations), sets or determines the mechanism for setting technical standards, and regulates interstate and international telecommunications, chiefly by overseeing rates and services. Since the Executive Branch has the power of appointment to the Commission (within the constraint that not more than three of the five commissioners may be from one political party) including appointment of the chair, the President holds considerable sway over the FCC. Moreover, FCC decisions are subject to the process of legal appeal before the Courts. Over the past ten or so years, the FCC has been the major government agency responsible for implementing the corporate demand that the marketplace rather than public interest regulation take precedence in communications regulation. The major conflicts before the Commission have been differences among private commercial interests as to the structure, timing and precise definition of market-based regulation.

The Congress

Since discussion of deregulation began in the late 1960s, major legislation has been limited to two measures. The 1984 Cable Communications Policy Act eliminated many cable regulations and limited the extent of local regulatory authority. Congress also supported legislation extending the amount of time that broadcasters could hold a license before coming up for renewal review. More importantly, over roughly the past decade, the communications subcommittees in each House have conducted regular hearings that have framed the agenda for deregulation.

The Congress has been the focus of concern from those who have been negatively affected by deregulation. Since the FCC is no longer identified as the arena for the expression of public interest concerns, people have directed their criticisms and pressures directly on the legislature. Trade unions, women's organizations, minority groups and others have demanded action to counter increases in local phone and cable television rates. Others, such as associations of rural residents, have made their concerns part of a wider protest against the impact of deregulation on the general decline in services, including loss of airline routes and diminished mail service. (Dempsey, 1987) In essence, the combination of reduced regulatory concern for the public interest and the growing importance of communications services has greatly politicized this area for the Congress. The lesson for deregulation is that because the policy does not address fundamental political and social concerns, it simply shifts the burden for addressing these concerns to the Congress, at the national level, and to state public utility commissions at the local level.

The Executive
The White House has acted most directly in the *international* policy arena, primarily by promoting the extension of domestic deregulation into the international arena. The Executive Branch impact on domestic policy matters has been felt most strongly in policies to diminish federal involvement in non-commercial media and information programs.

Several executive agencies are involved in the policy formation process. The major participants include: the Department of Defense—as Chapter Six noted, the single largest user, public or private, in the communication system; the Department of Justice, particularly active in issues of speech and press freedom and antitrust; the Office of Management and Budget, responsible for setting government information policies; the State Department, responsible for international matters; and the National Telecommunication and Information Administration (NTIA), a Commerce Department agency responsible for policy research and coordination.

NTIA represents the latest in a series of White House efforts to establish an agency for policy coordination. For decades, communication policy had a small presence in the White House, chiefly to coordinate government radio spectrum use. An executive office administered the work of the government Interdepartment Radio Advisory Committee (IRAC), to distribute that portion, typically one half, of the radio spectrum used by government. In 1970, after numerous blue ribbon panels called for better White House policy management in communications, President Nixon created the Office of Telecommunications Policy. OTP wavered between its official role as a policy research agency and its unofficial, but White House approved, role of publicly criticizing media allegedly critical of the Nixon Administration. OTP seemed to be constantly mired in controversy, stimulated by its recommendation, accepted by the President, that the White House veto funding for a public broadcasting system whose programming the President found particularly unsettling. President Carter shifted OTP from the White House to the Commerce Department in 1978 (and renamed it NTIA). Since that time, NTIA has limited its activities to support for domestic and international deregulation.

Numerous commentators have complained that there are too many agencies with overlapping jurisdictions in communications policy. But few have been as perceptive as Ahern, who pointed out that the multiplicity of policy points reflects an ultimately unsuccessful effort to separate out what are essentially major conflicts, particularly in the international domain, between an international security policy (Defense), an international diplomatic policy (State), and an international commercial policy (NTIA) (Ahern, 1984: 367-371). Even fewer have suggested that the lack of policy coordination means extensive reliance on the corporate sector for expertise. This is simply another instance of privatizing the policy process, particularly for participation in international bodies like the UN International Telecommunication Union, the Organization for Economic Cooperation and Development (OECD), and the General Agreement on Tariffs and Trade (GATT).

The Courts

The US court system has been far more extensively involved in communications policy matters than the courts of any other Western nation, including Canada. The right to appeal FCC decisions, the abstract language of the Communications Act (phrases such as "the public interest" and "fairness"), and also the tradition of settling issues of press and speech freedom through adjudication, make the courts central participants in the regulatory and policy process.

The courts have never been more central to the policy process than in recent years, with the extensive litigations against two of the world's largest communications companies, IBM and AT&T. The IBM case ended when the Reagan Administration decided to discontinue pursuing the decade old case charging the computer firm with unfairly controlling the computer marketplace. The AT&T case ended with the Modified Final Judgment which reflects the agreement reached between the phone giant and the government on terms for settling this monumental antitrust case.

The AT&T Judgement is the most substantial revision of telecommuniations policy in the United States since the Communications Act was put in place in 1934. Principally, it permits AT&T, shorn of its local operating companies, to enter new, unregulated markets for the first time in its modern history. The outcome of this will be felt for decades. If nothing else, the ruling stands as a major example of how the impetus to deregulation tends to shift rather than eliminate the regulatory burden. A federal court is now overseeing changes in industry structure, pricing, market entry, and access to services. These are all dimensions of the telecommunications system that, in the days of regulation, would have been the job of the FCC. There are basic differences. The court's mandate is limited, as is the amount of time it has to oversee the implementation of the agreement. Nevertheless, there is no guarantee that limits to its mandate or official time constraints will resolve the matter and diminish the court's role in communications policy.

Local Regulation

State and local public utility commissions (PUCs) oversee local and intrastate telecommunications rates and services. These agencies bear the burden of passing on the negative consequences of the AT&T ruling and of the general deregulatory policy. A principle outcome of restructuring the telecommunications system to conform to the interests of large domestic and international users is that lower costs for these corporate users means higher rates for local customers. PUCs are responsible for overseeing these local rate increases, which, according to the federal General Accounting Office, increased in 1984 and 1985 at over twice the rate of the Consumer Price Index. (US, GAO, 1986: 21-24). This can only exacerbate the problem of a society whose citizens increasingly depend on the telephone, but who are finding it less affordable. In March of 1986, twenty-five per cent of households officially classified as below poverty, lacked a telephone. (US, GAO, 1987a: 20).

The Development of Regulation: Mass Media

The following sections consider the state of regulation in the areas of mass media and telecommunications, as well as how these areas are influenced by developments in the increasingly overlapping domains of print and computer systems. It looks at how regulation evolved in these areas, the impact of recent changes in the regulatory regime, and major outstanding issues facing the government.

The US communications system, owing in part to the role of the press in the rebellion against British imperial rule, contains a strong prejudice supporting the rights to speech and press freedom, articulated in the first amendment to the Constitution. This differs somewhat from the Canadian system which is still influenced by a British legal tradition that maintained a stronger role for government protection of information

distribution (through the Official Sectrets Act) and government regulation of speech and print that might be considered harmful and offensive.
In the US, courts have taken a strong position in opposition to most
forms of prior restraint on publication. These include direct government
censorship or systems of taxation or licensing that would make it more
difficult to publish something.

US radio broadcasting began with a strong presumption in support of
the freedom to broadcast. This argument emerged over efforts to establish control by the US government, through the Navy, which pioneered
in ship to shore radio before and during World War I. Radio had been of
critical value in the war. At the time, it was uncertain precisely how the
medium would develop once the war ended. This changed rapidly in
the early 1920s, when fears of British control of radio (to match its control
of undersea cables) prompted US creation of RCA, which, as Chapter Six
described, was a government approved joint venture among electronics
giants AT&T, Westinghouse, and General Electric, and the major radio
user, the United Fruit Company, a conglomerate with plantation operations all over Latin America. The decision was to permit private radio
development, though with considerable government oversight, to overcome British control over global cable communications. This differs
from the Canadian broadcasting system which, from the earliest days of
radio, in part as a response to protests about excessive US programming, maintained a strong public presence. This continued with the
development of Canadian television, through the national CBC network
and provincial broadcasting systems such as TV Ontario.

Even in the US, radio differed from print, however, because radio
used a scarce resource, the electromagnetic spectrum. No single station
could broadcast on the same frequency or channel, at the same time,
over the same geographical area. When companies began to test the
commercial potential in radio broadcasting, they increasingly clashed
over the use of frequencies. Despite numerous industry meetings and
considerable government prodding, commercial radio stations could
not reach an agreement on how to allocate spectrum, assign channels,
and generally police compliance in order to minimize interference.

The federal government reluctantly took on the job of regulation
because industry self-regulation failed. The Radio Act of 1927 established the first broadcast regulatory agency. In 1934, the Communications Act supplanted the Radio Act by incorporating telecommunications regulation and establishing the Federal Communications Commission. The Act clearly supported a private broadcasting system, but

tempered this support with a permanent regulatory structure to assign scarce frequencies and oversee content in the public interest. Canada has had a similar system of regulation though with more explicit concerns about protecting the public broadcasting system and, because it is a problem in the Canadian and not the US system, protection of domestic programming content.

The US Communications Act has been applied, with minor modifications, to subsequent developments, including FM radio, broadcast television, and cable television. These modifications have mainly covered content regulations. Over the years the FCC has adopted controls on the amount of commercial advertising time. It has also instituted rules to provide time for news broadcasts, guarantee some degree of content diversity, make broadcasters ascertain community needs, and provide equal time to candidates for political office. Broadcast deregulation has eliminated most of these rules.

The FCC has been at the centre of criticism since the time of its founding (Mosco, 1979). The most recurrent of these criticisms is that the Commission has essentially defined the public interest as whatever is in the interest of the established radio and, now, television networks, including their owned and operated stations and affiliates. The drive to deregulate broadcasting began when those interests supporting new production and delivery systems, such as cable, developed sufficient power, in part by strategic alliances with some broadcasters, to challenge the complete power of the networks.

The Development of Regulation in Telecommunications

In both the US and Canada, telephone regulation grew from a different legal tradition than that of the mass media. Rather than the press model of competitive free speech, telecommunications regulation has its roots in postal road and railroad statutes that established the *common carrier* concept. Telephone, like its predecessor the telegraph, was considered an extension of the highway, a communications highway vital to business. There was considerable debate early on in the history of telephone about whether to extend the highway analogy completely and provide for complete government ownership of telecommunications. The early leader in the industry, AT&T, was sufficiently powerful to avoid nationalization and win regulated private monopoly status. This gave the government some influence over a growing corporate giant and avoided wasteful duplication involved in buiding and maintaining competing phone systems.

Government regulation of local (PUC), national, and international rates (eventually the FCC) would insure a reasonable return for the company and widespread public access at affordable rates. AT&T agreed to leave other communications media, like telegraphy and radio (except to provide lines for networking), and agreed to forego entering new businesses outside of telephony. In its essence, government made AT&T a regulated monopoly in return for providing near (today 92 per cent of US households) universal service. In Canada, a similar monoply position was extended to the Trans Canada Telephone System (TCTS) which is a consortium of private and provincial carriers such as Bell Canada, British Columbia Telephones, Saskatchewan Telephones, etc.

The history of telecommunications is filled with the conflicts and compromises over this agreement. The entire communications regulatory system, FCC, Congress, the Executive, and the Courts, has been involved in efforts to sort out the internal structure of AT&T. This is chiefly a process of assigning revenues and costs (called separations and settlements) between local and long distance divisions of the company. The process is a critical one because it determines the distribution of charges between local and long distance subscribers. As the geographical scope of business has grown, so too have the business pressures to see that revenue settlements increasingly favour the long distance side.

In addition to the division of revenues and costs, there is the determination of what comprises the capital base for the company. Since AT&T and its local operating companies were allowed to earn a percentage return on the value of their capital, this determination was critical to the company's level of profit. Like separations and settlements, the determination of the company's "revenue requirements" involved a massive amount of regulatory activity. It is not unfair to suggest that a great deal of this activity was largely ritualistic. The company itself controlled all evidence about its performance. The government simply did not have the budget to monitor the telecommunications system. Consequently, the regulator, federal or state, would typically respond to company rate increases with a symbolic toughness that would lead the company to accept less revenue. There was never a real determination of what would constitute efficient, equitable, or fair decisions. Regulators simply kept an eye on telephone penetration levels and, provided the numbers were acceptable, continued the regulatory ritual. Oettinger described the ritual best in a statement that would be as applicable to Canada as it is to the US:

... consider cost and price decisions as fairy tales whose merit lies in how well they meet the needs or the goals of various stakeholders—companies, regulators, politicians and so on.

Whatever contending theologies or party lines are in vogue, in practice the prevailing costing and pricing methods reflect more or less faithfully and with greater or lesser time lags the prevailing political balances of their day. At their best, costing and pricing methods are the means to policy ends, not the ends in themselves.

What policy ends? Those in harmony with whatever consensus or compromise is acceptable to the stakeholders and to the referees involved in the battle: providers, customers, competitors, regulators, legislators, the courts. (Oettinger, 1988)

Over the years, this system was buttressed by a number of legislative and regulatory decisions. For example, an amendment to the Communications Act established a mechanism for dividing international telephone and telegraph (record) service between AT&T and a cartel of private international record carriers. The 1956 Consent Decree between AT&T and the federal government maintained that AT&T would stay out of nonregulated businesses such as data processing in order for the company to maintain its integrated monopoly. Most recently, three FCC Computer Inquiries revisited the issue of AT&T entry into new markets by trying to distinguish betwen communication and computer markets, and between basic and enhanced services. In addition to these actions, government users, particularly the Pentagon, have been active over the years in making the case for the AT&T monopoly as an essential infrastructure for national defense and security.

Over the past six decades, regulation maintained a fragile balance in mass media and telecommunications. In the former, the balance consisted of a system led by an oligopoly of private networks who kept regulators off their backs by providing a modicum of public service to local communities. In telecommunications, the balance was struck between private monopoloy and widespread, if not universal, service. Changes in technology, particularly computers, satellites, and optical fibre, while changes in business organization, particularly globalization, created new communications opportunities. These opportunities brought pressure from new entrants, in both mass electronic media and telecommunications, and large users, mainly in telecommunications, to reconfigure communications systems. Regulators have responded to these pressures in recent years.

The Consequences of Deregulation in the United States

Mass Media

In the mass media, regulators slowly loosened restrictions on owner-ship concentration. This includes increasing the number of stations one owner can hold and the ability of a company to own different types of media in the same market (cross-ownership). They have also eliminated almost all content and monitoring responsibilities in radio and loosened content (the Fairness Doctrine and most advertising restrictions have been lifted) and community ascertainment rules in television. The latter aimed to guarantee that local broadcasters served their communities by demonstrating an effort to determine what were major local concerns and by programming to address them. Regulators have also removed the requirement that cable companies must carry all local television signals. This has led to the removal of public broadcasting stations from many cable systems that would rather fill the system with services, such as home shopping, which earn cable companies a percentage share of shopping revenues.

In addition to this, regulators have extended the duration for which regulators can hold a radio and television license, as well as making it considerably easier to renew a license. In radio, it can be done by post-card. There are fewer experiences of challenges to licenses or compara-tive hearings to determine whether a station should be punished with anything from a shorter term renewal to actual loss of its license.

The 1984 Cable Communications Policy Act deregulated much of the cable industry. It did so by limiting local government regulation, includ-ing restricting the grounds a municipality can use to deny a franchise renewal, and a phase out of municipal rate-regulation. Cable companies were also protected from cross ownership by local broadcast outlets and by telephone companies (except in certain underserved rural areas). In return for giving up effective regulation of this local monopoly, cities retained the right to maintain a levy on cable revenues, though this is limited to five per cent of the gross. These changes have strengthened the concentration of power among leading broadcasting and cable pro-viders, rendering broadcasting licenses and cable franchises to near pri-vate property status.

Electronic media providers have been freed from almost all content and hiring constraints. As a result, there is less money spent on low profit ends of the media business; many radio stations no longer broadcast news at all; less is spent on television news, public affairs, and children's programming; and deregulated cable rates have risen markedly. According to a study produced by the National Cable Television Association, the major industry lobby, cable subscribers paid an average of 6.7 per cent more for service six months after deregulatory provisions came into effect (*FCC Week*, November 30, 1987: 5).

Telecommunications

The AT&T decision reorganized the company by separating from the old Bell System, twenty-two basic operating companies (BOCs) which are now organized into seven Regional Holding Companies (RHCs). But AT&T has still retained control over its more profitable operations: long distance and international telephony, manufacturing, and research. Moreover, AT&T is now free to enter new markets such as electronic information services. The twenty-two BOCs are limited largely to the provision of regulated local service. The federal court has limited the expansion of BOC activities because it fears that these companies would take advantage of their regulated monopoly status in local service provision to cross-subsidize their entry into new markets such as information services. As a result, local voice customers would suffer. Backed by the deregulatory-minded FCC and NTIA, the local companies counter that without the freedom to enter more lucrative markets, their businesses, including the provision of basic local voice service, would suffer.

In addition to the AT&T ruling, the FCC has, over the last two decades, liberalized regulations on entry into equipment and service markets. As a result, numerous firms now offer a wide range of equipment, and several companies offer long distance voice and data services to the general public and, in customized networks, to business customers. Nevertheless, AT&T is still the major provider of switching equipment. Though it lost sales, principally to the Canadian firm Northern Telecom, in the first two years after divestiture, it rebounded in 1986 to increase its share of the market to close to 60 per cent of sales. Furthermore, AT&T still retains close to 80 per cent control of the long distance telephone market. MCI, Sprint and a few others essentially occupy niche markets. Moreover, despite considerable discussion of company efforts to *bypass* the local network with alternative systems and technologies, the RHCs retain over 99 per cent of local market share (*Trends in Communications Regulation*, December, 1987: 7).

Perhaps the FCC's most controversial action has been in the area of pricing. Traditionally, under the unified Bell System, the FCC and local regulators responded to rate requests from AT&T and its local companies, and thereby set local and long distance charges. There has been a longstanding debate about whether the division between local and long distance changes actually reflects the cost of providing the services. Many claim that long distance charges subsidized local services in order to maintain widespread access to telephony. Others argue that the reverse is the case. We can only be certain that there can be no definitive conclusion here. The decision-making process reflected political bargaining more than scientific decision-making, though elaborate regulatory rituals created the impression that this was the stuff of scientific economics. Since there was never any effort to verify the accuracy of company-provided data, no manner of rational thought could arrive at an independent decision. Regulators simply reached a price figure that would minimize complaints from shareholders and customers.

This system ended with divestiture because the long distance and local revenue bases were assigned to entirely different companies. The FCC, which still regulates long distance rates, has acted to stimulate competition in the long distance market. The Commission has permitted competitive entry and, more recently, instituted what it calls Customer Access Line Charges to put more of the cost burden on local subscribers. Officially, this is a fee that local subscribers pay for the right to have access to the long distance network, whether or not the subscriber uses the network. Offical regulatory rationalizations aside, the Access Charge is a means of shifting the cost burden to local subscribers, stimulating cuts in long distance rates, and thus gives in to the pressure from large businesses, the most extensive users of the long distance network, for low rates and better long distance service. Long distance charges *have*, in fact, declined (by about one-third) and local rates, have, increased (on average by about forty per cent) since divestiture. The beneficiaries of deregulation have clearly been big business users.

The FCC is also considering proposals that would change the method of regulating phone charges. Traditionally, the Commission used a rate base method, permitting the company to earn a percentage, set annually, of revenues. The leading alternative is price cap regulation, a method that would offer a wider range of latitude for the company to determine its own rate of return. The Commission hopes that competition would prevent excessive returns and that the phone companies would be in a better position to allocate resources more efficiently in response to market changes. However, examining historical data, the

Consumer Federation of America has concluded that employing even a conservative price cap method would have resulted in rates that were 20 per cent higher over five years and 50 per cent higher over ten (Consumer Federation of America, 1987).

The overall impact of deregulation has been higher rates for local customers—varying by region, the political clout of the local PUC, and the pressure of individual customers—lower rates for long distance customers and higher rates of return for telephone companies. Table 7.1 offers data for selected companies. According to the Consumer Federation, if companies were allowed to earn no more than other large corporations, ratepayers would have saved more than $6 billion over the past three years.

Table 7.1
Return on Equity
Telephone Companies Compared to Top 1000 Companies

Company	Year			
	1984	1985	1986	1987
Ameritech	14.1	14.5	15.0	14.9
Bell Atlantic	13.1	13.8	14.1	14.4
Bell South	13.4	14.2	14.4	13.8
NYNEX	12.9	13.3	13.9	13.7
Pactel	12.8	12.8	14.1	12.3
SW Bell	12.9	13.6	13.4	12.8
US West	13.3	13.3	12.7	12.9
Average for all RHCs	13.2	13.7	14.1	13.6
Top 1000 companies	13.2	11.4	10.4	10.9

Source: Consumer Federation of America, 1987: 2.

International Regulation

With considerable support from the Executive Branch, especially NTIA, the FCC has sought to "export" deregulation to the international arena by promoting this policy among foreign governments and in international fora. More concretely, the Commission has approved the petition of companies to compete in international satellite communication with the global Intelsat system. Companies such as PanAmSat and Orion have sought to operate discount services, primarily over lucrative North Atlantic routes. Intelsat complains that this would "skim the cream" from the profitable routes that Intelsat uses to provide what it considers to be subsidized prices for lesser trafficked routes, particularly to the Third World. This development raises to the global arena questions of cost and rate distribution that have been part of the domestic agenda for years.

The effort to export deregulation is part of a wider strategy to maintain US business supremacy in international communications. This supremacy was established after the Second World War when the US was left as the only developed nation with the capacity to shape global communication. The policy has continued since the War, though the political strategy to implement it has shifted with shifts in the international political arena.

Immediately after the War, the US established international organizations that would help coordinate the implementation of US policy worldwide. In communications, the US headed the creation of UNESCO and restructured the work of the International Telecommunications Union. These two agencies of the United Nations helped coordinate US international communication policy in mass media and telecommunications respectively. As long as the US continued to dominate these agencies, they accepted the democratic processes that governed their operation, including the principle of one nation, one vote. After all, democratic procedures gave legitimacy to decisions that accepted, in the name of such values as "the free flow of information," the spread of US transnational mass media and telecommunications companies around the world.

US openness to democratic procedures began to change as the number of new nations began to swell the ranks of UN organizations. These nations established independent organizations, principally the Non-Aligned Movement, which called for the implementation of national and regional communications policies that would promote development, even if that meant restrictions on the operations of transnational firms, including mass media and telecommunications companies. The US began to lose votes in international fora, including a memorable UN vote in which the entire General Assembly was lined up against the US in a vote that favoured restrictions on the unbridled commercial and governmental use of direct broadcasting satellites. The response of the US was to step up its criticism of what it described as the sudden politicization of these agencies. According to Secretary of State George Schultz, in a letter to then UNESCO Director General M'Bow:

For a number of years, as you know from statements we have made at the Executive Board and elsewhere, we have been concerned that trends in policy, ideological emphasis, budget and management of UNESCO were detracting from the organization's effectiveness. We believe these trends have led UNESCO away from the original purposes of its constitution. We feel that they have served the political purposes of member states, rather than the international vocation of UNESCO. (Schultz, 1984: 82-84)

Herbert Schiller has pointed to the contradiction in this US response:

In its formative days, when its membership was 28 states-for the most part Western countries who at the time were heavily dependent on US economic aid-politicization was practically a structural condition. Unquestioning acceptance of US initiatives was not seen by the domestic media *then* as politicization. (H. Schiller, 1984 *b*: 127)

After a modest effort to reassert its control over UNESCO through the implementation of a communications development project, the US decided that UNESCO was not sufficiently responsive and withdrew from the organization, as it had earlier withdrawn from the UN International Labour Organization.

In recent years, the US has put more emphasis on developing co-optive mechanisms that would permit it to operate in international organizations with some measure of controlling influence. The best example of this practice is within the International Telecommunication Union. Though the US has threatened withdrawing from the ITU, particularly when the organization threatened to expel Israel for its invasion of Lebanon, the US has decided to remain. This decision is based on the accurate assessment that the ITU differs from UNESCO in that the ITU holds substantive powers. These include the allocation of radio frequencies and the geostationary satellite orbit, both of which are essential for the conduct of international telecommunications. Furthermore, the ITU is responsible for setting global standards for radio and telecommunications equipment. Again, transnational business depends on standards agreements to establish markets and conduct business. In essence, the US needs the ITU, but it does not want to be subject to its democratic decision-making processes.

The US has used the same rhetoric in its ITU dealings as it did at

UNESCO. The ITU, in the US view, suffers from increasing politicization that detracts from the Union's technical mandate. Rhetoric aside, Codding has established that it is not so easy to separate technology from politics. According to him, the ITU has always been a political body. (Codding, 1984: 438). The inaugural conference of the ITU's predecessor, the International Telegraph Union, was held in Paris in 1865 to promote Napolean III's prestige. In 1868, colonial nations obtained extra votes for their territories over the protests of other members, a practice not abolished until 1973. For many years, the United States refused to join the ITU because it feared that an international union might restrict the activities of its private companies. In the 1950s, the United States and the Soviet Union battled over the membership of Latvia, Lithuania, and Estonia. Since 1959 development issues have played an increasingly significant role, though the issue today is not growing politicization, but rather the particular way politics is played at the ITU.

Recently, the US has sought to co-opt legitimate Third World concerns for development assistance by promoting a private-sector led agency that would offer such assistance. To do this, the US helped to establish the Independent Commission for World-Wide Telecommunications Development, also known for its chairman as the Maitland Commission. The Commission's recommendations offer insights into how the US and its Western allies promote a version of development conforming to the needs of their interests and those of transnational business. The Commission included among its membership the former Energy Secretary to Margaret Thatcher, the Chairman of the Board of the Japanese transnational NEC, and the past president of AT&T. Its work was aided by the world's major telecommunications and consulting firms and its recommendations reflect their interests.

First, Maitland calls for deploying state of the art digital technology throughout the Third World:

We believe that taken together the advantages of a wholly digital network are overwhelming and that every telecommunications planning decision should now be made with the creation of such a network in mind. (ITU, 1985: 33)

Digital equipment is extremely expensive to acquire, install, and maintain. Developing countries lack the technical expertise and resources to provide their own technicians to install and maintain such systems. Instead of installing less expensive telephone equipment that would adequately serve the needs of many developing countries for some time to come and could be maintained by their own administrations, such nations will be dependent on technological developments and competitive market forces at work in industrialized countries.

The Maitland Commission also proposed that the ITU provide a catalogue of all the choices offered by telecommunications equipment suppliers—operating in effect as a marketing vehicle:

> To help developing countries ... We recommend that the ITU, in conjuction with manufacturers of telecommunications equipment and components, should consider compiling a comprehensive catalogue of telecommunications suppliers and systems currently in use. (ITU, 1985: 35)

The Commission even goes so far as to point out how the developing countries represent a "fast growing and potentially the largest market for telecommunications equipment and should be highly attractive to manufacturers in industrialized countries." (ITU, 1985: 57) There is no intrinsic problem with providing a catalogue of available equipment. However, Third World analysts and policy makers may well ask whether their call for equity is being met by transforming the ITU into a marketing vehicle for the largest telecommunications manufacturers.

Finally, the Commission suggests that the management of telecommunications systems be taken out of public administrations and placed in the hands of private business, that is, privatization:

> These considerations can best be taken into account if telecommunications are run as a separate, self-sustaining enterprise, operated on business lines. The management of its operations and its finances should be separate from those of posts and similar undertakings, and from the structure and financial machinery of central government. (ITU, 1985: 38)

The Maitland Commission's activities may or may not succeed. The intransigence of Western business interests to any form of dealing with Third World concerns threatens to limit the amount of money made available to the Centre for Telecommunications Development that the Commission proposed and the ITU accepted. The Canadian government has generally supported this effort. In fact, the first head of the CTD was a Canadian telecommunications executive. Consequently, Canada stands to gain or lose international favour with the results of the Maitland inspired effort. Whatever the consequences, the Commission's recommendations reveal an alternative to the heavy-handed approach taken at UNESCO, essentially an alternative that seeks to co-opt calls for greater equity in international telecommunications.

Consequences

Recent regulatory and legal actions have reversed the long-established tendency to maintain a balance between economic and social values in broadcasting and telecommunications. Clearly putting the needs of large American businesses first, the government has made it easier for companies to make money from broadcasting, cable, and telephone operations by removing public interest controls. It has also increased the incentive of telecommunications companies to provide the low-cost, customized services that large manufacturing and service companies—particularly those operating in the international arena—demand. Unless political pressures on Congress mount, the situation is likely to continue. Price cap regulation and a continuation of the access charge rules only promise higher telephone rates. As the court eases up on its regulation of local phone companies, even local voice service will suffer. In broadcasting, television networks are already implementing plans to cut costs and restructure operations to maximize the profit goals of parent companies, while cable giants exercise their new freedom under the Cable Act to raise rates and limit their systems to profitable services. How well citizens groups mobilize to stop this remains a central political question in US communication policy. Whether Third World nations respond well to efforts co-opting their calls for greater global equity remains a central political question in international communication policy. Canada faces the fundamental problem of deciding how closely it will follow the US lead in applying deregulatory policy to its domestic communication system and in participating in the international effort to co-opt Third World calls for a New World Information and Communications Order.

Future Policy Issues

Deregulation does not eliminate government involvement. Rather, it tends to reshape issues and displace them onto different government bodies.

In mass media, technology and market forces converge, increasing the concentration of power in electronic information and entertainment services among a small number of companies. Deregulation proponents have tended to argue that first amendment protections prevent regulatory control, even if regulation is intended to increase the diversity of ideas. As a result, in the name of free speech we get fewer ideas. The alternatives include negative sanctions such as enforcement of antitrust statutes to break up excessive market concentration. Those who contend that such structural intervention provides no guarantee of diversity call for a more expansionary approach. This would include charging a fee for spectrum use or for a cable franchise and redistributing revenues to non-commercial and alternative media. Similarly, new services—such as low-powered television, teletext and videotex—and expanding old services, such as broadcast radio, might be required to reserve access for non-commercial interests.

In telecommunications, for the short term, regulators face the problem of monitoring and acting on price, industry structure, and service implications of the AT&T decision. This includes the impact on telephone universality. Supporters of universality and fairness have little cause for optimism here. The Congressional oversight agency, the General Accounting Office, has concluded that the FCC is simply incapable of protecting the public from the power of telephone firms to use regulated revenues to subsidize ostensibly competitive businesses. According to the GAO:

> The level of oversight FCC is prepared to provide will not, in GAO's opinion, provide telephone ratepayers or competitors positive assurance that FCC cost allocation rules and procedures are properly controlling cross-subsidy. (US, GAO, 1987b: 3)

Particularly significant issues are likely to surface at the boundaries of telecommunications. On the boundary between publishing and telecommunications, one can anticipate increased movement of AT&T and the RHCs into information services. Newspaper companies have repeatedly raised concerns about the impact of such a development on the production and distribution of information. The AT&T ruling put a moratorium on that company's entry into the information marketplace until the early 1990s. As well, the court has limited RHC entry to the storage of data and provision of "gateways" for information providers. But it is likely that policy makers in the 1990s will need to deal with the problem of carrier control over information services. In an environment where information is a vital commodity and in which the government has privatized a considerable amount of its data collection and storage, industry conflicts and questions of access are likely to be quite bitter.

At the computer-telecommunications boundary, regulators need to address the implications of the impending struggle between AT&T and IBM. Will they emerge as the primary forces in the electronic information services marketplace? What are the antitrust implications, the international implications? More generally, what are the implictions of an increasingly private sector run US international policy structure for US participation in what are largely government-based international fora such as the International Telecommunication Union.

Conclusion: Toward a Broader View of Policymaking

This chapter has provided an overview of the communications system in the United States from a regulatory perspective and identified the major elements of the system, including providers, users, technologies, and regulators. The system has traditionally been propelled by providers, though more recently, large, organized users have sought to take advantage of advances in technology to reshape the system for their interests.

Regulation has tended to react to problems. Historically, regulators have presided over a balance between corporate and socio-political goals. Recently, the balance has tipped decidedly in the direction of corporate needs. The view among regulators is that it is most beneficial to bring about the rapid introduction of new technology and services. Moreover, they contend that the best way to accomplish this would be by "unleashing" private companies in the marketplace. As a result, longstanding goals such as universal service and information diversity have been threatened, though interests supporting these goals have begun to pressure the US Congress for redress. In essence, deregulation does not eliminate longstanding values in the communications system. Rather, it displaces these values onto institutions that provide some support for them.

For the policy process to change, we need a political movement demanding that government take the active—rather than reactive— view that recent developments in communications systems offer opportunities the market is simply not equipped to realize. The chapter concludes with a series of questions that frame such an active policy position.

Deregulation represents an abdication of policy in favour of the marketplace. Nevertheless, limiting an alternative to universality of access to a specific technology like the telephone is only a partial response. Active policy starts with assessing the communications needs and requirements of citizens in an information society, and planning the appropriate mix of organizational resources and technologies to meet those needs and requirements.

An active policy would assess current communications usage and assess, through extensive survey, interview, and institutional research, how people perceive their communications needs, and what sorts of communications skills citizenship requires.

What policies promote citizenship rather than, simply, consumerism? How can we reconcile the right to communicate with the need for economic growth and universal access to fully diverse information at affordable rates? How can overwhelmingly centralizing tendencies in the technologies accommodate the need for local community control? And how do we address the demand for making information a commodity with the need to retain its value as a public good? How can we address the global demand for democratic communication?

Chapter Eight

Free Trade in Euphemisms:

The Impact of Exporting Deregulation

Metaphors, Incorporated

"Nothing unpatriotic intended," Townsend said. "But what is it the Americans really know how to make and sell? Not cars. Our cars are junk. Not rockets. Our rockets blow up. Not steel, or textiles, or furniture, or electronics. We can't afford to pay the help." Townsend kept smiling and shaking his head until the lesser consultants subsided into respectful silence. Murray was kind enough to ask the straight-man's question.

"O.K.," he said, "what is it that the Americans know how to make and sell better than anybody else in the world?"

Townsend drank deeply from his still tax-deductible drink, and then, after a majestic pause, he said: "Metaphors, my dear Murray. Metaphors and images and expectations."

If given a choice in the matter, he said, Americans prefer something that isn't there. They're in love with the idea of a thing, not the thing itself. Of those who buy jogging shoes, 70 per cent don't jog. The menu in most American restaurants is more interesting than the food. A television commercial is an artifact far more subtly made than the product it advertises. Apartments on Fifth Avenue sell for $4 million not because the buyers want a place to live but because they seek a state of grace. The diamond in the Tiffany box is infinitely more precious than the same diamond bought on West-Forty-seventh Street. Entire vocabularies of unintelligible jargon—literary as well as military and academic—describe kingdoms of nonexistent thought. Political promises belong to the realm of surrealist fiction. Like the government in Washington, the economy floats on the market in abstraction—on the credulity of people willing to pay, and pay handsomely, for a domino theory, a stock market tip, or any other paper moon with which to furnish the empty rooms of their desire. (Lapham, 1986: 8-10)

Deregulation is fast becoming one of the most important metaphors that the US produces today. One might debate whether the US is good at making *things*, but it has certainly succeeded in producing and exporting a model of policy making and managemement that has helped to open global markets to US transnational firms.

This chapter examines the impact of exporting deregulation and privatization on Canada, the largest US trading partner. Canada represents a challenge for US policy makers because of its stronger commitment to such goals as public control and universal access to media and telecommunications. Though there is already extensive private ownership of Canadian electronic media and a very substantial US influence, the major radio and television network, the CBC, is a public network accessible to most Canadians. Three of the country's provincial telephone systems are owned by their respective governments, which participate in the nationwide long distance telephone consortium (Telecom Canada) and thereby influence national telecommunications policy. Despite its much lower population density, 98 per cent of Canadian households have telephones compared to 92 per cent of US. A strong constituency led by the New Democratic Party, leading trade unions, educators, women's groups, cultural organizations, elderly and voluntary associations provide a significant force to defend the principle of universality, or full and equal access to services. They have been able to defeat several attempts by the majority Conservative government to undermine universality in such diverse areas as pensions and telecommunications.

The US would like to break down what it sees as barriers to US penetration of the Canadian marketplace. It would like to do so because the Canadian market represents a significant value in its own right. Moreover, the development of a privately controlled North American market in telecommunications and related industries would serve as a model for the US export of deregulation around the world. The goal is to eliminate any constraints on increased US penetration of the Canadian market. This would include statutes and regulations that respond to the Canadian concern that values other than marketability should shape the operation of communications systems. One way to accomplish this is through a bilateral agreement such as the Canada-US trade deal. More subtle measures may be even more effective. These include pressure on the Canadian government to harmonize its regulatory and policy structure to reflect the US emphasis on revamping a communications system to meet US corporate needs.

In other words, even if Canada were to succeed in retaining the current minimal protection it gives its own cultural industries, Canadian adoption of the US model for deregulation and privatization will still likely create the conditions for integrating the media, telecommunications, and information sectors of both societies. Deregulation in this sense is a euphemism for achieving free trade without a free trade agreement. Although the trade agreement is important, it is one item in a set of policies aimed at integrating US and Canadian markets. Stopping the trade agreement is therefore not likely, in itself, to free Canada from incorporation into a North American marketplace.

Ma Bell's Revenge

Not too long ago, a magazine article offered concrete and personal evidence that deregulation is indeed a metaphor, though not a very pleasant one. "Ma Bell's Revenge" reports on the plight of one writer, a would be pioneer of the information society, who moved into a house with a backyard cabin that he planned to use as an office. As a man who made his living from communication and presumably a father of the '80s, he approached his wife with a great idea: "We'll put in a phone with an intercom to the phones in the house and if you or the baby need anything—*presto*." His wife, concluding that, to paraphrase the AT&T lingo, "telecommunity" is the next best thing to being there, agreed: "Great," she said, "Let's call the phone company." After several weeks of careening through the maze of telephone companies, or "dial providers" as they are now called, and equipment firms that offered him deals "for roughly the price of fixing the O-rings on the space shuttle," we find this would be computer age Davy Crockett or *voyageur* lugging 15 ten-foot pipes across his back yard and concluding that the words "Let's call the phone company" are the second worst in the English language; "the worst word in the English language is deregulation." (*The New York Times Sunday Magazine*, March, 1987: 12)

Though this is not a universal reaction to deregulation in the US, it is far from an unusual response for individual customers who have seen local telephone rates increase, according to a 1986 GAO study, by about 40 per cent since deregulation and who must confront a bewildering number of firms in the marketplace. (US, General Accounting Office, 1986) Moreover, deregulation has done nothing to help those groups in the United States that could make best use of the telephone, but who cannot afford one. According to the GAO (1987a), 25 per cent of Americans below the poverty line do not have telephone service. The same is the case for 31 per cent of food stamp households and 24 per cent of households whose children participate in subsidized lunch programs. Universal service is simply not a reality for a large per centage of America's poor, perhaps the group that could benefit most from the service. So, for the vast majority of Americans, deregulation means paying more for the same level of telephone service, or worse. Consequently, it is hard for many people to understand why deregulation is so popular in US policy circles and increasingly a central item on the policy agendas of other industrial nations, including Canada, when the individual response has been far from supportive.

The response has not been greatly different in Britain where the privatized British Telecom has experienced enormous service problems. According to one account, the company has been hit with "a flood of complaints—about shoddy service, unfathomable billing and a corporate imperiousness unchanged from its former incarnation as a Government-owned utility." (*Toronto Globe and Mail*, September 9, 1987: B19). As criticism mounted, the chairman of the company was forced to resign. Here is how one British industrialist summarized the experience with BT:

I always regarded Britain's telephone system as the worst in Europe or America, thus I had vaguely imagined that, with privatization it could only get better. How wrong I was: the performance of British Telecom has plumbed depths hitherto undiscovered by their previous managers ... and the conceited mandarins who run this awful organization have the gall to fund advertising campaigns saying what a wonderful lot they are. (*Ibid.*)

This feeling would easily be shared by one BT subscriber who received no response from the company when he queried it about why he had been billed for calls allegedly made four months after his house had burned down and by another who gets fifty to one hundred calls a day for the national prison service because BT mistakenly assigned him the same number.

What sort of policy is it, people wonder, that leads individual customers to pay more for a lower quality service? To understand why policy makers like deregulation, we need to situate the policy within the wider context of a changing international information order.

The Western New World Information Order

Over the past thirty years, the nations of the Third World have called for the development of a New World Information Order. Such a development would overturn the domination of advanced Western economies in mass media, telecommunications and information systems. The Third World would take a leadership role in the production and distribution of communication, data, and information. Third World and Non-aligned nations have invested substantial political resources to realize this goal, though success has been limited.

In fact, one might argue that as the rhetoric for and against the demands of Third World nations has risen and fallen, developed Western nations, led by the US, but including Canada, Western Europe, and Japan, have been busily constructing their own global information order. This order is founded on the establishment of global digital information networks that would take best advantage of the ability to make information both a commodity for sale and a tool for organizational and social control.

The stakes are so high in this development that businesses with very little historical experience in the information industries have taken an active role in the promotion of corporate controlled global networks. User organizations like the International Communication Association in the US and the Canadian Business Telecommunications Association (which represents such diverse companies as the Canadian Imperial Bank of Commerce, General Foods, Dylex, and Ontario Hydro) are increasingly challenging the established players in this field.

In addition to noticeable changes in the stakes and the configuration of players, we can identify significant changes in the arenas in which these players contend. Not too long ago one could speak about discrete markets in culture, media, telecommunications, and information because neither the technologies nor the providers were significantly integrated across these industries. Though it is never easy to say precisely when a change in degree becomes a change in kind, we can speak more comfortably today about an increasingly integrated arena for the provision of electronic services. The electronic services arena results from the integration of processing, distribution, and reception technologies *and* from the growing vertical, horizontal and global integration of companies in the electronic services marketplace. Major providers of media, culture, and information are companies with names like General Motors, the Royal Bank of Canada, Lockheed, General Electric, American Express, and Sears.

The Thrust to Deregulation

For years, regulators in the United States equivocated on changes in the stakes, players, and arenas. On the one hand, they wanted to support technological change and marketplace control; on the other, they did not want to jeopardize a system that for decades maintained a steady flow of information and entertainment controlled by private enterprise, albeit organized as monopolies and oligopolies, but subject to such public interest constraints as fairness in broadcasting and universal service in telephone. More recently, particularly since the resolution of the AT&T case in 1982, the regulatory and policy apparatus has promoted deregulation and privatization.

In essence, deregulation is a metaphor, more appropriately a euphemism. But this is not to conclude that it is inconsequential. Far from that, deregulation is an instrument to carry out the national and global restructuring of an industry that encompasses culture, media, telecommunication and information. Moreover, it involves a particular kind of restructuring: one that supports technological integration with little consideration for social or national consequences, and networks tailored to the cost and service demands of large users. One finds scant attention paid to the growing cost and diminished service quality available to small users. With metaphors like this to export, who needs a steel industry?

Exporting Deregulation and Privatization

Canada
From 1984 to 1988, the Canadian government has sold off $4.6 billion in assets. (Figure 8.1) This includes federal privatizations totalling $2.1

billion and provincial sales by the right-wing Social Credit government in British Columbia ($1.1 billion), the Liberal government in Quebec ($827 million) and the Conservative government in Saskatchewan ($430 million). In total, about 40 governmental organizations in Canada have been sold entirely or in part since 1984.

Figure 8.1
Privatization in Canada, Europe and Japan

Canada
Eldorado Nuclear *
Air Canada
Northwest Tel and Terra Nova Tel
Northern Canada Power Commission
CN Hotels
Teleglobe Canada
Fishery Products International
Canadair
CN Route
Nanisivik Mines
Canada Development Corporation
Canadian Arsenals
Pecheries Canada
de Havilland Aircraft of Canada
Northern Transportation

Britain
Associated British Ports
British Gas
British Telecom
Sea Link
National Bus Co.
British Airways
British Airports Authority *
British Petroleum
Cable and Wireless
Britoil
Enterprise Oil
British Aerospace
Jaguar

Inmos
Amersham International
International Aeradio
British Sugar Corp.
Uniparts *
Shorts *
Rolls-Royce *
Royal Ordnance
North Sea Oil License
Land
Council House

Germany
I.V.G. *
Veba
Viag
Volkswagen *
Deutsche Pfandbriefanstait *
Deutsche Siedlungs
    und Landesrentenbank *
Deutsche Verkehrskreditbank *

Japan
Nippon Telegraph & Telephone
Japan National Railway *
Japan Air Lines *
Japan Tobacco Corp. *

France
TF 1
Elf-Aquitaine
St. Gobain
Paribas *
AGF *
CGCT *

Italy
Alitalia *
Aeritalia
Sirti
Selenia
Alfa Romeo *
Banco Nazionale del Lavoro *

Spain
GESA
Iberia *
SEAT
Secoinsa
Textil Tarazona
SKF
ENTURSA
Vlajes Marsans

Netherlands
KLM *

Austria
Graz-Koflacher Eisenbahn
    und Bergau GmbH *
OMV *
Bayou Steel Co.
Fepla-Hirsch GmbH *
Futurit Werk AG *

Denmark
Kryolitselskabet

* Indicates Prospective Privatization

Europe

The US has achieved some success in exporting deregulation and privatization to Europe. Cable and satellite delivered television now brings private, advertiser sponsored programming to nations that for years provided nothing but public broadcasting. According to the media director for Coca-Cola, a major sponsor of rock videos across Europe, "The whole European spectrum is opening up." (Marcom, 1987) The London based transnational advertising agency Saatchie & Saatchie predicts that ad spending on television will increase 22 per cent by 1990. This could not be achieved without deregulation and privatization of European public broadcasting systems.

The US has also succeeded in loosening the controls that European PTTs—government controlled Post, Telephone and Telecommunications agencies—exert on communication equipment and service markets. Private broadcasters, telecommunications providers and information service companies have made major inroads, particularly in Britain. British Telecom represents one of numerous privatizations.

The US has had its impact on the continent as well. France is privatizing CGE and selling a chunk of it to ITT. In December 1987 the European Economic Community (EEC) presented a set of deadlines for implementing the June 1987 "Green Paper" which called for an extensive round of privatization in the telecommunications market. US communications companies such as AT&T, ITT, and IBM are likely to increase their influence on European markets.

There is a lesson here for the Canadian debate on free trade with the United States. The US. has not needed a free trade agreement to make major inroads in European markets. It has been able to do so by promoting its home-grown policy of deregulation and privatization.

Deregulation and Privatization in Canadian Communications
Though there has been less of an explicit effort to deregulate Canadian mass media as had been the case in the US, the Report of the Task Force on Broadcasting Policy has pointed out that the CRTC has taken an increasingly permissive approach to new programming that has favored US services. As the report concludes, "it seems to us clear that access to more services has won out thus far over a stronger Canadian presence." (Canada, Report of the Task Force, 1986: 177). This is a euphemistic way of saying that Canadian policy makers have generally given in to the pressures applied by both US and Canadian interests for more US material. For example, in Kingston, Ontario, the local cable company, Cablenet, offers subscribers the three major US networks out of Syracuse, two additional network affiliates (one PBS) out of Watertown, one out of Utica, and these US cable networks: Cable News, Headline News, Arts and Entertainment, the Nashville Network, and extensive US programming on the Canadian channels. This is more US programming than is available in most American cities. Moreover, the government policy to cut back on funding for public broadcasting services further erodes the Canadian dimension of Canadian broadcasting. In addition, the Canadian regulator, the CRTC, has followed the FCC lead in taking a permissive attitude to industry mergers and the oversight of cable industry rates and services. Canada achieves effective deregulation by making it easier for private US networks to reach Canadians with their programming.

There has been extensive discussion in Canadian policy circles, again following the US lead, about auctioning off, rather than licensing with oversight, scarce radio spectrum channels. If this is not enough, efforts are still pending to weaken CRTC regulatory authority even further by permitting the government to intervene directly in the regulatory decision-making process.

Canada has also moved to deregulate and privatize elements of its telecommunications system, though at a slower pace than the US. In 1979, the CRTC permitted CNCP to provide private line long distance telephone and data communications services using the public network. In 1981, the CRTC approved the sale of privately owned terminal equipment. In a related development, the government supported the reorganization of Bell Canada into Bell Canada Enterprises, a move which enables the company to enter a range of new markets, but which has also made all the more complex the task of regulating telephone rates for a company that is heavily involved in non-regulated activities. Supporters of deregulation received a blow in 1985, when extensive public pressure, from the opposition New Democratic Party and a coalition of trade unions, voluntary associations, and small businesses successfully pressured the CRTC to reject a CNCP bid to compete in the public telephone market. Nevertheless, the Canadian government supports a long term strategy of harmonizing the Canadian and US telecommunications systems. (Pike and Mosco, 1986) A 1985 cabinet memo, reported on in the press, charted a US-like course to competitiveness and so-called cost-based pricing in telecommunications. It recognizes the implications:

> This will require gradual decreases in cross-subsidization and therefore increased local rates. This will hit residential and small business users hardest, while big business users will benefit.

The memo calls for a million-dollar public relations campaign to sell this idea to the public and "establish the credibility of the government as protector of the consumer and the champion of universal service." (Musumeci and Parkinson, 1986) Consequently, most analysts consider the CNCP defeat to be a temporary setback.

The federal government has taken steps to further advance the deregulation of privately owned companies, a policy that erodes the position of provincially owned firms and increases the likelihood of privatization. These steps include the 1987 proposal for restructuring the telecommunications industry to strengthen federal authority, at the expense of provincial regulation, and to expand competition. Additionally, in a sign that Canada can also produce snappy euphemisms, Bell Canada proposes to institute "rate rebalancing" as it and the government call what is essentially a means to raise local rates and lower long distance charges. Experts forecast that, as a likely result, thousands of subscribers would no longer be able to afford basic telephone service. The government claims that in the absence of following the American lead, Canadian businesses would simply use the cheaper US long distance network and bypass the Canadian system. To date most analysts have discounted this as nothing more than a convenient reason for instituting the policy. (Mansell, 1985) In essence, we have free trade in euphemisms.

The US exports the policy euphemism—deregulation; and Canada exports the euphemism that implements it—rate rebalancing.

Two current efforts take Canadian deregulation explicitly into the international domain: the ongoing effort to deregulate the Canadian banking industry and thereby free financial services companies to enter new markets, and the privatization of Teleglobe, the former crown corporation that ran global telecommunications services for Canadian customers. These developments will go a long way to harmonize Canadian activities in the electronic services market, whether or not a free trade agreement takes lasting effect.

The Trade Implications

What does all this mean for free trade in culture? First we can no longer separate out the cultural from the media, telecommunications or information sectors. These are all part of an electronic services market that both the technology and the providers inextricably intertwine. Consequently, when the then International Trade Minister stated in the House of Commons that "We want to have free trade in intellectual property. We want free trade in services" and then argued that cultural policies will not be part of an agreement, she was at best shortsighted or is operating with a very narrow conception of culture. (Toronto *Globe and Mail*, March 17, 1987)

Second, given the present US commitment to deregulation and privatization, and to the creation of privately controlled global communication and information networks for the transmission of culture, Canada is under enormous pressure to conform and bring its policy and regulatory structures into harmony with US systems. The US Congress has proposed to retaliate against countries like Canada that fail to harmonize markets with those of the US. The House version of a general trade bill called for telecommunications import restrictions unless countries provide "fully competitive market opportunities." The Senate version called for "substantially equivalent competitive opportunities." The Senate Finance Committee even singled out Canada for its analysis:

> Canada is one of the few countries that allows even a limited amount of competition in its domestic market. ... It is the Committee's hope that reciprocal trade in telecommuncations products and services can be achieved through free trade area talks, thereby satisfying the requirement of this legislation. However, failure to achieve satisfactory results through the free trade

area makes the use of this legislation's leverage with respect to Canada no less important. (Cited in Roseman, 1987: 31).

Canada has begun to conform by supporting its own version of deregulation and privatization. In essence, without a free trade agreement, Canada is implementing policy principles that produce *de facto* free trade in communication and culture.

The Canada-US Trade Agreement

The Canada-US free trade agreement speeds the process of harmonizing regulation and policy in the North American telecommunications marketplace. Much has been made of the fact that the agreement did not roll back any of the protections the Canadian government has put in place to protect cultural industries. But this is hardly a victory for Canadian nationalism. There were very few protections in place to begin with. The US publishing, film, and broadcasting industries already dominate their respective Canadian counterparts. For this "victory," Canada gives up the right to take future steps to protect its cultural industries. The general "notwithstanding" clause, which applies to the entire agreement, allows a party to take measures "of equivalent commercial effect" in response to such Canadian intervention. Concretely, if the Canadian government were to take steps to provide some degree of support for Canadian film distribution, the US could retaliate for the amount of money the US would lose from such a Canadian action. In essence, the agreement holds the line at a very low level of Canadian self-protection and makes it more difficult for a future Canadian government to strengthen that protection.

The telecommunications sections of the agreement seek to phase-in the elimination of tariffs on equipment sales between the countries. More importantly, the deal guarantees "national treatment" to enhanced service providers for each country. In other words, an American company providing enhanced telecommunications services—such as voice mail or call accounting—would be treated in Canada as if it were a Canadian firm. The same would be the case for a Canadian company operating in the United States. Basic telephone service—local and long distance voice service—are not explicitly covered by the agreement. A major loophole, however, one that may turn out to be large enough for US companies like AT&T and MCI to move into the Canadian marketplace, hinges on the definition of an enhanced service. The US regulator's definition of enhanced services has typically been broader than that of the Canadian, encompassing what the CRTC has identified as basic service. Should the CRTC revise its definition, US companies would be in a better position to move into the Canadian market, taking with them the heightened pressures to deregulate. Though Canadian firms might be hurt by the additional competition, such competition would provide them with added reason to break free of their commitments to low-cost service to all Canadians, i.e., universality. It would also enable Canadian policy makers to put in place a deregulatory strategy that is very unpopular with many Canadians, as the defeat of CNCP's long distance petition showed, without taking responsibility for the policy. Deregulation could be defined in the more politically palatable rhetoric of one of the necessary consequences of a bilateral agreement, not the explicit policy of the Canadian government. The government would thereby achieve the goals of its large business user constituency at the same time it distances itself from the likely political fallout.

The pressures to realize this have mounted. In fact, Canadian business has learned a lesson from the US experience by setting up its own stalking horse to promote the liberalization strategy. Just as MCI was used as a vehicle for opening up competition in US telecommunications, the Canadian company, Call-Net, is being used as one means to deregulate the Canadian marketplace.

Call-Net Telecommunications Ltd. is a small company; its revenues are only about $7 million. The Toronto-based company leases lines from Bell Canada and CNCP and resells call time to customers in the Toronto and Montreal area. Call-Net provides its subscribers, mainly lawyers and accountants, with a service that keeps detailed records of calls made on behalf of clients and monitors employee calls. Call-Net considers its Customer Dialed Account Recording to be an enhanced service permissible under Canadian regulations. The CRTC ruled against Call-Net, arguing that this was simply a case of leasing lines to provide a basic service. Call-Net appealed to the federal Cabinet which equivocated. The company was given first one, then another extension, on a deadline to amend its service to conform with CRTC regulations. The opposition New Democratic Party and the coalition of groups opposed to deregulating the Canadian telephone system contend that the government is using this case to expand the definition of an enhanced service in order to open the way for US entry into the Canadian market and exporting to Canada US style deregulation. One cannot be certain about how this specific case will be resolved. However, this case is not as important as what it reveals about the writing "between the lines" of the free trade agreement. An agreement that carries benign language, that even appears to say nothing has changed, can actually be used to restructure a national telecommunications system.

Conclusion: Are Rosencrantz and Guildenstern Dead?

If observing the US policy situation is a lot like sitting through *Hamlet*, the Canadian policy process is a lot like the feeling of sitting through a performance of Tom Stoppard's play *Rosencrantz and Guildenstern are Dead*. The play focusses on two of the minor characters in Hamlet. In a sense, it turns Hamlet inside out by making these minor players the centre of attention. In fact, of course, they are not the centre of attention. Though they have most of the dialogue, they mainly talk about Hamlet. In reality, most of the play is still about Hamlet, but only from a different angle of vision, the "vision," as Stoppard's Guildenstern puts it "of two blind men looting a bazaar for their own portraits."

The Canadian policy process is often taken up with finding the Canadian portrait. But the policy makers are easily blinded by the US presence. Canadian policy making is officially about Canada, but is mainly about the United States. Lately, it has been about how best to implement US models of deregulation, privatization, and a general reliance on private markets, even at the expense of such principles as universality and strong public institutions, values that have traditionally distinguished Canada from the United States. In fact, they have been vital for preserving what independence Canadians enjoy.

Ironically, though it is too soon to weigh their significance, there are signs that the US government is taking another look at the political wisdom of its deregulatory policy. Complaints are growing about the demise of broadcast news as a result of a deregulated and profit-conscious management that has eliminated thousands of news jobs in the US and Canadian broadcasting networks (*The New York Times*, Sunday, November 2, 1986, Section 3; Toronto *Globe and Mail*, February 24, 1987; Kingston *Whig Standard*, March 14, 1987). They have even led to a series of unprecedented Congressional hearings, in the spring of 1987, on the sorry state of broadcast news. As complaints mount about rising phone bills and poor service (Ma Bell's revenge), a *Business Week* cover headlines: "Has the FCC Gone Too Far?"

One can certainly overemphasize these developments. Nevertheless, they do suggest questions that are vital to Canadian interests. Can we anticipate a future prospect of exporting reregulation or some suitable euphemism? What does this say about Canadians who are scrambling to import a policy that Americans are beginning to question. Perhaps most importantly of all: *What do all these things tell us about the ability of governments in general to cope with fundamental divisions brought about by the growth of technology, the demands of international business and the needs of its citizens?*

Reference List

Partial references are cited in full elsewhere in this reference list.

Ahern, Veronica. "Policy Research in International
Telecommunications: The Poor Naked Emperor." In V. Mosco (ed.)
Policy Research in Telecommunications. Norwood, New Jersey: Ablex,
1984, pp. 367-371.

Alford, Robert R. and Friedland, Roger. *Powers of Theory*. Cambridge
University Press, 1985.

Allen, Jeanne. "The Industrialization of Culture: The Case of the Player
Piano." In Mosco and Wasko (Eds.), 1985.

Althusser, Louis. "Ideology and Ideological State Apparatuses." In
Lenin and Philosophy and Other Essays. London: New Left Books, 1971,
pp. 121-173.

American Library Association. *Less Access to Less Information by and
about the US Goverment: A 1981-1987 Chronology*. Washington, D.C.:
ALA, 1988.

Atwood, Rita and McAnany, Emile G. (Eds.) *Communication and Latin
American Society*. Madison: University of Wisconsin Press, 1986.

Aufderheide, Patricia. "Universal Service: Telephone Policy in the
Public Interest." *Journal of Communication*. 37 (1) (Winter, 1987), 81-

96.

Babbage, Charles. *On the Economy of Machinery and Manufactures.* London, 1832.

Babe, Robert. *Canadian Television Broadcasting: Structure Performance and Regulation.* Ottawa: Supply and Services, 1979.

———. *The Political Economy of Canadian Telecommunications.* forthcoming.

Bagdikian, Ben H. *The Media Monopoly.* Boston: Beacon Press, 2nd revised edition, 1988.

Bamford, James. *The Puzzle Palace.* Boston: Houghton Mifflin, 1982.

Barker, Colin. "A Note on the Theory of the State." *Capital and Class.* 4 (1978), 120-124.

Barnouw, Erik. *Tube of Plenty.* New York: Oxford University Press, 1975.

Beatty, Jack. "In Harm's Way." *The Atlantic Monthly* (May, 1987), pp. 37-53.

Bell, Daniel. *The Coming of Postindustrial Society.* New York: Basic, 1973.

———. *The Cultural Contradictions of Capitalism.* New York: Basic, 1976.

Beltran, L.R. and Fox, E. "Latin America and the United States: Flaws in the Free Flow of Information." In Nordenstreng and Schiller (Eds.), 1979, pp. 33-64.

Benda, Charles G. "State Organization and Policy Formation: The 1970 Reorganization of the Post Office Department." *Politics and Society,* 9 (1979), 123-151.

Beniger, James R. *The Control Revolution.* Harvard University Press, 1986

Bernard, Elaine. *The Long Distance Feeling.* Vancouver: New Star, 1982.

Bjorn-Andersen, N., et al. (eds.) *Information Society: For Richer, For Poorer.* Amsterdam: North Holland, 1982.

Bluestone, Barry and Harrison, Bennett. *The Deindustrialization of America.* New York: Basic, 1982.

Bolter, J. David. *Turing's Man.* Chapel Hill: The University of North Carolina Press, 1984.

Boot, W. "NASA and the Spellbound Press." *Columbia Journalism Review.* (July/August, 1986).

Bowles, Samuel and Gintis, Herbert. *Democracy and Capitalism.* New York: Basic Books, 1986.

Brand, Stuart. *The Media Lab.* New York: Penguin, 1987.

Braverman, Harry. *Labor and Monopoly Capital.* New York: Monthly Review, 1974.

Bresnahan, Rosalind. "Mass Communication, Mass Organizations, and Social Participation in Revolutionary Cuba and Nicaragua." In Mosco and Wasko (Eds.), 1985.

Brittan, Samuel. *The Economic Consequences of Democracy.* London: Temple, Smith, 1977.

Broad, William J. "Star Wars is Coming, But Where is it Going." *The New York Times Magazine.* December 6, 1987.

Brooks, Harvey. "Technology, Competition, and Employment." *The Annals of the American Academy of Political and Social Science,* 470 (November, 1983), 115-122.

Browne, Malcolm. "The Star Wars Spinoff." *The New York Times Magazine.* August 24, 1906.

Bruce, R.R., Cunard, J.P., and Director, M.D. *From Telecommunications to Electronic Services.* Toronto: Butterworths, 1986.

Burnham, James. *The Rise of the Computer State.* New York: Random House 1980.

Butsch, Richard. "The Commodification of Leisure: The Model Airplane Hobby and Industry." In Mosco and Wasko (Eds.), 1985.

Butsch, Richard and Glennon, Lynda M. "Social Class: Frequency Trends in Domestic Situation Comedy, 1946-1978." *Journal of Broadcasting,* 27 (1983) (1), 77-81.

Calhoun, Craig. "Comments on 'Democracy in an Information Society.'" *The Information Society,* IV (1,2), (1986), 115-122.

Canada, Department of Communication. *Communications for the Twenty-First Century.* Ministry of Supply and Services, 1987.

Canada, Department of Communication. *Instant World.* Ottawa: Ministry of Supply and Services, 1971.

Canada, Department of Communication. "The Development of SHARP: A Proposal to Industry." Draft. June 3, 1988.

Canada, *Report of the Task Force on Broadcasting Policy.* Ottawa: Supply and Services Canada, 1986.

Canada, Royal Commission on Newspapers. *Final Report.* Ottawa: Supply and Services, 1981.

Canada, Science Council of Canada. *Planning Now For an Information Society.* Ottawa: Ministry of Supply and Services, 1982.

Cannon, W.B. *The Wisdom of the Body.* New York: Norton, 1932.

Carrington, Tim. "Pentagon Panel Urges Better Strategies to Deal with Conflicts in Third World." *The Wall Street Journal.* January 12, 1988.

Castells, Manuel. "High Technology, Economic Restructuring, and the Urban-Regional Process in the United States." In Castells (ed.), *High*

Technology, Space, and Society. Beverly Hills, Sage, 1985.

Chambliss, William J. and Ryther, Thomas E. *Sociology: The Discipline and its Direction.* New York: McGraw Hill, 1975.

Chapple, Steve and Garofalo, Reebee. *Rock 'N' Roll is Here to Pay.* Chicago: Nelson-Hall, 1977.

Charles, Daniel. "Star Wars Fell on Alabama." *The Nation.* December 19, 1987.

Chomsky, Noam and Herman, Edward. *The Political Economy of Human Rights.* 2 Vols. Boston: South End Press, 1979.

Chorbajian, Levon. "Mass Media Coverage of Olympic Boycotts." In Mosco and Wasko (Eds.), 1985.

Clement, Andrew, "Electronic Management: The New Technology of Workplace Surveillance," *Proceedings of CIPS Session 84,* Calgary, Alberta, May 9-11, 1984.

———. "Office Automation and the Technical Control of Information Workers." In Mosco and Wasko (eds.), 1988, 217-246.

Cleveland, Harlan. "The Twilight of Hierarchy: Speculations on the Global Information Society," in Bruce R. Guile (ed.) *Information Technologies and Social Transformation,* Washington, D.C.: National Academy of Sciences Press, 1985, 55-80.

Codding, George. "Politicization of the International Telecommunications: Nairobi and After." In V. Mosco (ed.), 1984.

Cohen, Sam. "Use Star Wars Weapons in Ground Wars." *The Wall Street Journal.* April 20, 1988.

Committee on the Constitutional System. *A Bicentennial Analysis of the American Political Structure.* Washington, D.C.: CCS, 1987.

Consumer Federation of America. *Divestiture Plus Four.* Washington, D.C.: CFA, 1987.

Crozier, Michel J., Huntington, Samuel P., and Watanuki, Joji. *The Crisis of Democracy.* New York University Press, 1975.

Dahl, Robert A. *A Preface to Democratic Theory.* Chicago: University of Chicago Press, 1956.

———. *Dilemmas of Pluralist Democracy.* New Haven: Yale University Press, 1982.

Danilean, N.R. *The AT&T.* New York: Vanguard, 1939.

Demac, Donna A. "Hearts and Minds Revisited: The Information Policies of the Reagan Administration." In Mosco and Wasko (eds.), 1988.

———. *Keeping America Uninformed: Government Secrecy in the 1980s.* New York: Pilgrim Press, 1984.

Dempsey, Paul Stephen. "The Dark Side of Deregulation: Its Impact on Small Communities." *Administrative Law Review* (Fall, 1987), 445-465.

Derthick, Martha and Quirk, Paul J. *The Politics of Deregulation.* Washington, D.C.: The Brookings Institution, 1985.

Disch, Thomas. "The Road to Heaven: Science Fiction and the Militarization of Space." *The Nation.* May 10, 1986.

Dizard, Wilson. *The Coming Information Age.* New York: Longman, 1982.

Dorfman, Ariel. *The Empire's Old Clothes.* New York: Pantheon, 1983.

Dorfman, Ariel and Mattelart, Armand. *How to Read Donald Duck.* London: International General, 1975.

Douglas, Sara. *Labor's New Voice: Unions and the Mass Media.* Norwood, New Jersey: Ablex, 1986.

Downing, John. *Radical Media.* Boston: South End Press, 1984.

Draper, Roger. "The Golden Arm." *New York Review of Books.* October 24, 1985, 46-52.

Dreier, Peter. "The Position of the Press in the US Power Structure." *Social Problems*, 29 (1982) (3), 293-310.

DuBoff, Richard. "The Rise of Communications Regulation: The Telegraph Industry, 1844-1880." *Journal of Communication*, 34 (1984) (3), 52-66.

Easton, David. *A Framework for Political Analysis.* Englewood Cliffs, New Jersey: Prentice Hall, 1965.

Edwards, Paul N. "Border Wars: The Science, Technology, and Politics of Artificial Intelligence." Working Paper of the Silicon Valley Research Group, University of California, Santa Cruz, December, 1984.

Eisenstein, Elizabeth. *The Printing Press as an Agent of Change.* Cambridge University Press, 1979.

English, H.E. (Ed.) *Telecommunications for Canada.* Toronto: Methuen, 1973.

Enzensberger, Hans Magnus. *The Consciousness Industry.* The Seabury Press, 1974.

Ewen, Stuart. *Captains of Consciousness.* New York: McGraw Hill, 1976.

Ewen, Stuart and Ewen, Elizabeth. *Channels of Desire: Mass Images and the Shaping of American Consciousness.* New York: McGraw Hill, 1982.

Federation of American Scientists. *What's Up In Space.* Washington, D.C.: Federation of American Scientists, 1987.

Fejes, Fred. *Imperialism, Media, and the Good Neighbor.* Norwood, New Jersey: Ablex, 1986.

Flacks, Richard and Turkel, Gerald. "Radical Sociology." *Annual*

Review of Sociology. Vol. IV (1978), pp. 193-238.

Flamm, Kenneth. *Targeting the Computer: Government Support and International Competition.* Washington,D.C.: The Brookings Institution, 1987.

Foucault, Michel. *Power/Knowledge.* New York: Pantheon, 1980.

Frederick, Howard. "La Guerra Radiofònica: Radio War Between Cuba and the United States." In Mosco and Wasko (eds.), 1984.

Freiberg, J.W. *The French Press: Class,State and Ideology.* New York: Praeger, 1981.

Fuentes, Annette and Ehrenreich, Bárbara. *Women in the Global Factory.* Boston: South End Press, 1983.

Galbraith, John Kenneth. *The Affluent Society.* Boston: Houghton Mifflin, 1958.

Galtung, Johan. "The Real Star Wars Threat." *The Nation.* February 28, 1987.

Gandy, Oscar. *Beyond Agenda Setting: Information Subsidies and Public Policy.* Norwood, New Jersey: Ablex, 1982.

———. "The Political Economy of Communications Competence," in Vincent Mosco and Janet Wasko (eds.), 1988, 108-124.

Ganley, Oswald H. and Ganley, Gladys D. *Information Implications of United States Communications and Information Resources.* Cambridge, Mass.: Harvard University Program on Information Resources Policy, 1981.

Garnham, Nicholas. "Contribution to a Political Economy of Mass Communication." *Media Culture and Society,* 1 (1979) (2), 122-146.

Gaudemar, J.P. de. *La Mobilisation Générale.* Paris: Editions du Champ Urbain, 1979.

Gervasi, Paul. *The Myth of Soviet Military Supremacy.* New York: Harper and Row, 1986.

Giddens, Anthony. *A Contemporary Critique of Historical Materialism.* Berkeley: University of California Press, 1983.

Ginsberg, Benjamin. *The Captive Public.* New York: Basic, 1986.

Gitlin, Todd. "The Greatest Story Never Told." *Mother Jones.* (June/July, 1987).

———. "Prime Time Ideology: The Hegemonic Process in Television Entertainment." In Newcomb (Ed.), 1982, pp. 426-454.

———. *The Whole World is Watching: Mass Media in the Making and Unmaking of the New Left.* Berkeley: University of California Press, 1980.

Glasgow Media Group. *Bad News.* London: Routledge and Kegan Paul,

1977.

———. *More Bad News.* London: Routledge and Kegan Paul, 1980.

Goldhaber, Michael. *Reinventing Technology.* New York: Routledge and Kegan Paul, 1986.

Gouldner, Alvin. *The Future of Intellectuals and the Rise of the New Class.* London: Macmillan, 1979.

Gramsci, Antonio. *Selections from the Prison Notebooks.* London: Lawrence and Wishart, 1971.

Gray, Colin. *Nuclear Defense and Strategic Planning.* Philadelphia: Foreign Policy Research Institute, 1984.

Gregory, Judith. "Technological Change in the Office Workplace and the Implications for Organizing." in Kennedy, Craypo, and Lehman (Eds.). *Labor and Technology: Union Responses to Changing Environments.* Department of Labor Studies, Pennsylvania State University, 1982.

Grinberg, Maximo Simpson. "Trends in Alternative Communications Research in North America." In Atwood and McAnany (eds.)., 1986.

Gruneau, Richard. *Class, Sports and Social Development.* Amherst, MA: University of Massachusetts Press, 1983.

Guback, Thomas. "The Evolution of the Motion Picture Theater Business in the 1980s." *Journal of Communication* 37 (Spring, 1987) 2, 60-77.

———. *The International Film Industry: Western Europe and America Since 1945.* Bloomington, Ind.: Indiana University Press, 1969

———. "Theatrical Film." In Benjamin Compaine, et al. *Who Owns the Media?* 2nd Edition. White Plains, New York: Knowledge Industries Publications, 1982.

Gurevitch, M., Bennet, T., Curran, J. and Woolacott, J. *Culture, Society and the Media.* London: Methuen, 1982.

Guyon, Janet. "AT&T Profits on Price-Cap Alternative." *The Wall Street Journal,* September 2, 1987.

Habermas, Jurgen. *Legitimation Crisis.* Boston: Beacon Press, 1973.

Hacker, Andrew. "Women at Work." *New York Review of Books.* August 14, 1986, 26-32.

Haight, Timothy R. and Weinstein, Laurie R. "Changing Ideology on Television by Changing Telecommunications Policy: Notes on a Contradictory Situation." In McAnany, Schnitman, and Janus (eds.), 1981.

Hall, Stuart. "The Rediscovery of Ideology: Return of the Repressed in Media Studies." In Gurevitch, et al.(eds.), 1982.

Hamelink, Cees J. *Cultural Autonomy in Global Communications*. New
    York: Longman, 1983.
Hardin, Herschel. *Closed Circuits: The Sellout of Canadian Television*.
    Vancouver: Douglas and McIntyre, 1985.
Harris, William B. "The Electronic Business." *Fortune*. (April, 1957),
    pp. 137-226.
Hartmann, Heidi I. (Ed.). *Comparable Worth: New Directions for Research*.
    Washington, D.C.: National Academy Press, 1985.
Hartung, W. and Nimroody, R. "Cutting Up the Star Wars Pie." *The
    Nation*. September 14, 1985.
Harvard University, Program on Information Resources Policy,
    Seminar on Command, Control, Communications and Intelligence,
    Cambridge, MA, 1982.
Head, Sidney with Sterling, Christopher H. *Broadcasting in America*.
    Fourth Edition. Boston, MA: Houghton-Mifflin, 1982.
Held, David. *Models of Democracy*. Stanford, CA: Stanford University
    Press, 1987.
Herman, Edward S. *The Real Terror Network*. Boston: South End Press,
    1982.
Herman, Edward S. and Brodhead, Frank. *Demonstration Elections*
    Boston: South End Press, 1984.
Herman, Edward S. and Chomsky, Noam. *Manufacturing Consent: The
    Political Economy of the Mass Media*. New York: Pantheon, 1988.
Hewlett, Richard and Duncan, Francis. *The Nuclear Navy*. Chicago:
    University of Chicago Press, 1974.
Hirschman, Albert O. *Exit, Voice and Loyalty*. Cambridge, MA: Harvard
    University Press, 1970.
Horowitz, Irving Louis. *Communicating Ideas: The Crisis of Publishing in
    a Post-industrial Society*. New York: Oxford University Press, 1986.
Horwood, David and Grogono, Peter. "Software Shows Star Wars
    Can't Ensure Safe World." *Toronto Globe and Mail*. March 17, 1987.
Howard, Robert. *Brave New Workplace*. New York: Viking, 1985.
IAM. *A Technology Bill of Rights*. Washington, D.C.: IAM, 1981.
Innis, Harold. *Empire and Communications*. University of Toronto Press,
    1972.
International Telecommunication Union, Independent Commission for
    Worldwide Telecommunications Development, *The Missing Link*.
    Geneva: ITU, 1985.
Janisch, H.N. "Winners and Losers: The Challenges Facing
    Telecommunications Regulation." In W.T. Stanbury (Ed.), 1986, 307-

400.

Janus, Noreene. "Advertising and the Creation of Global Markets: the Role of the New Communication Technologies." In Mosco and Wasko (Eds.), 1984.

―――. "Transnational Advertising: Some Consideration on the Impact on Peripheral Societies." In Atwood and McAnany (Eds.), 1986.

Jessop, Bob. *The Capitalist State.* Oxford: Martin Robertson, 1982.

Johnston, Bennett and Proxmire, William. "SDI's Broken Promises." *The Wall Street Journal.* August 28, 1987.

Kattenburg, David. "Sneaking Canada into SDI." *The Nation.* February 27, 1988.

Kellner, Douglas. "TV, Ideology, and Emancipatory Popular Culture." In Newcomb (Ed.), 1982.

Kennan, George. "In the American Mirror." *The New York Review of Books,* November 6, 1986, 3-6.

Kilman, Scott. "An Unexpected Result of Airline Decontrol is Return to Monopolies." *The Wall Street Journal,* July 20, 1987, 1 and 13.

Kinsley, Michael. *Outer Space and Inner Sanctums.* New York: Wiley Interscience, 1976.

Kling, Rob, "The Struggles for Democracy in an Information Society," *The Information Society,* IV (1, 2), (1986), 1-7.

Kling, Rob and Kraemer, Kenneth. *The Dynamics of Computing.* New York: Columbia University Press, 1985.

Knight, G. "News and Ideology." *Canadian Journal of Communication.* 8 (1982) (4), 15-41.

―――. "Strike Talk: A Case Study of News." *Canadian Journal of Communication.* 8 (1982) (3), 61-79.

Kozol, Jonathan. *Illiterate America.* New York: Doubleday, 1985.

Kraft, Philip and Dubnoff, Stephen. "Job Content, Fragmentation, and Control in Computer Software." *Industrial Relations* 25 (Spring, 1986), 2, 184-196.

Landes, David S. *Revolution in Time.* Cambridge, MA: Harvard University Press, 1983.

Lapham, Louis. "Paper Moons." *Harper's Magazine,* December, 1986, pp. 8-10.

Lasch, Christopher. *The Culture of Narcissism.* New York: Norton, 1978.

Lazarsfeld, Paul. "Remarks on Administrative and Critical Communications Research." *Studies in Philosophy and Social Sciences,* 9 (1), 1941.

Lazarsfeld, Paul and Merton. Robert K. "Mass Communication, Popular Taste and Organized Social Action," In *The Communication of Ideas*. New York: Institute for Religious and Social Studies, 1949.

Leggett, J., et al. *Allende His Exit and Our Times*. New Brunswick, New Jersey: New Brunswick Cooperative Press, 1978.

Leiss, William; Kline, Stephen and Jhally, Sut, *Social Communication in Advertising*. Toronto: Methuen, 1986.

Lemann, Nicholas. "The Peacetime War." *Atlantic Monthly*. (October, 1984).

Lindblom, Charles E. *Politics and Markets*. New York: Basic, 1977.

Lowe, Graham. S. *Women in the Administrative Revolution*. Toronto: University of Toronto Press, 1987.

Lowi, Theodore J. and Lytel, David, "Comments on 'Democracy in an Information Society': Making It a Real Revolution," *The Information Society*, IV (1,2), (1986), 91-99.

Luhmann, Niklas. *The Differentiation of Society*. New York: Columbia University Press, 1982.

Macpherson, C.B. *The Life and Times of Liberal Democracy*. Oxford University Press, 1977.

Mahoney, Eileen. "The Intergovernmental Bureau For Informatics: An International Organization Within the Changing World Political Economy." In Mosco and Wasko (eds.), 1988, 297-315.

Malcomson, Robert. "Exposing Nuclear Fallacies: An Interview with Robert Malcomson." *Studies in Political Economy*. 20 (Summer, 1986).

Mander, Jerry. *Four Arguments for the Elimination of Television*. New York: Morrow, 1978.

Manno, Jack. *Arming the Heavens*. New York: Dodd, Mead, 1983.

Mansell, Robin. "The Telecommunications Bypass Threat: Real or Imagined?" Paper presented at the Conference of the Canadian Communication Association, Montreal, P.Q., May 31-June 2, 1985.

Marcom, John. "Cable and Satellites are Opening Europe to TV Commercials." *The Wall Street Journal*. December 22, 1987.

Markusen, Ann; Hall, Peter, and Glasmeier, Amy. *High Tech America*. Boston: Allen and Unwin, 1986.

Marx, Gary T., "The Iron Fist and the Velvet Glove: Totalitarian Potentials Within Democratic Structures," in J. Short (ed.) *The Social Fabric*, Beverly Hills: Sage, 1986, 89-108.

Marx, Karl. *Capital*. Vol. 1. London: Everyman's Library, 1972.

Mattelart, Armand and Siegelaub, Seth. (Eds.). *Communication and Class Struggle. Vol.1: Capitalism, Imperialism*. New York: International

General, 1979.

———. *Communication and Class Struggle. Vol.2: Liberation, Socialism.* New York: International General, 1983.

McAnany, Emile G. "The Logic of Cultural Industries in Latin America: The Television Industry in Brazil." In Mosco and Wasko (eds.), 1984, pp. 185-208.

McAnany, Emile G., Schnitman, Jorge, and Janus, Noreene. (Eds.). *Communication and Social Structure.* New York: Praeger, 1981.

McClellan, S.T. *The Coming Computer Industry Shakeout.* New York: John Wiley, 1984.

Meehan, Eileen R. "Technical Capability vs. Corporate Imperatives: Towards a Political Economy of Cable Television and Information Diversity." In Mosco and Wasko (eds.), 1988.

———. "Towards a Third Vision of an Information Society." *Media Culture and Society.* 6 (1984), 257-272.

Mills, C. Wright. *The Sociological Imagination.* New York: Oxford, 1959.

Mosco, Vincent. *Broadcasting in the United States: Innovative Challenge and Organizational Control.* Norwood, New Jersey: Ablex, 1979.

———. "The Communications System from a Regulatory Perspective." Paper prepared for the US Congress, Office of Technology Assessment, 1987a.

———. (Ed.). *Policy Research in Telecommunications.* Norwood, New Jersey: Ablex, 1984.

———. *Pushbutton Fantasies: Critical Perspectives on Videotex and Information Technology.* Norwood, New Jersey: Ablex, 1982.

———. "Star Wars is Already Working." *Science as Culture* (May, 1987a), 12-24.

Mosco, Vincent and Wasko, Janet.(Eds.). *The Critical Communications Review. Vol.1: Labor, the Working Class, and the Media.* Norwood, New Jersey: Ablex, 1983. (Eds.). *The Critical Communications Review. Vol.2: Changing Patterns of Communication Control.* Norwood, New Jersey: Ablex, 1984. (Eds.). *The Critical Communications Review. Vol.3: Popular Culture and Media Events.* Norwood, New Jersey: Ablex, 1985. (Eds.). *The Political Economy of Information* Madison: University of Wisconsin Press, 1988.

Mosco, Vincent and Zureik, Elia. *Computers in the Workplace.* Report to the Federal Department of Labour, Canada, 1987.

Mowshowitz, Abbe, "On the Social Relations of Computers," *Human Systems Management,* 5 (1985) 99-110.

Murdock, Graham and Golding, Peter. "For a Political Economy of

Mass Communications." In Ralph Miliband and John Saville (Eds.). *Socialist Register.* London: Merlin Press, 1974.

Musumeci, R. and Parkinson, B. *A Study of Change and Development of Communications in Canada, the USA & Great Britain.* Australian Telecommunications Employees Association, 1986.

Naisbitt, John. *Magatrends.* New York: Warner, 1982.

Nash, June and Fernandez-Kelly, Maria Patricia (Eds.). *Women and Men in the International Division of Labor.* Albany: State University of New York Press, 1983.

Nielson, Mike. "Toward a Worker's History of the US Film Industry." In Mosco and Wasko (eds.), 1983.

Nelson, Joyce. *The Perfect Machine: TV in the Nuclear Age.* Toronto: Between the Lines, 1987.

Newcomb, Horace. (Ed.). *Television: The Critical View.* 3rd Edition. New York: Oxford, 1982.

Nichols, William J. *Ideology and the Image.* Bloomington: Indiana University, 1981.

Noam, Eli M. "The Public Telecommunications Network: A Concept in Transition." *Journal of Communication.* 37 (1), (Winter, 1987), 30-48.

Noble, David. *Forces of Production.* New York: Knopf, 1984.

Noll, Roger (Ed.). *Regulatory Policy and the Social Sciences.* Berkeley: University of California Press, 1987.

Nora, Simon and Minc, Alain. *The Computerization of Society.* Cambridge, MA: MIT, 1980.

Nordenstreng, Kaarle. *Informational Mass Communication.* Helsinki: Tammi, 1974.

Nordenstreng, Kaarle and Schiller, Herbert (Eds.). *National Sovereignty and International Communication.* Norwood, New Jersey: Ablex, 1979.

Nozick, Robert. *Anarchy, State, and Utopia.* New York: Basic, 1974.

Oettinger, Anthony G. "Information Resources: Knowledge and Power in the 21st Century." *Science,* 209 (4 July 1980), 191-198.

———. "The Formula is Everything: Costing and Pricing in the Telecommunications Industry." Cambridge, MA: Harvard University, Program on Information Resources Policy, 1988.

Offe, Claus. *Contradictions of the Welfare State.* Cambridge, Mass.: MIT, 1984.

———. *Disorganized Capitalism.* Cambridge, Mass.: MIT, 1985.

Parenti, Michael. *Inventing Reality.* New York: St. Martin's Press, 1986.

Parnas, David. "Software Aspects of Strategic Defense Systems." University of Victoria, Department of Computer Science, DCS-47-IR,

July, 1985.

Parsons, Talcott. *The Social System*. Glencoe, Illinois: The Free Press, 1951.

———. *Societies*. Englewood Cliffs, New Jersey: Prentice-Hall, 1966.

Pendakur, Manjunath. "United States-Canada Relations: Cultural Dependence and Conflict." In Mosco and Wasko (eds.), 1984, pp. 165-184.

Pike, Robert M. and Mosco, Vincent. "Canadian Consumers and Telephone Pricing: From Luxury to Necessity and Back Again?" *Telecommunications Policy*, X (1), March, 1986, pp. 17-32.

Pool, Ithiel de Sola. *Technologies of Freedom*. Harvard University Press, 1983.

Posner, Richard A. "Theories of Economic Regulation." *Bell Journal of Economics and Management Science*. 5 (2) (1974), 335-358.

Poulantzas, Nicos. *State, Power, and Socialism*. London: New Left Books, 1978.

Raboy, Marc. *Movements and Messages: Media and Radical Politics in Quebec*. Toronto: Between the Lines, 1984.

Rada, Juan F. "The Microelectronics Revolution: Implications for the Third World." *Development Dialogue*, 2 (1981), 41-67.

Rand Corporation. *Preliminary Design for a World-Circling Spaceship*. Santa Monica: Rand, 1946.

Reed, F. "The Great Star Wars Swindle." *Harpers* (May, 1985).

Reich, Robert. *Tales of a New America*. New York: Times Books, 1987.

Reinecke, Ian. *Connecting You*. Penguin, 1985.

Reiter, Ester. "Life in a Fast-Food Factory." In Craig Herron and Robert Storey (eds.). *On the Job*. Kingston and Montreal: McGill-Queen's Press, 1986.

Reyes Matta, Fernando. "Alternative Communication: Solidarity and Development in the Face of Transnational Expansion." In Atwood and McAnany (eds.), 1986, 190-214.

———. "A Model for Democratic Communication." *Development Dialogue*, 2 (1981), 79-97.

Rips, G. "The Campaign Against the Underground Press." In A. Janowitz and N.J. Peters (Eds.). *Unamerican Activities*. San Francisco: City Light Books, 1981.

Robins, Kevin and Webster, Frank. "Cybernetic Capitalism: Information Technology, Everyday Life." In Mosco and Wasko (eds.), 1988, 44-75.

Rohatyn, Felix. "On the Brink." *The New York Review of Books*, July 11,

1987, 3-6.

Rollings, Jerry. "Mass Communications and the American Worker." In Mosco and Wasko (eds.), 1983.

Roncagliolo, Rafael and Janus, Noreene. "Advertising and the Democratization of Communications." *Development Dialogue,* 2 (1981), 31-40.

Roseman, Daniel. "Telecommunications Trade: Exporting Deregulation," *International Economic Issues* (September, 1987), pp. 27-34.

Rosenberg, Emily S. *Spreading the American Dream.* New York: Hill and Wang, 1982.

Roszak, Theodore. *The Cult of Information.* New York: Pantheon, 1986.

Rumberger, Russell W. and Levin, Henry M., "Forecasting the Impact of New Technologies on the Future Job Market," *Technological Forecasting and Social Change,* 27 (1985), 399-417.

Salter, Liora. "Two Directions on a One-Way Street: Old and New Approaches in Media Analysis in Two Decades." In Thelma McCormack (ed.). *Studies in Communications.* Greenwich, CT: JAI Press, 1980.

Schiller, Anita R. and Schiller, Herbert I., "Libraries, Public Access to Information, and Commerce," in Vincent Mosco and Janet Wasko (eds.), Madison: University of Wisconsin Press, 1988, 146-166.

Schiller, Dan. "How to Think About Information." In Mosco and Wasko (Eds.), 1988.

————. *Objectivity and the News* Philadelphia: University of Pennsylvania Press, 1981.

————. *Telematics and Government.* Norwood, New Jersey: Ablex, 1982.

————. "The Emerging Global Grid: Planning for What?" *Media Culture & Society,* Vol. 7, No. 1 (January, 1985), 105-125.

Schiller, Herbert I. *Communication and Cultural Domination.* White Plains, New York: International Arts and Sciences Press, 1976.

————. *Information in the Crisis Economy.* Norwood, New Jersey: Ablex, 1984a.

————. *Mass Communication and American Empire.* Boston: Beacon Press, 1969.

————. *The Mind Managers.* Boston: Beacon Press, 1973.

————. "The US Decision to Withdraw from UNESCO." *Journal of Communication.* 34 (Autumn, 1984a), 4.

————. *Who Knows: Information in the Age of the Fortune 500.* Norwood, New Jersey: Ablex, 1981.

Schmitter, Phillipe. "Modes of Interest Intermediation and Models of Societal Change in Western Europe." *Comparative Political Studies.* 10 (1977), 7-38.

Schnitman, Jorge. "Economic Protectionism and Mass Media Development: Film Industry in Argentina." In McAnany, Schnitman, and Janus (eds.), 1981.

Schultz, George. "The US Decision to Withdraw from UNESCO." *Journal of Communication.* 34 (Autumn, 1984) 4.

Schumpeter, Joseph. *Capitalism, Socialism, and Democracy.* London: Allen and Unwin, 1943.

Shaffer, Ed. "Militarism and the Economy." *Studies in Political Economy.* 24 (Autumn, 1987), pp. 87-104.

Shaiken, Harley. *Work Transformed.* New York: Holt, Rinehart, and Winston, 1984.

Shannon, C. and Weaver, W. *The Mathematical Theory of Communication.* University of Illinois Press, 1959.

Sheff, David. "Portrait of a Generation." *Rolling Stone.* May 5, 1988.

Shepherd, William G. "Concepts of Competition and Efficient Policy in the Telecommunications Sector." In Eli M. Noam (Ed.). *Telecommunications Regulation: Today and Tomorrow.* Harcourt Brace Jovanovich, 1983, 79-120.

Shore, Larry. *The Crossroads of Business and Music: The Music Industry in the United States and Internationally.* Doctoral Dissertation. Stanford University, Stanford, CA, 1983.

Siegel, Lenny and Markoff, John. *The High Cost of High Tech.* New York: Harper and Row, 1985.

Skocpol, Theda. *States and Social Revolutions.* Cambridge University Press, 1979.

Slack, Jennifer D. *Communication Technologies and Society.* Norwood, New Jersey: Ablex, 1983

———. "The Information Revolution as Ideology." *Media Culture and Society.* 6 (1984), 247-256.

Smith, Jeff. "Reagan, Star Wars, and American Culture." *Bulletin of the Atomic Scientists.* (January/February, 1987), pp. 19-25.

Smith, Merrit Roe. (Ed.). *Military Enterprise and Technological Change.* Cambridge, MA: MIT Press, 1985.

Smythe, Dallas W. "Communications: Blindspot of Western Marxism." *Canadian Journal of Political and Social Theory,* I (1977),3, 1-27.

———. *Dependency Road: Communication, Capitalism, Consciousness and Canada.* Norwood, New Jersey: Ablex, 1981.

————. "Radio Spectrum Policy and World Needs." Paper presented to the First Canberra Conference on International Communications, Canberra, Australia, December, 1986.

————. *The Structure and Policy of Electronic Communications.* Urbana: University of Illinois Press, 1957.

Somavia, Juan. "The Democratization of Communications: From Minority Social Monopoly to Majority Social Representation." *Development Dialogue,* 2 (1981), 13-30.

Stanbury, W.T. (Ed.) *Telecommunications Policy and Regulation.* Montreal: The Institute for Research on Public Policy, 1986.

Stares, Paul. *Space and National Security.* Washington, D.C.: The Brookings Institution, 1987.

Sterling, Theodor D. "Democracy in an Information Society," *The Information Society,* IV (1,2), (1986), 9-47.

Sussman, Gerald. "Global Telecommunications and the Third World: Theoretical Considerations." *Media Culture and Society,* 6 (1984), 289-300.

————. "Information Technologies For The ASEAN Region: The Political Economy of Privatization." In Mosco and Wasko, (eds.), 1988.

Swedish Center for Working Life. *The Utopia Project: An Alternative in Text and Images,* Stockholm, 1985.

Telecom Australia. *Capital and Policy Requirements for the 1980s.* (The McKinsey Report), 1980.

Thompson, E.P. and Thompson, B. *Star Wars: Self-Destruct Incorporated.* London: Merlin, 1985.

Toffler, Alvin. *The Third Wave.* New York: William Morrow, 1980.

Toles, Terry. "Videogames and American Military Ideology." In Mosco and Wasko (Eds.), 1985.

Tran van Dinh. *Independence, Liberation, Revolution: An Aproach to the Understanding of the Third World.* Norwood, New Jersey: Ablex, 1987.

Tunstall, Jeremy. *The Media are American.* New York: Columbia Univesity Press, 1977.

UNESCO, International Commission for the Study of Communication Problems, *Final Report.* Paris: UNESCO, 1979.

US, Congress, House, Commitee on Science and Technology. *Japanese Technological Advances and Possible United States Responses Using Research Joint Ventures.* 98th Cong., lst Sess., June 29, 30, 1983. Washington, DC: Government Printing Office, 1984.

US, Congress, Office of the Budget. *The Benefits and Risks of Federal Funding for Sematech.* Washington, D.C.: Congressional Budget

Office, 1987.

US, Congress, Office of Technology Assessment. *Science, Technology and the Constitution.* Washington, D.C.: OTA, 1987a.

————. *The Electronic Supervisor: New Technology, New Tensions.* Washington, D.C.: OTA, 1987b.

————. *Strategic Defense.* Princeton, New Jersey: Princeton University Press, 1986.

US, Congress, Senate, Committee on Foreign Relations. *Strategic Defense and Anti Satellite Weapons.* 98th Cong., 2d Sess., April 25, 1984, Washington, D.C.: Government Printing Office, 1984.

US, Defense Advanced Research Projects Agency. *Strategic Computing.* Washington, D.C.: DARPA, 1983.

US, Department of Defense. *Discriminate Defense.* Report of the Commission on Integrated Long-Term Strategy, Fred C. Iklé and Albert Wohlstetter, co-chairmen, Washington, D.C.: GPO, January, 1988.

US, General Accounting Office. *Telephone Communications: The FCC's Monitoring of Residential Telephone Service,* GAO / RCED-86-146, Washington, D.C.: Government Printing Office, 1986.

————. *Telephone Communications: Cost and Funding Information on Lifeline Telephone Service,* GAO / RCED-87-189, Washington, D.C.: Government Printing Office, 1987a.

————. *Telephone Communications: Controlling Cross Subsidy Between Regulated and Competitive Services,* GAO / RCED-88-34, Washington, D.C.: Government Printing Office, 1987b.

Wasko, Janet. *Movies and Money: Financing the American Film Industry.* Norwood, New Jersey: Ablex, 1982.

————. "Trade Unions and Broadcasting." In Mosco and Wasko (eds.), 1983.

Wasko, Janet and Mosco, Vincent (Eds.). *Democratic Communication in an Information Age,* forthcoming.

Webb, James H. Jr. "US Military: Strength Through Flexibility." *The Wall Street Journal,* January 18, 1988.

Weber, Max. *Economy and Society.* Berkeley: University of California Press, 1978.

Webster, Frank and Robins, Kevin. *Information Technology: A Luddite Analysis.* Norwood, New Jersey: Ablex, 1986.

Weinhaus, Carol and Oettinger, Anthony G. "Behind the Telephone Debates-2 Concepts: Understanding Debates Over Competition and Divestiture." Cambridge, MA: Program on Information Policy

Research, Harvard University, 1987.

Weinstein, James. *The Corporate Ideal and the Liberal State, 1900-1918.* Boston: Beacon Press, 1968.

Weizenbaum, Joseph. "Once More, The Computer Revolution." In Forester (Ed.). *The Micrelectronics Revolution.* Cambridge: MIT Press, 1981.

Wiener, Norbert. *Cybernetics.* Cambridge: MIT Press, 1948.

———. *The Human Use of Human Beings.* Garden City: Anchor Books, 1954.

Williams, Raymond. *Culture.* London: Fontana, 1981.

———. *Problems in Materialism and Culture.* London: Verso, 1980.

———. *Television, Technology and Cultural Form.* London: Fontana, 1975.

Wilson, James Q. (Ed.). *The Politics of Regulation.* New York: Basic, 1980.

Wilson, Kevin. *Technologies of Control.* Madison: University of Wisconsin Press, 1988.

Winner, Langdon. *Autonomous Technology.* Cambridge, MA: MIT, 1977.

Winston, Brian. *Misunderstanding Media.* Cambridge, MA: Harvard University Press, 1986.

Wolfe, Alan. *The Limits of Legitimacy.* New York: The Free Press 1977.

Woodrow, R. Brian and Woodside, Ken B. "Players, Stakes and Politics in the Future of Telecommunications Regulation in Canada." In W.T. Stanbury (Ed.), 1986, 101-288.

Woodward, C. Vann. "The President—And Us." *The New York Times Book Review.* January 11, 1987.

Zimbalist, Andrew, "Technology and the Labor Process in the Printing Industry." In Andrew Zimbalist (ed.). *Case Studies in the Labor Process.* New York: Monthly Review, 1979.

Zuboff, Shoshana. *In the Age of the Smart Machine.* New York: Basic Books, 1988.

Subject Index

237

Author Index